PLA[...]

BOOK OF SHOTS

STERLING, the Sterling logo, STERLING INNOVATION, and the Sterling Innovation logo are
registered trademarks of Sterling Publishing Co., Inc.

Library of Congress Cataloging-in-Publication Data Available

2 4 6 8 10 9 7 5 3 1

Published by Sterling Publishing Co., Inc.
387 Park Avenue South, New York, NY 10016
© 2010 by Sterling Publishing Co., Inc.

This book is comprised of the following titles:
Playboy Bartender's Guide © 1971, 1979 by Thomas Mario, published by Barnes & Noble, Inc.,
under license from Playboy Enterprises International, Inc.
10,000 Drinks © 2007 by Paul Knorr, published by Sterling Publishing Co., Inc.

Distributed in Canada by Sterling Publishing
c/o Canadian Manda Group, 165 Dufferin Street
Toronto, Ontario, Canada M6K 3H6
Distributed in the United Kingdom by GMC Distribution Services
Castle Place, 166 High Street, Lewes, East Sussex, England BN7 1XU
Distributed in Australia by Capricorn Link (Australia) Pty. Ltd.
P.O. Box 704, Windsor, NSW 2756, Australia

Design by Mike Rivilis
Playboy and Rabbit Head design are trademarks of Playboy Enterprises International, Inc.

Printed in China
All rights reserved

Sterling ISBN 978-1-4027-6954-2

For information about custom editions, special sales, premium and
corporate purchases, please contact Sterling Special Sales
Department at 800-805-5489 or specialsales@sterlingpublishing.com.

PLAYBOY
BOOK OF SHOTS

Paul Knorr and the Editors of *Playboy*

Illustrations by LeRoy Neiman

STERLING INNOVATION
An imprint of Sterling Publishing Co., Inc.

New York / London
www.sterlingpublishing.com

Contents

Introduction

Drinking, like so many of the finer things in life, changes with the times but never goes out of style. So, while the ancient Teutonic custom of quaffing beer out of vessels made from the skulls of your enemies might raise a few eyebrows at a keg party today, the old proverb still applies: *Essen und Trinken hält Leib und Seele zusammen* ("Eating and drinking holds body and soul together"). And we've come a long way since the days of Prohibition, when it was definitively proved that not even outlawing alcohol with a Constitutional Amendment could keep Americans from drinking the stuff with abandon. Indeed, in the span of thirty years since Playboy's first bartender's guide, *Playboy's Bar Guide*, was published, the popularity and availability of different wines and spirits have exploded, and new drinking habits have proliferated among the cognoscenti with positively revolutionary fervor.

The Playboy Book of Shots is offered in the belief that whenever two or more people touch glasses, it isn't just the liquor stirring up fun—it's the appetite for life and the excitement felt at the many ways of satisfying that appetite. Encouraging this joie de vivre is not only Playboy's primary mission, it is also the raison d'être for this book.

À votre santé!

Glassware

All you really need are shot glasses, but there's no rule that says you have to serve shots strictly as shooters.

Glassware generally falls into three categories:

1. **Tumblers**—Glasses of cylindrical shape, sometimes with a heavy or "sham" bottom, which adds stability
2. **Footed glasses**—Glasses of cylindrical or bowl shape that rest on a round pedestal or foot but with no stem
3. **Stemware**—Glasses with a bowl, stem, and foot

Shot glasses fall into the first category. So it tends to make the most sense to try other tumblers in place of shot glasses if you want to mix things up. However, here's a list of all the glassware that's out there:

Old-fashioned, or **on-the-rocks**—No drinking vessel gets a bigger play these days than the old-fashioned, or on-the-rocks, glass. Over the years the old-fashioned glass has blossomed into an all-purpose glass, bearer of any drink from a Scotch Old-Fashioned to a Bourbon Mist to a Black Russian. It may have straight flared sides or be barrel-shaped or footed. Double old-fashioned glasses holding up to 15 ounces are great labor savers for hosts because demands for seconds are spaced further apart.

Highball, **collins**, and **cooler**—The straight, tall, thin glass ranging in size from 8 to 12 ounces is sometimes called the shell glass and is used not only for highballs but also for Gin and Tonics, Collins drinks, Cobblers, Daisies, Screwdrivers, Bloody Marys, beer, and other drinks. More elegant is the weighted-bottom glass. Glasses of the same tall shape that hold up to 21 ounces are known as coolers and can accommodate king-size Collinses, extra-long juleps, Polynesian rum drinks, and other long summer libations.

Delmonico or **sour**—This glass may be footed or straight-sided and varies in size from 4 ½ to 7 ounces. Used for Whiskey, Rum, or Brandy Sours, it doubles for fruit juice, Sherry Flips, Port Flips, and morning-after pick-me-ups.

Liqueur, **cordial**, and **pony**—These 1-ounce capacity glasses may be rounded or straight sided. The latter is called a pousse-café and can hold a rainbow's spectrum of different liqueurs in layers.

Whiskey shot, or **jigger**—No modern host should buy a shot glass that holds less than 1 ½ ounces. Used more frequently for measuring than drinking, it's the proper glass for a Boilermaker (straight whiskey followed by beer). The heavy-bottomed type provides stability; the extra-long sham bottom sometimes seen in public bars is out of place in your pad.

Brandy and **brandy snifter**—These glasses have a rounded bowl for retaining their liquor's rich, volatile fragrance. Glasses range in size from 2 ounces to a sensible 8-ounce size, comfortable for holding as well as nosing, to large balloon styles holding up to 25 ounces, which are considered completely affected by professional brandymen.

All-purpose wine—The tulip shape is designed for trapping the wine's bouquet and enables you to comfortably eye the wine's color, swirl the wine, and nose it. Volumes range from 8 to 11 ounces; the glass is never more than half-filled. Used for both red and white table wines as well as champagne.

Burgundy and **Rhine wine**—For most Dionysian delights, the all-purpose wineglass will be very satisfying. But the host who makes a continuing avocation of buying wines for his own cellar and laying down vintage wines for later years may also like to own the balloon-shaped red-wine glass, beloved by Burgundians, or the graceful, tall-stemmed glass for Rhine wines or Moselles.

Port and **sherry**—Although port in both England and the United States is frequently sipped from the squat port glass and sherry from the Y-shaped glass, neither of these glasses is as satisfying as the dock glass, which can be used for either port or sherry and is favored by both sherrymen in Spain and port connoisseurs in Oporto. For Madeira, too, the dock glass is recommended.

Champagne—The glass that is the darling of most enlightened champagne drinkers is a slightly narrower version of the all-purpose wineglass but with a taller stem. It is never more than half-filled. Saucer champagne glasses allow a somewhat faster release of bubbles and are customarily used for champagne cocktails. The long throat of the hollow-stemmed champagne glass is designed to show continuing life in bubbly; it's also used for sparkling Burgundy.

Beer—The trumpet-shaped pilsner glass retains cold and fizz as long as possible and is the proper glass for a Black Velvet (Guinness stout and champagne). The heavy glass stein is a perfect suds container at bull sessions and bachelor parties. The glass tankard with graceful lines is made with a weighted bottom. The silver or pewter tankard with glass bottom is in the best English tradition for leisurely sipping ale or stout.

How many glasses should you own? It depends on the maximum number of people your pad can comfortably contain at any one time. Double that number to account for drop-ins and for normal glassware breakage. Thus, if you usually invite eight for a party, stock sixteen of each kind of glass that you'd be most likely to use.

Other Tools of the Trade

Below is a tableau of bar gadgetry showing some of the most useful implements for the conveniences and pleasures of party drinking.

- **Long tongs** snugly grip ice cubes, although in many wet circles of society, hands are de rigueur for picking up rocks from an ice bucket.

- A **cork bottle-stopper** with a no-drip pouring end is useful for dispensing anything from crème de cassis to vermouth.

- A **coil-rimmed strainer** for the cocktail mixing glass is a good trap against ice floes tumbling into the cocktail glass.

- A small glass **compote dish** is a convenient vessel for cherries, olives, and onions.

- A **long-handled bar spoon/stirrer** is used either in a cocktail mixing glass or as a substitute for a glass Martini stirrer, as well as for stirring all long, deep potations—coolers, pitchers, punches, and Zombies.

- An **ice pick** may be used for chipping large ice blocks into suitable sizes for punch bowls and is also useful for unsticking ice cubes in an ice bucket.

- A **jigger** with ½- and 1½-ounce measures is ideal for measuring liquor.

- An **olive**, **onion**, or **cherry grabber** will find its mark even in the most stubborn bottle.

- A **nutmeg grater** is welcome for long, year-end partying when flips, nogs, grogs, and gloggs are flowing.

- A sturdy metal **bottle stopper** is less likely to get lost than a common plastic disc. Keeps anything from club soda to bitter lemon sparkling from one night to the next.

- Both drinking glass and drink look better when placed on an attractive **coaster**. The trouble with most shoddy coasters isn't that they disappear but that they don't disappear fast enough.

- This stainless steel **knife cum-opener** has a pronged edge for stabbing fruit and other garnishes.

- A sturdy, capacious **cutting board** is less likely to warp than a small thin version; the board doubles as kitchen equipment.

- A heavy-duty **lime** or **lemon squeezer** is indispensable for squeezing fruit into fizzes, tonics, and tall mixtures with juniper juice.

- The fang of a heavy-duty **can opener** sinks easily into metal.

- A set of standard **measuring spoons** is indispensable in formulas calling for small quantities of flavoring liqueurs, juices, or bitters.

- A sharp, well-balanced **French knife** is best for slicing fruit.

- A folding-flat waiter's **corkscrew** is good for itinerant bartenders carrying pocket equipment to beaches and mountain sites for fun and games.

- A **bottle-cap opener** of the husky type provides good leverage.

- A **shaker**—stainless steel is preferred—is a must for making those cocktails that call for eggs, cream, heavy liqueurs, or other hard-to-mix ingredients.

- A **wing-type corkscrew** permits you to use both hands for extracting stubborn corks. (Many hosts have abandoned the conventional corkscrew in favor of the CO_2 bottle opener. A small charge of CO_2 —which has no effect whatsoever on a wine's flavor—gently raises the cork out of the bottle without wrenching muscles.)

All the Trimmings

The applied art of mixing alcoholic drinks depends on many things that aren't alcohol. Alcohol must be made tart, sweet, rich, bitter, foamy, and in countless other ways congenial to sophisticated taste buds. Frequently a drink (a shot included!) is garnished in a manner that accents its appearance as well as its flavor and aroma—as with the olive in the Martini, the cucumber peel in the Pimm's Cup, or the strawberry in the champagne cocktail.

The number of accessories you choose to acquire for mixing will depend on whether you're going in for mass drinking or for more modest quenching.

The checklist that follows should be consulted not only for setting up a basic bar stock but also every time you're hosting a drinking party of sizable dimensions. Items that belong in any basic bar are marked with an asterisk to differentiate them from those less frequently used.

Mixing Aids

Almonds—Use them whole for Scandinavian glogg, sliced or julienne for floating on punches and tall summer drinks.

Almond syrup—Called orgeat when made in France, orzata when made in Italy. Some liqueurs with a vivid almondlike flavor—such as amaretto, made from apricot pits—may be used in place of the nonalcoholic almond syrup.

Apple juice—Often found in congenial company with vodka. The space-saving frozen concentrate variety is handy for parties. (*See also Cider.*)

Apricots—Whole peeled canned apricots are better than the fresh for velvety blender drinks.

Bananas—They should always be speckled ripe for bar purposes. They're turned to best account in Banana Daiquiris.

*****Bitter lemon**—A superior mixer in high esteem among the Gin and Tonic crowd.

Bitter lemon concentrate—An essence that may be added to plain club soda in an emergency.

*****Bitters**—Best known is Angostura from Trinidad, but orange bitters are sometimes preferred for drinks that benefit from a soupçon of citrus. It's a good idea to keep Peychaud's bitters (obtainable in some areas only in liquor stores) on hand for making New Orleans Sazeracs.

Butter—Use fresh sweet butter for a mellow glow in hot buttered rum.

Cassis—This black currant syrup—simpatico with vermouth—is similar to crème de cassis, except it contains no alcohol.

*Cherries—Most common are the maraschino, with or without stems. Mint-flavored cherries provide a green decorative note; brandied pitted red cherries and pitted black cherries, with or without rum flavor, complete the cherry constellation.

Cider—In groceries, "apple cider" and "apple juice" are synonymous terms for pasteurized juice of the apple. Country cider, sold at roadside stands, is often partially fermented apple juice. Hard cider is apple juice fermented to the wine stage.

Cinnamon sticks (or stick cinnamon)—Used for both stirring and flavoring hot mulled mixes. Buy the extra long sticks for drinks in deep mugs.

Cloves—Add them whole (not ground) to hot winter wassail.

*****Club soda**—Buy it in splits for individual drinks, the 12-ounce size for several highballs, and quarts for parties or punch bowls. Most brands have good bite and can keep their fizz locked up overnight or even for several days. Generally, club soda provides more zing than seltzer water.

Cocktail mixes—(Not to be confused with bottled premixed cocktails.) Nonalcoholic mixes are never equal to the fresh ingredients, but many hosts like to keep them on hand as reserve ammunition. Mixes for the Bloody Mary, Daiquiri, Mai Tai, Manhattan, Navy Grog, Scorpion, and Whiskey Sour have become standard items in many home bars. While all bottles have specific mixing directions on their labels, try varying the alcohol-mix ratio to suit your own taste.

Coffee—Brew it fresh and strong for steaming Irish Coffee.

Cranberry juice—Adds brilliant color and eye-opening tartness to punches and vodka drinks.

Cream—Use heavy sweet cream for Alexanders and dessert drinks.

Currant syrup—Red currants (rather than black cassis berries) go into this tart extract. It's not a substitute for grenadine but a flavoring component in its own right.

Eggs—There would be no nog without them—nor a number of frothy confections such as Clover Clubs, Silver Fizzes, and the like. Use a small size for individual drinks. (Note: Raw eggs can pose a food safety hazard; if your recipe calls for raw or lightly cooked eggs, be sure to buy pasteurized eggs. Never use an egg that has a cracked shell.)

Falernum—A delightful West Indian syrup made from almonds and spices.

*Frothee Creamy Head—A few splashes of this egg-white concentrate will give mixed drinks the creamy cap supplied otherwise by fresh egg whites; however, the head tends to disappear faster than an egg-white head.

*Ginger ale—The drier the better for modern tastes.

Ginger beer—The second-fiddle catalyst in a Moscow Mule.

Grapefruit juice—The one fruit juice that's better canned or frozen than fresh, undoubtedly because the latter is often quite insipid and varies so much in flavor. The unsweetened variety is best for drink making.

Grape juice—One of vodka's many compatible consorts. The frozen concentrate form is a space saver.

Grenadine—A bright red syrup made from the pulp of pomegranates, it's used in the Jack Rose, Clover Club, Bacardi, and many other cocktails, as well as in punches and tall drinks. Unlike most additives, it can be stored on the shelf for long periods without losing its tint or tartness. Grenadine liqueur, made by Leroux, may be used in place of its non alcoholic cousin.

Guanabana nectar—The luscious juice of the soursop, moderately sweetened, makes a delicious partner in rum drinks.

Guava jelly—Melted down to syrup, it's used for sweetening Caribbean rum drinks.

Honey—Use a light-colored honey for bar purposes. If granulation occurs, place the jar in hot water for a few minutes and then stir until the granules disappear.

Lemon juice—The bottled juice, whether in glass or plastic containers, never equals the fresh-squeezed variety and should be kept on hand for emergency use only.

*Lemons—They should be firm and green stemmed. The size of the fruit is not too important because most recipes calling for lemon juice use ounce measurements. Before squeezing, using the palm of the hand, lean on the fruit on a cutting board, rolling it back and forth to make squeezing easier and to extract more juice.

Lime juice—As with lemon juice, the bottled product should be used only in emergencies.

*Lime juice, sweetened—The best-known brand, Rose's, is actually a tart syrup rather than a substitute for fresh lime juice, and is an essential ingredient in a Gimlet.

*Limes—A far-from-silent partner in almost all rum drinks. Choose limes with smooth green skin rather than yellow.

Mangoes or mango nectar—An exotic ingredient in some tall rum drinks.

Maple syrup—Used occasionally as a drink sweetener.

Milk—Essential in many brandy drinks, milk punches, and eggnogs. Use whole milk rather than skim for best results.

Mint, fresh—Mint leaves are best if taken from the mint patch directly to julep cups or glasses. When using fresh mint, choose leaves that are deep green rather than yellowed, and use small, tender leaves rather than large.

Nutmeg—Used in flips, nogs, mulls, and other warmed cold-weather drinks. Buy the whole nutmeg for grating rather than the ground.

*Olives—Although the small pitted variety is a standard bar ingredient, many Martini drinkers prefer the unpitted, stuffed colossal, or supercolossal. There are also almond-, anchovy-, and onion-stuffed olives, all of which are delightful and even pitted black olives are used in some Martini-type drinks. Be sure to store recapped jars in the refrigerator; olives should be kept in their own brine and washed just before serving. The flavor of the olives will deteriorate if stored for more than a few weeks.

Onions, cocktail or pearl—The sine qua non of the Gibson cocktail. Buy them in small jars and store in the refrigerator after opening. Bottled in vinegar or in vermouth and vinegar.

Orange-flower water—A clear distillation of orange blossoms that is an essential ingredient in a Ramos Gin Fizz; sometimes labeled fleur d'orange. Available in gourmet food shops and in some liquor stores.

Oranges—Juice from fresh oranges is always better than frozen juice or the kind that comes in cartons or bottles, even though the fresh fruit varies widely in sweetness and color throughout the year. (Frozen juice also varies in quality and flavor from one brand to the next. If you must use it, say, for large blowouts, select the best brand you can find.)

Orange slices—Actually wedges rather than slices, they're packed in syrup in jars. They provide a rich garnish for an Old-Fashioned.

Orgeat (from France) or **orzata** (from Italy)—Nonalcoholic almond syrups. (*See Almond syrup.*)

Papaya syrup or **nectar**—One of the tropical juices occasionally called for in Polynesian rum drinks.

Passion fruit juice or **nectar**—A pleasantly tart mixer used in rum drinks.

Peaches—Sliced fresh in season, they make an elegant adornment for champagne, sparkling Rhine wine, and wine cups. Elbertas—frozen or canned—are best for crushed-ice blender drinks.

Pineapple—When buying, check for ripeness: the top-center leaves should come out easily and the fruit should have a heavy, musky pineapple aroma. Pineapple cocktail sticks in syrup are a pleasant cocktail garnish.

Pineapple juice—Best for bar purposes is the frozen concentrate, followed by the canned, unsweetened variety. If canned juice is stored in the refrigerator after opening, be sure to pour it into a glass jar and cover tightly to ward off refrigerator aromas.

Quinine concentrate—Used for making quinine water (commonly known as tonic) by adding to seltzer water or club soda; it's useful on boats and in other cramped bar quarters.

*Quinine water (a.k.a. tonic) —A staple bar item that you should keep on hand in quantity for warm-weather drinks.

Raspberries—Use fresh or frozen in summer wine cups, punch bowls, and blender drinks.

not as tart as grenadine, has
vor.

y Marys, Bloody Marias,
the Bloody genre and in
ed with lemon is packed
andy when applying the

eldom has the liveliness
dge charge for permanent
ough rarely seen today.

carbonated lemon drinks, it can
e potable.

d ginger ale, sodas with flavors
d grapefruit are pleasant tall-

Strawberries—Fresh berries make a colorful garnish for May wine, wine cups, fancy drinks, and summer fruit bowls. Frozen ones can be used in blender drinks with crushed ice.

Strawberry syrup—This is one of the brightest members in the family of red bar sweeteners. Be sure it's a natural, not artificial, fruit flavor—and don't keep it too long on the shelf.

*Sugar—For the bar, superfine sugar, which dissolves quickly, is preferred to plain granulated, but if kept too long after the box is opened, it will tend to lump, in which case it should be put through a fine sieve. Do not use confectioners' sugar. Brown sugar is rarely called for except in hot mulled drinks.

Sugar syrup (simple syrup)—Some of the commercially prepared table syrups may be too thick for easy blending. Exceptions are Wuppermann's bar syrup and rock-candy syrup. Or make your own: bring 1 cup of water to a boil and stir in 1 cup of sugar; simmer 1 ½ minutes. The mixture should reduce to approximately 1 cup, making it possible to substitute equal amounts of syrup for sugar in any bar recipe in which it may be preferred. Pour any leftovers into a bottle or syrup container and store at room temperature. There may be some crystallization of the sugar in time, but that won't affect the syrup's usefulness.

Tea—Punch bowls of colonial times often called for brewed tea as part of the liquid. Brew it for five minutes, then let it cool at room temperature to prevent the drink from clouding.

*Tomato juice—The base for Bloody Marys and many other pick-me-ups. Buy straight tomato juice rather than tomato-juice cocktails such as V-8, Clamato, etc. (Personal preference may vary, of course,

as mentioned below in Vegetable juice.) Jars rather than cans are best for refrigerator storage.

*Tonic water—Without this staple, there would be no Gin and Tonics. (See Quinine water.)

Vegetable juice—Sometimes preferred to tomato juice in a Bloody Mary because its blend of flavors lends a somewhat livelier, more interesting flavor to the drink.

*Water—At out-of-the-way picnics and lonely beach sites, a bottle of this offbeat ingredient is sometimes desirable as an additive to Scotch. In localities where tap water is rusty or has a pronounced taste of chlorine, use bottled spring water.

Worcestershire sauce—A snappy accent for Prairie Oysters, Bloody Marys, and the like.

Barmanship

Familiarize yourself with the basic barman's skills that follow and consult them for special potables, and every time you pour drinks, you'll generate among your guests the mood described superlatively by novelist Henry Fielding as "one universal grin."

Icemanship

Every barman—amateur or pro—should insist that his ice is clean, hard, and dry, and he should make each drink or batch of drinks with fresh ice. Hoard your ice in the freezer until you actually need it. Use ice buckets with vacuum sides and lids; plastic-foam ice tubs are convenient for throwaway service. When you empty your ice trays, don't run water over them unless it's absolutely necessary to spring the ice free—the water will cause them to stick together after they're put in the bucket. Or you may have a refrigerator that not only makes ice cubes automatically but turns them out and stores them night and day—a comforting thought when one is party planning. If the water in your fiefdom is heavily chlorinated, use bottled spring water for ice. Finally, as a host, be the most prodigal of icemen. If you're gambling on the fact that you may just possibly get by with two buckets of ice at a summer fling, don't gamble. Provide at least three or four bucketfuls for supercooling your crowd. If your ice-making equipment is somewhat limited, find out before your rumpus takes place where you can buy additional ice.

The Mechanics of Mixing and Pouring

Filling the shaker Ice should always go into the shaker first, alcohol last. By giving ice first place, all the ingredients that follow will be cooled on their way down. Furthermore, once you acquire the habit of adding the liquor last, it's unlikely that you'll inadvertently double the spirits or, worse yet, forget them altogether, both possible errors for hosts taking jolts along with their guests. The order of ingredients between ice and alcohol follows no dogmatic ritual; whether sugar should precede the lemon juice or vice versa isn't important so far as the final drink is concerned. One useful control for drinking hosts is to put the correct number of glasses for the needed drinks in front of the shaker before adding anything—a clear reminder of how many dashes of bitters, how many spoons of this or jiggers of that are necessary. Finally, never fill a shaker to the brim; allow enough room for all ingredients to be tossed back and forth—to set up the clear, pleasant rattle of ice.

Measuring Guests at a pour-it-yourself bar should feel free to pour as many fingers as they please, but if the host himself is preparing any kind of mixed drink, he should trust the jigger rather than his eye, just as the best professional bartenders always do.

Stirring To keep their icy clarity, cocktails such as Martinis, Manhattans, Rob Roys, and Gimlets should always be stirred, not shaken. (However, it's no major disaster—and sometimes a matter of preference—if you unwittingly shake rather than stir a Martini; it will turn cloudy, but only for a few minutes.) For proper dilution, stir every batch of cocktails at least twenty times. When carbonated water is added to tall drinks, stir as briefly as possible; most of the liquor rises to the top automatically, and excessive stirring only dissipates the sparkle in the water.

Shaking

Shake the shaker, not yourself. Don't just rock it—hold it well out in front of you and move it diagonally from lower left to upper right, or in any other convenient motion, with a pistonlike rhythm. In time the icy feel of the cocktail shaker will tell you that the drinks are ready for pouring. Shake one round of drinks at a time and rinse the shaker thoroughly after each use.

Pouring When drinks have been shaken, pour them at once; don't let the cocktail shaker become a watery grave. If extra liquid is left in the shaker, strain it off at once; the so-called dividends left standing in ice will be weak replicas of the original drinks. When garnishes such as orange slices and pineapple sticks are being used, allow sufficient room to add them without causing the drink to overflow. When pouring more than one mixed drink, line up the glasses rim to rim, fill them half full, then pour again to the same height in each glass.

Special Effects

Floating liqueurs Drinks are sometimes served with a spoonful of liqueur or 151-proof rum floating on top; usually such toppings are merely poured slowly from a spoon against the side of the glass. The Pousse-Café, on the other hand, is a multilayered after-dinner drink whose rainbow effect can be created in any one of four ways: (1) first pour the heaviest liqueur slowly against the side of the glass, following it in turn with progressively lighter liqueurs, a procedure that can be learned through trial and error or by following the drink recipes included in this book; (2) pour the liqueurs over an inverted small spoon held at the top of the glass; (3) pour the liqueurs down the side of a mixing rod held in the glass; or (4) pour the liqueurs slowly into the glass in any sequence you desire, place the glass in your refrigerator, and in time each liqueur will find its own weight level, forming distinct layers.

Flaming liquors Occasionally brandy or liqueurs are set aflame in a drink. For this bit of showmanship, the liquor should be preheated briefly—not boiled, which causes the alcohol to evaporate, but simply made hot enough so that when a flame is held to the liquor, it will begin to blaze quietly.

Say When

A Short Course in the Math of Mixology

The shots in this book are measured in "parts," as in 1 part this and 2 parts that. This serves two purposes. First, it makes the recipes work even if you're metrically challenged, and there's no need to convert between ounces and centiliters. The other reason for listing is to allow for different glassware. Different glasses might call for different amounts, but proportionally the ingredients are always the same: 1 part this and 2 parts that.

This said, you have to choose your unit or measurement. Here's a basic guide:

Undoubtedly the traditional 1 ½-ounce bar jigger will continue to be the standard unit for mixing or measuring individual drinks. Other units of liquid measurement from a dash to a nip, as well as old and new bottle sizes, are described below. They should help you take a recipe for a single drink and magnify it at will, or reduce a giant-size punch bowl to the desired amount of wassail.

Dash—For all drink recipes in this book, a dash means ⅛ teaspoon; two dashes will thus fill a ¼-teaspoon measure. Theoretically, a dash is the amount of liquid that squirts out of a bottle equipped with a dash stopper. Stoppers, however, vary in size, and to different liquor dispensers a dash means anything from three drops up, but dashes have potent flavor or they wouldn't be dashes, so it's important to be as accurate as possible. Thus, if you're making Sazeracs for sixteen people and you need sixteen times a dash of Pernod, a little calculating will quickly tell you that you need 2 teaspoons of Pernod, and it's best to measure it exactly rather than make a clumsy guess.

Teaspoon—Equals ⅓ tablespoon, or ⅙ ounce. Use a measuring spoon, not a long-handled bar spoon, which is designed for mixing rather than measuring.

Tablespoon—Equals 3 teaspoons, or ½ ounce.

Pony—Equals 1 ounce, or the small end of a double-ended measuring jigger. Also equals the normal capacity of the liqueur glass or the pousse-café glass.

Jigger—Equals 1½ ounces. Also called a bar measuring glass, it's the standard measure for mixing individual drinks, though generous hosts use a 2-ounce jigger. Although jiggers are supposed to provide exact measurements, they're sometimes grossly inaccurate, so it's a good idea, if possible, to check any new jigger you buy against a lab measuring glass.

Wineglass—Used as a measuring term, it equals 4 ounces, which is the amount of an old-fashioned wineglass filled to the brim. But today wine is generally served in a much larger glass—one-third full to permit the wine to be swirled for releasing its bouquet—though the wineglass as a 4-ounce measure still appears in some drink recipes and in food recipes.

Split or nip—Equals 6 to 8 ounces, about the same as a half-pint, or the standard 1-cup measure. One refers to a split of champagne, but the same quantity of stout is called a nip.

Pint—Measures 16 ounces, ½ quart, or two standard measuring cups.

Fifth—Measures 25.6 ounces, ⅘ quart, ⅕ gallon, or 750 milliliters.

Quart—Measures 32 ounces, 2 pints, 4 cups, ¼ gallon. Not to be confused (in Canada and England) with the imperial quart, which equals 38.4 ounces, or (in continental Europe) with the liter, which equals 33.8 ounces. (Most standard wine and champagne bottles contain 750 milliliters, or 25.6 fluid ounces, the same as a fifth.)

Magnum—Measures about 52 ounces, or double the size of a standard champagne bottle.

Keep Your Spirits Up

Let's assume you're planning to stock a home bar and you don't as yet own an ounce of the straight stuff. It's always a comfortable if not sumptuous feeling to buy your liquor leisurely rather than under the pressure of some sudden emergency at the liquor cabinet. But when stocking a bar for the first time or building up your present liquor inventory, don't attempt to range the gamut of the spirit world from anisette to zubrovka; consider rather the tastes of the group that socializes casually with you. If the drinking companions in your neck of the woods have a habitual thirst for Sloe Gin Fizzes, you'll want to have sloe gin on hand even though it isn't mentioned in any of the combinations that follow. If there are those in your crowd who are happy only with Harvey Wallbangers (orange juice, vodka, and Galliano liqueur), you'll need Galliano—and ignore the liquor adviser who tells you that Galliano is only an after-dinner liqueur.

At the outset, a typical supply might reasonably consist of the following bottled goods (assume the list indicates liters, except for assorted liqueurs and aperitifs, for which a smaller size should suffice).

- **Whiskey** or **Whisky**—Irish or American, respectively

- **Scotch**—Quality blended or single malt (unblended)

- **Gin**—English, Dutch, Damrak (citrus flavored with a touch of honeysuckle)

- **Vodka**—Finnish, Polish, Norwegian, Russian, zubrovka, many-flavored

- **Rum**—Bacardi, Virgin Islands, Jamaican, añejo, 151 proof

- **Brandy**—Cognac, Armagnac, apple, German, Greek Metaxa, ouzo

- **Liqueurs**—From straight flavors like apricot or banana to proprietary brands like Southern Comfort, Wild Turkey, Grand Marnier, Cointreau, Chartreuse, Drambuie, Benedictine, Peter Heering, etc.

- **Aperitifs**—Amer Picon, Byrrh, Cinzano, Cynar, Lillet, Punt e Mes

Going still further one might wish to add:

- **Whiskey**—Japanese Suntory

- **Unaged brandies**—Aquavit,
  slivovitz, kirschwasser

Finally, a few sensible reminders:
Your bar may be a movable one on wheels,
a built-in piece of sectional furniture, the
shelves above a clothes closet, a tea wagon,
or a wicker hamper in the back of your station
wagon. Reserve supplies may be stashed away
wherever it's convenient—in cellar or attic.
But within easy reach, close to your mixing
counter, there should be one bottle of each
commonly used liquor. Your inventory isn't an
old rock collection to be hunted for behind

bookshelves, nor is a host normally able to pop fifths Houdini-like out of a silk hat. Keep everything arranged conveniently so that you can find the liquor you're looking for without fumbling or squinting at labels. For big blowouts and punch-bowl parties, fill in your stock well in advance of the fest itself. Don't get caught scrounging for replacements at the eleventh hour.

A host may commence many things; he may finish few. But every host at his home-bar base learns that the one thing that always gets finished is liquor. Still, you may now and then find an odd bottle that has reached the aged-in-the-coffin stage. Take such oddments, supplement them with fresh liquors, and turn them into coolers, pitchers, or punches. It's fun to invent them and to make room simultaneously for new liquors that may readily become a going concern.

Bar Starter Kit

- 3 Vodka
- 2 Blended whiskey, U.S.
- 2 Gin
- 1 Dry vermouth
- 1 Sweet vermouth
- 2 Rum
- 3 Assorted liqueurs
  (fruit, coffee, crème de
  menthe, etc.)

- 2 Bourbon
- 2 Scotch
- 1 Canadian whiskey
- 2 Tequila
- 1 Brandy, U.S.
- 1 Aperitif
  (Campari, Dubonnet,
  etc.)

Shots & Shooters

10 LB. SLEDGEHAMMER

- 1 part Tequila
- 1 part Jack Daniel's®
- Shot Glass

Pour ingredients into glass neat (do not chill)

24 SEVEN

- 2 parts Melon Liqueur
- 1 part Green Chartreuse®
- 4 parts Pineapple Juice
- ½ part Sweetened Lime Juice
- Shot Glass

Shake with ice and strain

252

- 1 part 151-Proof Rum
- 1 part Wild Turkey® 101
- Shot Glass

Pour ingredients into glass neat (do not chill)

3 WISE MEN

- 1 part Jack Daniel's®
- 1 part Johnnie Walker® Black Label
- 1 part Jim Beam®
- Shot Glass

Pour ingredients into glass neat (do not chill)

40 SKIT AND A BENT JANT

- 1 part Blue Curaçao
- 1 part Jägermeister®
- 1 part Citrus-Flavored Vodka
- 1 part Peach Schnapps
- 1 part Cranberry Juice Cocktail
- 1 part Pineapple Juice
- splash Lime Juice
- Shot Glass

Shake with ice and strain

49ER GOLD RUSH

- 1 part Goldschläger®
- 1 part Tequila
- Shot Glass

Shake with ice and strain

649

- Various Ingredients (see below)
- Shot Glass

Stand facing the bar and count off the bottles: 6th from right, 4th from left, and 9th from right. Pour equal parts of each into a shot glass neat (do not chill).

8 BALL

- 4 parts Coconut-Flavored Rum
- 4 parts Peach Schnapps
- 4 parts Raspberry Liqueur
- 4 parts Vodka
- splash Lemon-Lime Soda
- 1 ½ parts Cranberry Juice Cocktail
- 1 ½ parts Sour Mix
- splash Grenadine
- Shot Glass

Shake with ice and strain

8 SECONDS

- 1 part Jägermeister®
- 1 part Goldschläger®
- 1 part Hot Damn!® Cinnamon Schnapps
- 1 part Rumple Minze®
- Shot Glass

Shake with ice and strain

911

- 1 part 100-Proof Peppermint Schnapps
- 1 part 100-Proof Cinnamon Schnapps
- Shot Glass

Pour ingredients into glass neat (do not chill)

A-BOMB

- 1 part Vodka
- 1 part Coffee
- 1/2 part Cold Coffee
- Shot Glass

Shake with ice and strain

ABSOHOT

- 1/2 part Absolut® Peppar Vodka
- splash Hot Sauce
- 1 Beer
- Shot Glass

Mix Vodka and Hot Sauce in a shot glass. Serve with beer chaser.

ABSOLUT® ANTIFREEZE

- 1 part Melon Liqueur
- 2 parts Absolut® Citron Vodka
- 2 parts Lemon-Lime Soda
- Shot Glass

Shake with ice and strain

ABSOLUT® ASSHOLE

- 2 parts Vodka
- 1 part Sour Apple Schnapps
- Shot Glass

Shake with ice and strain

ABSOLUT® HUNTER

- 2 parts Vodka
- 1 part Jägermeister®
- Shot Glass

Shake with ice and strain

ABSOLUT® PASSION

- 2 parts Vodka
- 1 part Passion Fruit Juice
- Shot Glass

Shake with ice and strain

ABSOLUT® PEPPARMINT

- 1 part Absolut® Peppar Vodka
- splash Peppermint Schnapps
- Shot Glass

Shake with ice and strain

ABSOLUT® TESTA ROSSA

- 1 part Vodka
- ½ part Campari®
- Shot Glass

Shake with ice and strain

ABSOLUTELY FRUITY

- 1 part Vodka
- 1 part 99-Proof Banana Liqueur
- 1 part Watermelon Schnapps
- Shot Glass

Shake with ice and strain

ABSOLUTELY SCREWED

- 1 part Orange-Flavored Vodka
- 1 part Orange Juice
- Shot Glass

Shake with ice and strain

ACID COOKIE

- 1 part Irish Cream Liqueur
- 1 part Butterscotch Schnapps
- 1 part Hot Damn!® Cinnamon Schnapps
- splash 151-Proof Rum
- Shot Glass

Shake with ice and strain

THE ACTION CONTRACTION

- 1 part Banana Liqueur
- 1 part Peppermint Schnapps
- 1 part Sambuca

- splash Lemon Juice
- Shot Glass

Shake with ice and strain

ADAM BOMB

- 1 part Sour Apple Schnapps
- 1 part Goldschläger®

- Shot Glass

Shake with ice and strain

ADIOS, MOTHERFUCKER

- 1 part Vodka
- 1 part Gin
- 1 part Rum
- 1 part Tequila
- 1 part Triple Sec
- 2 parts Sour Mix
- splash Cola
- splash Blue Curaçao
- Shot Glass

Shake with ice and strain. *Note: Because this recipe includes many ingredients, it's easier to make in volume, about 6 shots.

ADULT LIT

- 1 part Dry Gin
- 1 part Vodka
- 1 part Triple Sec
- 1 part Light Rum
- Shot Glass

Shake with ice and strain

AFFAIR SHOT

- 1 part Strawberry Liqueur
- 1 part Orange Juice
- Shot Glass

Shake with ice and strain

AFTER EIGHT® SHOOTER

- 1 part Crème de Cacao (White)
- 1 part Crème de Menthe (White)
- 1 part Vodka
- Shot Glass

Shake with ice and strain

AFTERBURNER

- 1 part After Shock® Cinnamon Schnapps
- 1 part 151-Proof Rum
- Shot Glass

Pour ingredients into glass neat (do not chill)

AFTERBURNER #2

- 1 part Pepper-Flavored Vodka
- 1 part Coffee
- 1 part Goldschläger®
- Shot Glass

Pour ingredients into glass neat (do not chill)

AIRHEAD

- 1 ½ parts Peach Schnapps
- fill with Cranberry Juice Cocktail
- Shot Glass

Shake with ice and strain

ALABAMA SLAMMER

- 1 part Coffee Liqueur
- 1 part Tequila
- 1 part Lemon-Lime Soda
- Shot Glass

Shake with ice and strain

ALABAMA SLAMMER #2

- 1 part Southern Comfort®
- 1 part Jack Daniel's®
- 1 part Amaretto
- splash Orange Juice
- splash Grenadine
- Shot Glass

Shake with ice and strain

ALASKAN OIL SLICK

- 1 part Blue Curaçao
- 1 part Peppermint Schnapps
- splash Jägermeister®
- Shot Glass

Chill Blue Curaçao and strain into shot glass. Float Jägermeister® on top.

ALASKAN PIPELINE

- 1 part Yukon Jack®
- 1 part Amaretto
- Shot Glass

Shake with ice and strain

ALCOHOLIC PEPPERMINT PATTIE

- 1 part Rumple Minze®
- ½ part Chocolate Syrup
- Shot Glass

Pour Chocolate Syrup into your mouth, followed by a shot of Rumple Minze®. Shake it around and swallow.

ALICE FROM DALLAS SHOOTER

- 1 part Coffee Liqueur
- 1 part Mandarine Napoléon® Liqueur
- 1 part Tequila Reposado
- Shot Glass

Shake with ice and strain

ALIEN

- 1 part Blue Curaçao
- splash Irish Cream Liqueur
- Shot Glass

Pour the Blue Curaçao into a chilled shot glass, then pour the Irish Cream into the center

ALIEN SECRETION

- 1 part Vodka
- 1 part Melon Liqueur
- 1 part Coconut-Flavored Rum
- 1 part Pineapple Juice
- Shot Glass

Shake with ice and strain

ALMOND COOKIE

- 1 part Amaretto
- 1 part Butterscotch Schnapps
- Shot Glass

Shake with ice and strain

ALPINE BREEZE

- 1 part Pineapple Juice
- 1 part Grenadine
- ½ part Crème de Menthe (White)
- ½ part Dark Rum
- Shot Glass

Shake with ice and strain

AMARETTO CHILL

- 1 part Vodka
- 1 part Amaretto
- 1 part Lemonade
- 1 part Pineapple Juice
- Shot Glass

Shake with ice and strain

AMARETTO KAMIKAZE

- 1 part Vodka
- 1 part Amaretto
- fill with Sour Mix
- Shot Glass

Shake with ice and strain

AMARETTO LEMONDROP

- 1 part Vodka
- 1 part Amaretto
- fill with Lemonade
- Shot Glass

Build over ice and stir

AMARETTO PIE

- 1 part Amaretto
- 1 part Orange Juice
- 1 part Pineapple Juice
- Shot Glass

Shake with ice and strain

AMARETTO SLAMMER

- 1 part Amaretto
- 1 part Lemon-Lime Soda
- Shot Glass

Combine in a shot glass. Cover with your hand, slam on the bar, and drink.

AMARETTO SLAMMER #2

- 1 part Amaretto
- 1 part Cherry-Flavored Schnapps
- Shot Glass

Shake with ice and strain over ice

AMARETTO SOURBALL

- 1 part Vodka
- 1 part Amaretto
- 1 part Lemonade
- 1 part Orange Juice
- Shot Glass

Shake with ice and strain

AMARETTO SWEET TART

- 1 part Vodka
- 1 part Amaretto
- 1 part Cherry Juice
- 1 part Wild Berry Schnapps
- fill with Lemonade
- Shot Glass

Shake with ice and strain

AMENIE MAMA

- 3 parts Irish Whiskey
- 1 part Amaretto
- Shot Glass

Shake with ice and strain

AMERICAN APPLE PIE

- 1 part Cinnamon Schnapps
- 1 part Apple Juice
- Shot Glass

Shake with ice and strain

AMERICAN DREAM

- 1 part Coffee Liqueur
- 1 part Amaretto
- 1 part Frangelico®
- 1 part Crème de Cacao (Dark)
- Shot Glass

Shake with ice and strain

ANABOLIC STERIODS

- 2 parts Triple Sec
- 2 parts Melon Liqueur
- 1 part Blue Curaçao
- Shot Glass

Shake with ice and strain

ANDIES

- 1 part Crème de Cacao (Dark)
- 1 part Crème de Menthe (White)
- Shot Glass

Shake with ice and strain

ANGEL WING

- 1 part Crème de Cacao (White)
- 1 part Brandy
- Shot Glass

Shake with ice and strain

ANGEL'S LIPS

- 1 part Irish Cream Liqueur
- 2 parts Benedictine®
- Shot Glass

Shake with ice and strain

ANGEL'S RUSH SHOOTER

- 1 part Cream
- 1 part Frangelico®
- Shot Glass

Shake with ice and strain

THE ANGRY GERMAN

- 1 part Amaretto
- 1 part Black Haus® Blackberry Schnapps
- 1 part Jägermeister®
- 2 parts Lime Juice
- dash Salt
- Shot Glass

Shake with ice and strain

ANITA

- 1 part Apricot Brandy
- 1 part Maraschino Liqueur
- 1 part Grenadine
- 1 part Campari®
- 1 part Cream
- Shot Glass

Shake with ice and strain. *Note: Because this recipe includes many ingredients, it's easier to make in volume, about 6 shots.

ANONYMOUS

- 1 part Southern Comfort®
- 1 part Raspberry Liqueur
- 1 part Sour Mix
- Shot Glass

Shake with ice and strain

ANTIFREEZE

- 1 part Crème de Menthe (Green)
- 1 part Vodka
- Shot Glass

Shake with ice and strain

APPLE AND CINNAMON JOY

- 1 part Sour Apple Schnapps
- splash Goldschläger®
- Shot Glass

Pour ingredients into glass neat (do not chill)

APPLE AND SPICE SHOOTER

- 1 part Sour Apple Schnapps
- 1 part Spiced Rum
- Shot Glass

Shake with ice and strain

APPLE COBBLER

- 1 part Sour Apple Schnapps
- 1 part Goldschläger®
- 1 part Irish Cream Liqueur
- Shot Glass

Shake with ice and strain

APPLE FUCKER

- 1 part Sour Apple Schnapps
- 1 part Vodka
- Shot Glass

Shake with ice and strain

APPLE JOLLY RANCHER®

- 1 part Melon Liqueur
- 1 part Sour Mix
- 1 part Crown Royal® Whiskey
- Shot Glass

Shake with ice and strain

APPLE KAMIHUZI

- 1 part Tequila
- 1 part Sour Apple Schnapps
- splash Sour Mix
- Shot Glass

Shake with ice and strain

APPLE KAMIKAZE

- 1 part Vodka
- 1 part Sour Apple Schnapps
- splash Sour Mix
- Shot Glass

Shake with ice and strain

APPLE LEMONDROP

- 1 part Vodka
- 1 part Sour Apple Schnapps
- splash Lemonade
- Shot Glass

Shake with ice and strain

APPLE MULE

- 1 part Amaretto
- 1 part Jack Daniel's®
- 1 ½ parts Lime Juice
- 2 parts Orange Juice
- 1 part Southern Comfort®
- 1 part Triple Sec
- Shot Glass

Shake with ice and strain. *Note: Because this recipe includes many ingredients, it's easier to make in volume, about 6 shots.

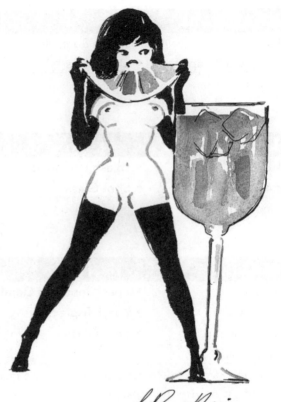

APPLE PIE SHOT

- 1 part Irish Mist®
- 1 part Cinnamon Schnapps
- 1 part Frangelico®
- 1 part Amaretto
- Shot Glass

Shake with ice and strain

APPLE CAKE

- 1 part Licor 43®
- 1 part Apple Brandy
- 1 part Milk
- Shot Glass

Shake with ice and strain

ARCTIC BRAIN FREEZE

- 1 part Amaretto
- 1 part Melon Liqueur
- Shot Glass

Shake with ice and strain

ARIZONA ANTIFREEZE

- 1 part Vodka
- 1 part Melon Liqueur
- 1 part Sour Mix
- Shot Glass

Shake with ice and strain

ARIZONA TWISTER

- 1 part Vodka
- 1 part Coconut-Flavored Rum
- 1 part Tequila
- splash Orange Juice
- splash Pineapple Juice
- splash Crème de Coconut
- splash Grenadine
- Shot Glass

Shake with ice and strain. *Note: Because this recipe includes many ingredients, it's easier to make in volume, about 6 shots.

ARKANSAS RATTLER

- 1 part Cinnamon Schnapps
- 1 part Tequila
- Shot Glass

Pour ingredients into glass neat (do not chill)

ARMY GREEN

- 1 part Goldschläger®
- 1 part Jägermeister®
- 1 part Tequila
- Shot Glass

Shake with ice and strain

ARTURROS' BURNING MINDTWISTER

- 1 part Scotch
- 1 part Tequila
- Shot Glass

Shake with ice and strain

ASTRONAUT SHOOTER

- 1 part Vodka (chilled)
- 1 Lemon Wedge
- dash Sugar
- dash Instant Coffee Granules
- Shot Glass

Coat the Lemon with Sugar on one side and Instant Coffee on the other, suck Lemon and drink the chilled Vodka

THE ATOMIC SHOT

- 1 part Tequila Silver
- 1 part Goldschläger®
- 1 part Absolut® Peppar Vodka
- splash Club Soda
- Shot Glass

Shake with ice and strain

AUBURN HEADBANGER

- 1 part Jägermeister®
- 1 part Goldschläger®
- Shot Glass

Shake with ice and strain

AVALANCHE SHOT

- 1 part Crème de Cacao (Dark)
- 1 part Coffee Liqueur
- 1 part Southern Comfort®
- Shot Glass

Shake with ice and strain

AWWWWWWW

- 1 part Gold Rum
- 1 part Triple Sec
- dash Bitters
- Shot Glass

Pour ingredients into glass neat (do not chill)

AZURRA

- 1 part Light Rum
- splash Crème de Cacao (White)
- splash Blue Curaçao
- Shot Glass

Shake with ice and strain

B-2 BOMBER

- 1 part Rum
- 1 part Southern Comfort®
- 1 part Lemon-Lime Soda
- 1 part Gatorade®
- Shot Glass

Shake with ice and strain

B-52

- 1 part Amaretto
- 2 parts Irish Cream Liqueur
- 1 part Rum
- Shot Glass

Pour the Amaretto, then the Irish Cream Liqueur, and then, carefully, the Rum. Light the shot on fire and drink it with a straw, or slap it to extinguish the flame and then drink.

B-54

- 1 part Irish Cream Liqueur
- 1 part Crème de Menthe (Green)
- 1 part Grand Marnier®
- 1 part Coffee Liqueur
- Shot Glass

Shake with ice and strain

BACK SHOT

- 1 part Vodka
- 1 part Raspberry Liqueur
- 2 parts Sour Mix
- Shot Glass

Shake with ice and strain

BACK STREET ROMEO

- 2 parts Whiskey
- 1 part Irish Cream Liqueur
- Shot Glass

Shake with ice and strain

BACKDRAFT SHOOTER

- 1 part Rum
- 1 part Cinnamon Schnapps
- Shot Glass

Pour ingredients into glass neat (do not chill)

BALD EAGLE SHOOTER

- 1 part Crème de Menthe (White)
- 1 part Tequila Reposado
- Shot Glass

Shake with ice and strain

BALL AND CHAIN

- 1 part Rumple Minze®
- 1 part Goldschläger®
- splash Jägermeister®
- Shot Glass

Shake with ice and strain

BALL HOOTER

- 1 part Tequila
- 1 part Peppermint Schnapps
- Shot Glass

Shake with ice and strain

BANAMON

- 1 part Pisang Ambon® Liqueur
- ½ part Amaretto
- ½ part Ginger Ale
- Shot Glass

Stir gently with ice and strain

BANANA BOAT SHOOTER

- 1 part Crème de Menthe (White)
- 1 part Coffee
- 1 part Ponche Kuba®
- Shot Glass

Shake with ice and strain

BANANA BOOMER SHOOTER

- 1 part Vodka
- 1 part Crème de Banana
- Shot Glass

Shake with ice and strain

BANANA CREAM PIE

- 1 part Banana Liqueur
- 1 part Crème de Cacao (White)
- 1 part Vodka
- 1 part Half and Half
- Shot Glass

Shake with ice and strain

BANANA LEMON SURPRISE

- 1 part Banana Liqueur
- 3 parts Lemon Juice
- Shot Glass

Shake with ice and strain

BANANA LICORICE

- 1 part Banana Liqueur
- ½ part Cherry Brandy
- ½ part Sambuca
- Shot Glass

Shake with ice and strain

BANANA POPSICLE® SHOOTER

- 1 part Vodka
- 1 part Crème de Banana
- 1 part Orange Juice
- Shot Glass

Shake with ice and strain

BANANA SLUG

- 3 parts 99-Proof Banana Liqueur
- 1 part Pineapple Juice
- Shot Glass

Shake with ice and strain

BANANA SPLIT SHOOTER

- 1 part Banana Liqueur
- 1 part Vodka
- Shot Glass

Shake with ice and strain

BANANA SWEET TART

- 1 part Vodka
- 1 part Banana Liqueur
- 1 part Cherry Juice
- fill with Lemonade
- Shot Glass

Shake with ice and strain

BANANAS AND CREAM

- 1 part Coffee Liqueur
- 1 part Irish Cream Liqueur
- 1 part 99-Proof Banana Liqueur
- Shot Glass

Shake with ice and strain

BANDERAS

- 1 part Tomato Juice
- 1 part Tequila Silver
- 1 part Lime Juice
- Shot Glass

Line up the shots to represent the Mexican flag: Tomato (red), Tequila (white), and Lime (green). Consume quickly in order.

BANSHEE SHOOTER

- 1 part Crème de Cacao (White)
- 1 part Cream
- 1 part Crème de Banana
- Shot Glass

Shake with ice and strain

BARBADOS BLAST

- 1 part Dark Rum
- 1 part Triple Sec
- 1 part Ginger Liqueur
- Shot Glass

Shake with ice and strain

BARBED WIRE

- 1 part Goldschläger®
- 1 part Sambuca
- Shot Glass

Shake with ice and strain

BARBIE® SHOT

- 1 part Coconut-Flavored Rum
- 1 part Vodka
- 1 part Cranberry Juice Cocktail
- 1 part Orange Juice
- Shot Glass

Shake with ice and strain

BARE ASS

- 1 part Amaretto
- splash Peach Schnapps
- 1/2 part Pineapple Juice
- Shot Glass

Shake with ice and strain

BARFING SENSATIONS

- 1 part Blackberry Liqueur
- 1 part Peach Schnapps
- 1 part Vodka
- 1 part Apple Brandy
- 1 part Raspberry Liqueur
- Shot Glass

Shake with ice and strain. *Note: Because this recipe includes many ingredients, it's easier to make in volume, about 6 shots.

BARNEY® ON ACID

- 1 part Blue Curaçao
- 1 part Jägermeister®
- splash Cranberry Juice Cocktail
- Shot Glass

Shake with ice and strain

BARTENDER'S WET DREAM

- 1 part Grenadine
- 1 part Coffee Liqueur
- 1 part Irish Cream Liqueur
- Shot Glass

Shake with ice and strain. Top with whipped cream.

BAYOU JUICE

- 1 part Coconut-Flavored Rum
- 1 part Spiced Rum
- 1 part Amaretto
- 1 part Cranberry Juice Cocktail
- 1 part Pineapple Juice
- Shot Glass

Shake with ice and strain

BAZOOKA® BUBBLE GUM

- 1 part Southern Comfort®
- 1 part Banana Liqueur
- 1 part Cream
- 1 part Grenadine
- Shot Glass

Shake with ice and strain

BAZOOKA JOE®

- 1 part Banana Liqueur
- 1 part Blue Curaçao
- 1 part Grand Marnier®
- Shot Glass

Shake with ice and strain

BAZOOKA MOE

- 1 part Blue Curaçao
- 1 part Crème de Banana
- Shot Glass

Shake with ice and strain

BEAR DOZER

- 1 part Tequila
- 1 part Whiskey
- 1 part Cherry Brandy
- Shot Glass

Shake with ice and strain

BEARDED BOY

- 1 part Southern Comfort®
- 1 part Vodka
- 1 part Water
- splash Grain Alcohol
- Shot Glass

Shake with ice and strain

BEAVER DAM

- 1 part Vodka
- 1 part Peach Schnapps
- 1 part Gatorade®
- Shot Glass

Shake with ice and strain

BEAVIS AND BUTT-HEAD®

- 1 part Sour Apple Schnapps
- 1 part Cinnamon Schnapps
- Shot Glass

Shake with ice and strain

A BEDROCK

- 1 part Sambuca
- 1 part Coffee Liqueur
- splash Milk
- Shot Glass

Shake with ice and strain

BELFAST CAR BOMB

- 1 pint Guinness® Stout
- 1 part Irish Cream Liqueur
- 1 part Scotch
- Shot Glass

Drop a shot glass filled with Scotch into a pint of Guiness and float an ounce of Irish Cream Liqueur on top.

BEND ME OVER SHOOTER

- 1 part Crown Royal® Whiskey
- 1 part Amaretto
- 1 part Sour Mix
- Shot Glass

Shake with ice and strain

BEOWULF

- 1 part Blue Curaçao
- 1 part Vodka
- Shot Glass

Shake with ice and strain

THE BERRY KIX®

- 2 parts Currant-Flavored Vodka
- 1 part Sour Mix
- Shot Glass

Shake with ice and strain

BERUBE'S DEATH

- 1 part Cinnamon Schnapps
- 1 part Black Sambuca
- 1 part Jägermeister®
- 1 part Rumple Minze®
- Shot Glass

Shake with ice and strain

BETTY COME BACK

- 2 parts Tequila Silver
- 1 part Triple Sec
- 1 part Parfait Amour
- Shot Glass

Shake with ice and strain

THE BIANCA POP

- 1 part Coconut-Flavored Rum
- 1 part Amaretto
- Shot Glass

Shake with ice and strain

BIG BALLER

- 2 parts Vodka
- 1 part Gin
- 1 part Triple Sec
- splash Lemon Juice
- Shot Glass

Shake with ice and strain

BIG PINE PUSS

- 1 part Spiced Rum
- ½ part Banana Liqueur
- splash Lime Juice
- splash Grenadine
- splash Cranberry Juice Cocktail
- Shot Glass

Shake with ice and strain

BIG RED

- 1 part Irish Cream Liqueur
- 1 part Goldschläger®
- Shot Glass

Shake with ice and strain

BIG ROLLER

- 1 part Amaretto
- 1 part Coffee
- 1 part Crème de Banana
- Shot Glass

Shake with ice and strain

BIG TIME

- 1 part Cognac
- 1 part Pernod®
- Shot Glass

Shake with ice and strain

BIG UNIT

- 2 parts Tequila
- 1 part Blue Curaçao
- Shot Glass

Shake with ice and strain

THE BIG V

- 1 part Vodka
- 1 part Crème de Cacao (White)
- 1 part Blue Curaçao
- 1 part Sour Mix
- Shot Glass

Shake with ice and strain

BIGLOWER

- 2 parts Dark Rum
- 1 part Crème de Cacao (Dark)
- 1 part Amaretto
- Shot Glass

Shake with ice and strain

BILLY BAD ASS

- 1 part 151-Proof Rum
- 1 part Tequila
- 1 part Jägermeister®
- Shot Glass

Shake with ice and strain

BIRD SHIT

- 1 part Blackberry Brandy
- splash Tequila
- splash Milk
- Shot Glass

Fill shot glass about ¾ full with Blackberry Brandy. Float the Tequila on top of Brandy. Pour in a little bit of Milk for effect.

BITE OF THE IGUANA

- 1 part Tequila
- 1 part Triple Sec
- ½ part Vodka

- 2 parts Orange Juice
- 2 parts Sour Mix
- Shot Glass

Shake with ice and strain

BLACK AND BLUE SHARK

- 2 parts Jack Daniel's®
- 1 part Gold Tequila
- 1 part Vodka

- 1 part Blue Curaçao
- Shot Glass

Shake with ice and strain

BLACK APPLE

- 1 part Blackberry Liqueur
- 1 part Sour Apple Schnapps
- splash Lemon-Lime Soda

- splash Sour Mix
- Shot Glass

Shake with ice and strain

BLACK BLOOD

- 2 parts Blue Curaçao
- 1 part Jägermeister®
- 1 part Ruby Red Grapefruit Juice
- Shot Glass

Shake with ice and strain

BLACK DEATH

- 1 part Jack Daniel's®
- 1 part Tequila
- Shot Glass

Shake with ice and strain

BLACK DEATH #2

- 3 parts Vodka
- 1 part Soy Sauce
- Shot Glass

Shake with ice and strain

BLACK FOREST CAKE

- 1 part Cherry Brandy
- 1 part Coffee Liqueur
- 1 part Irish Cream Liqueur
- Shot Glass

Shake with ice and strain

BLACK GOLD SHOOTER

- 1 part Black Sambuca
- 1 part Cinnamon Schnapps
- Shot Glass

Shake with ice and strain

BLACK HOLE

- 1 part Jägermeister®
- 1 part Rumple Minze®
- Shot Glass

Shake with ice and strain

BLACK ORGASM

- 1 part Vodka
- 1 part Sloe Gin
- 1 part Blue Curaçao
- 1 part Peach Schnapps
- Shot Glass

Shake with ice and strain

BLACK PEPPER

- 1 part Pepper-Flavored Vodka
- splash Blackberry Brandy
- Shot Glass

Shake with ice and strain

BLACKBERRY SOURBALL

- 1 part Vodka
- 1 part Blackberry Liqueur
- splash Lemonade
- splash Orange Juice
- Shot Glass

Shake with ice and strain

BLAZING SADDLE

- 3 parts Blackberry Brandy
- 1 part 151-Proof Rum
- Shot Glass

Shake with ice and strain

BLEACHER CREATURE

- 1 part Butterscotch Schnapps
- 1 part 151-Proof Rum
- Shot Glass

Pour ingredients into glass neat (do not chill)

BLEEDIN' HELL

- 1 part Vodka
- 1 part Strawberry Liqueur
- 1 part Lemonade
- Shot Glass

Shake with ice and strain

BLISS

- 1 part Vanilla Liqueur
- 1 part Vanilla-Flavored Vodka
- 1 part Vanilla Cola
- splash Honey
- Shot Glass

Shake with ice and strain

BLISTER

- 1 part 151-Proof Rum
- 1 part Wild Turkey® Bourbon
- 1 part Blue Curaçao
- splash Pineapple Juice
- splash Orange Juice
- Shot Glass

Shake with ice and strain

BLISTER IN THE SUN

- 2 parts Canadian Whiskey
- 1 part Raspberry Liqueur
- 1 part Orange Juice
- 1 part Lemon Juice
- 1 part Lemon-Lime Soda
- Shot Glass

*Shake with ice and strain. *Note: Because this recipe includes many ingredients, it's easier to make in volume, about 6 shots.*

BLOOD BATH

- 1 part Tequila Silver
- 1 part Strawberry Liqueur
- Shot Glass

Shake with ice and strain

BLOOD TEST

- 1 part Tequila Reposado
- 1 part Grenadine
- Shot Glass

Shake with ice and strain

BLUE BALLS

- 2 parts Blue Curaçao
- 2 parts Coconut-Flavored Rum
- 1 part Peach Schnapps
- splash Sour Mix
- splash Lemon-Lime Soda
- Shot Glass

Shake with ice and strain. *Note: Because this recipe includes many ingredients, it's easier to make in volume, about 6 shots.

BLUE BALLS SHOT

- 1 part Blue Curaçao
- 1 part Dr. McGillicuddy's® Mentholmint Schnapps
- Shot Glass

Shake with ice and strain

BLUE BANANA

- 1 part Crème de Banana
- 1 part Blue Curaçao
- Shot Glass

Shake with ice and strain

BLUE BASTARD

- 2 parts Triple Sec
- 1 part Blueberry Schnapps
- splash Lime Juice
- splash Simple Syrup
- Shot Glass

Shake with ice and strain

BLUE CABOOSE

- 1 part Irish Cream Liqueur
- 1 part Whiskey
- 1 part Amaretto
- Shot Glass

Shake with ice and strain

BLUE GHOST

- 1 part Banana Liqueur
- 1 part Blue Curaçao
- 1 part Coconut-Flavored Rum
- 1 part Vodka
- 1 part Crème de Cacao (White)
- 1 part Light Rum
- 1 part Triple Sec
- 4 parts Cream
- Shot Glass

*Shake with ice and strain. *Note: Because this recipe includes many ingredients, it's easier to make in volume, about 6 shots.*

BLUE MARLIN

- 1 part Light Rum
- ½ part Blue Curaçao
- 1 part Lime Juice
- Shot Glass

Shake with ice and strain

BLUE MEANIE

- 1 part Blue Curaçao
- 1 part Vodka
- 1 part Sour Mix
- Shot Glass

Shake with ice and strain

BLUE MOTHERFUCKER

- 1 part Blue Curaçao
- 1 part 151-Proof Rum
- Shot Glass

Pour ingredients into glass neat (do not chill)

BLUE PEACH

- 1 part Peach Schnapps
- 1 part Blue Curaçao
- Shot Glass

Shake with ice and strain

BLUE POLAR BEAR

- 1 part Vodka
- 1 part Avalanche® Peppermint Schnapps
- Shot Glass

Shake with ice and strain

BLUE RAZZBERRY KAMIKAZE

- 2 parts Raspberry Vodka
- 1 part Blue Curaçao
- splash Lime Cordial
- Shot Glass

Shake with ice and strain

BLUE SLAMMER

- 1 part Blue Curaçao
- 1 part Sambuca
- 1 part Vodka
- splash Lemon Juice
- Shot Glass

Pour ingredients into glass neat (do not chill)

BLUE SMURF® PISS

- 1 part Jägermeister®
- 1 part 151-Proof Rum
- 1 part Rumple Minze®
- 1 part Goldschläger®
- 1 part Blue Curaçao
- Shot Glass

Shake with ice and strain into shot glass. *Note: Because this recipe includes many ingredients, it's easier to make in volume, about 6 shots.

BLUE SPRUCE

- 1 part Maple Syrup
- 1 part Vodka
- Shot Glass

Pour ingredients into glass neat (do not chill).

BLURRICANE

- 1 part Blue Curaçao
- 1 part Rumple Minze®
- 1 part Goldschläger®
- 1 part Jägermeister®
- 1 part Wild Turkey® Bourbon
- 1 part Ouzo
- Shot Glass

*Shake with ice and strain. *Note: Because this recipe includes many ingredients, it's easier to make in volume, about 6 shots.*

BODY BAG

- 1 part 151-Proof Rum
- 1 part Goldschläger®
- 1 part Jägermeister®
- 1 part Rumple Minze®
- Shot Glass

Pour ingredients into glass neat (do not chill)

BODY SHOT

- 1 part Vodka
- dash Sugar
- 1 Lemon Wedge
- Shot Glass

Using a partner, lick his or her neck, then pour the Sugar onto the moistened shot. Place the wedge of Lemon in his or her mouth with the skin pointed inward. Lick the Sugar from his or her neck, shoot the Vodka, then suck the Lemon from his or her mouth (while gently holding back of the neck).

BOMB

- 1 part Coffee Liqueur
- 1 part Goldschläger®
- 1 part Irish Cream Liqueur
- Shot Glass

Shake with ice and strain

BOMB #2

- 1 part Sour Apple Schnapps
- 1 part Peach Schnapps
- 1 part Banana Liqueur
- 1 part Pineapple Juice
- 1 part Lemon-Lime Soda
- Shot Glass

Mix with ice and strain. *Note: Because this recipe includes many ingredients, it's easier to make in volume, about 6 shots.

BOMBSHELL

- 2 parts Irish Cream Liqueur
- 1 part Cointreau®
- splash Aquavit
- Shot Glass

Shake with ice and strain

BONG WATER

- 1 part Melon Liqueur
- 1 part Orange Juice
- 1 part Jägermeister®
- Shot Glass

Shake with ice and strain

BONNIES BERRY'S

- 1 part Vodka
- 1 part Amaretto
- 1 part Raspberry Liqueur
- Shot Glass

Shake with ice and strain

BOOGERS IN THE GRASS

- 1 part Melon Liqueur
- 1 part Peach Schnapps
- splash Irish Cream Liqueur
- Shot Glass

Shake all but Irish Cream with ice and strain into the glass.
Place a few drops of Irish Cream in the center of the drink.

BOOM BOX

- 1 part Vodka
- 1 part White Wine
- 1 part Hot Coffee
- Shot Glass

Pour ingredients into glass neat (do not chill)

BOOMER

- 1 part Tequila
- 1 part Triple Sec
- 1 part Crème de Banana
- 1 part Orange Juice
- 1 part Sour Mix
- Shot Glass

Shake with ice and strain

BOOMERANG SHOT

- 1 part Jägermeister®
- 1 part Yukon Jack®
- Shot Glass

Shake with ice and strain

BOOSTER SHOT

- 1 part Cherry Brandy
- 1 part Chocolate Liqueur
- 1 part Lemon-Lime Soda
- Shot Glass

Shake with ice and strain into a chilled shot glass

BOOT TO THE HEAD

- 1 part Drambuie®
- 1 part Jack Daniel's®
- 1 part Tequila Silver
- Shot Glass

Shake with ice and strain

THE BOOTLEGGER

- 1 part Jack Daniel's®
- 1 part Southern Comfort®
- 1 part Sambuca
- Shot Glass

Shake with ice and strain

BORDER CONFLICT SHOOTER

- 2 parts Vodka
- 2 parts Crème de Menthe (White)
- 1 part Grenadine
- Shot Glass

Shake with ice and strain

BOTTLE CAP

- 1 part Butterscotch Schnapps
- 1 part Raspberry Liqueur
- 1 part Lime Juice
- Shot Glass

Shake with ice and strain

BRAIN DAMAGE

- 1 part 151-Proof Rum
- 1 part Amaretto
- splash Irish Cream Liqueur
- Shot Glass

Shake all but Irish Cream with ice and strain into the glass. Place a few drops of Irish Cream in the center of the drink.

BRAIN DEAD

- 1 part Vodka
- 1 part Sour Mix
- 1 part Triple Sec
- Shot Glass

Shake with ice and strain

BRAIN ERASER

- 1 part Jägermeister®
- 1 part Peppermint Schnapps
- Shot Glass

Shake with ice and strain

BRAIN HEMORRHAGE

- 1 part Peach Schnapps
- 1 part Irish Cream Liqueur
- splash Grenadine
- Shot Glass

Shake all but Grenadine with ice and strain into the glass.
Place a few drops of Grenadine in the center of the drink.

BRAINMASTER

- 2 parts Light Rum
- 1 part Coconut-Flavored Liqueur
- 1 part Crème de Cacao (White)
- splash Apricot Syrup
- Shot Glass

Shake with ice and strain

BRASS BALLS

- 1 part Grand Marnier®
- 1 part Peach Schnapps
- 1 part Pineapple Juice
- Shot Glass

Shake with ice and strain

BRAVE BULL SHOOTER

- 1 part Tequila
- 1 part Coffee Liqueur
- Shot Glass

Pour ingredients into glass neat (do not chill)

BRAVEHEART

- 1 part Vodka
- splash Blue Curaçao
- Shot Glass

Shake with ice and strain

BREAST MILK

- 1 part Chocolate Liqueur
- 1 part Irish Cream Liqueur
- 1 part Butterscotch Schnapps
- splash Half and Half
- Shot Glass

Shake with ice and strain

BREATH FRESHENER

- 1 part Vodka
- 2 parts Peppermint Schnapps
- Shot Glass

Shake with ice and strain

BREATHALIZER

- 1 part Peppermint Schnapps
- 1 part Light Rum
- Shot Glass

Shake with ice and strain

BRODY'S ICY ALIEN

- 1 part Rum
- 1 part Melon Liqueur
- 1 part Rumple Minze®
- splash Cream
- Shot Glass

Shake with ice and strain

BROWN LION

- 1 part Crème de Cacao (Dark)
- 1 part Coffee Liqueur
- Shot Glass

Shake with ice and strain

BRUISED HEART

- 1 part Vodka
- 1 part Raspberry Liqueur
- 1 part Peach Schnapps
- 1 part Cranberry Juice Cocktail
- Shot Glass

Shake with ice and strain

BUBBA HUBBA BOOM BOOM

- 1 part Crème de Cacao (White)
- 1 part Crème de Menthe (White)
- Shot Glass

Shake with ice and strain

BUBBLE GUM

- 1 part Melon Liqueur
- 1 part Vodka
- 1 part Crème de Banana
- 1 part Orange Juice
- Shot Glass

Shake with ice and strain

BUCA BEAR

- 1 part Butterscotch Schnapps
- 1 part Sambuca
- Shot Glass

Shake with ice and strain

BULL SHOT SHOOTER

- 1 part Tequila Silver
- 1 part Coffee
- 1 part Dark Rum
- Shot Glass

Shake with ice and strain

BULL'S MILK

- 1 part Brandy
- 1 part Dark Rum
- 1 part Cream
- Shot Glass

Shake with ice and strain

BUONA SERA SHOOTER

- 1 part Amaretto
- 1 part Coffee
- 1 part Vanilla Rum
- Shot Glass

Shake with ice and strain

BURIED UNDER AN AVALANCHE

- 1 part Ouzo
- 1 part Rumple Minze®
- Shot Glass

Shake with ice and strain

BURNING CHERRY

- 1 part George Dickel Whiskey
- 1 part Irish Cream Liqueur
- 1 part Jim Beam®
- splash Grenadine
- Shot Glass

Pour ingredients into glass neat (do not chill)

BURNING WORM

- 1 part Mescal
- 1 part Goldschläger®
- Shot Glass

Pour ingredients into glass neat (do not chill)

BUSTED CHERRY

- 1 part Coffee Liqueur
- 1 part Cherry Brandy
- Shot Glass

Shake with ice and strain

BUTTERBALL

- 1 part Coffee Liqueur
- 1 part Irish Cream Liqueur
- splash Butterscotch Schnapps
- Shot Glass

Pour ingredients into glass neat (do not chill)

BUTTERFUCKER

- 1 part Jägermeister®
- 1 part Butterscotch Schnapps
- 1 part Irish Cream Liqueur
- Shot Glass

Shake with ice and strain

BUTTERNUT RUM LIFESAVER

- 1 part Irish Cream Liqueur
- 1 part Butterscotch Schnapps
- 1 part Coconut-Flavored Rum
- 1 part Pineapple Juice
- Shot Glass

Shake with ice and strain

BUTTERY NIPPLE

- 1 part Sambuca
- 1 part Butterscotch Schnapps
- Shot Glass

Shake with ice and strain

BUZZARD'S BREATH

- 1 part Crème de Menthe (White)
- 1 part Amaretto
- 1 part Coffee Liqueur
- Shot Glass

Shake with ice and strain

BUZZARD'S BREATH #2

- 1 part Amaretto
- 1 part Peppermint Schnapps
- 1 part Coffee Liqueur
- Shot Glass

Shake with ice and strain

CACTUS JACK SHOOTER

- 1 part Coffee
- 1 part Light Rum
- Shot Glass

Shake with ice and strain

CACTUS THORN

- 2 parts Tequila
- 1 part Crème de Menthe (Green)
- 1 part Lime Juice
- Shot Glass

Shake with ice and strain

CALIFORNIA SURFER

- 1 part Jägermeister®
- 1 part Coconut-Flavored Rum
- 2 parts Pineapple Juice
- Shot Glass

Shake with ice and strain

CAMEL DRIVER

- 1 part Sambuca
- 1 part Irish Cream Liqueur
- Shot Glass

Shake with ice and strain

CANADIAN HUNTER

- 1 part Yukon Jack®
- 1 part Wild Turkey® 101
- Shot Glass

Shake with ice and strain

CANADIAN MOOSE

- 1 part Coffee Liqueur
- 1 part Irish Cream Liqueur
- 1 part Crown Royal® Whiskey
- Shot Glass

Shake with ice and strain

CANADIAN SNAKEBITE

- 1 part Crème de Menthe (White)
- 1 part Canadian Whiskey
- Shot Glass

Shake with ice and strain

CANDY APPLE

- 1 part Crown Royal® Whiskey
- 1 part Sour Apple Schnapps
- splash Cranberry Juice Cocktail
- Shot Glass

Shake with ice and strain

CANDY KILLER WITH A KISS

- 1 part Ouzo
- 1 part Jägermeister®
- 1 part Goldschläger®
- Shot Glass

Shake with ice and strain

CAPTAIN LOUIE

- 1 part Spiced Rum
- 1 part Coffee Liqueur
- splash Vanilla Extract
- Shot Glass

Pour ingredients into glass neat (do not chill)

CARAMILK

- 2 parts Crème de Cacao (White)
- 1 part Crème de Banana
- 1 part Coffee Liqueur
- Shot Glass

Shake with ice and strain

CAROLINA VAGINA

- 2 parts Coconut-Flavored Rum
- 1 part Irish Cream Liqueur
- 1 part Coffee Liqueur
- splash Grenadine
- Shot Glass

Shake with ice and strain

CATFISH

- 3 parts Bourbon
- 1 part Peach Schnapps
- Shot Glass

Shake with ice and strain

CATTLE PROD

- 1 part Butterscotch Schnapps
- 1 part Crown Royal® Whiskey
- Shot Glass

Pour ingredients into glass neat (do not chill)

CAYMAN SHOOTER

- 1 part Crème de Banana
- 1 part Melon Liqueur
- 1 part Irish Cream Liqueur
- Shot Glass

Shake with ice and strain

CHAMPERELLE

- 1 part Triple Sec
- 1 part Anisette
- 1 part Cognac
- Shot Glass

Shake with ice and strain

CHARIOT OF FIRE

- 1 part Vodka
- 1 part Sambuca
- Shot Glass

Shake with ice and strain

CHE GUEVARA

- 1 part Goldschläger®
- 1 part Tequila
- 1 part Jägermeister®
- Shot Glass

Shake with ice and strain

CHEESECAKE

- 1 part Cranberry Juice Cocktail
- 1 part Vanilla Liqueur
- Shot Glass

Shake with ice and strain

CHERRY BLOW POP®

- 1 part Southern Comfort®
- 1 part Amaretto
- 1 part Grenadine
- Shot Glass

Shake with ice and strain

CHERRY BOMB

- 1 part Vodka
- 1 part Crème de Cacao (White)
- 1 part Grenadine
- Shot Glass

Shake with ice and strain

CHERRY BOMB #2

- 2 parts Vodka
- 1 part Goldschläger®
- 1 part Light Rum
- 1 Maraschino Cherry
- Shot Glass

Shake with ice and strain

CHERRY LIFESAVER®

- 1 part Southern Comfort®
- 1 part Amaretto
- 2 parts Sour Mix
- splash Grenadine
- Shot Glass

Shake with ice and strain

CHERRY RIPE SHOOTER

- 1 part Kirschwasser
- 1 part Coconut-Flavored Rum
- 1 part Irish Cream Liqueur
- Shot Glass

Shake with ice and strain

CHI PHI

- 1 part Peach Schnapps
- 1 part Southern Comfort®
- Shot Glass

Shake with ice and strain

CHICK LIT

- 1 part Dr. McGillicuddy's® Mentholmint Schnapps
- 1 part Southern Comfort®
- Shot Glass

Shake with ice and strain

CHICKEN DROP

- 1 part Jägermeister®
- 1 part Peach Schnapps
- 1 part Orange Juice
- Shot Glass

Shake with ice and strain

CHILLY GIRL

- 1 part Melon Liqueur
- 1 part Gin
- 1 part Cream
- Shot Glass

Shake with ice and strain

CHINESE MANDARIN

- 1 part Mandarine Napoléon® Liqueur
- 1 part Lychee Liqueur
- Shot Glass

Shake with ice and strain

CHIP SHOT

- 1 part Spiced Rum
- 1 part Cranberry Juice Cocktail
- 1 part Pineapple Juice
- Shot Glass

Shake with ice and strain

CHIQUITA

- 1 part Vodka
- 2 parts Crème de Banana
- 1 part Milk
- Shot Glass

Shake with ice and strain

CHOCOLATE BANANA SHOT

- 1 part Crème de Cacao (White)
- 1 part Crème de Banana
- Shot Glass

Shake with ice and strain

CHOCOLATE CAKE

- 1 part Frangelico®
- 1 part Vodka
- 1 Lemon Wedge
- dash Sugar
- Shot Glass

Shake Frangelico® and Vodka with ice and strain into a shot glass. Moisten hand and sprinkle Sugar onto it, drink the shot, lick the Sugar and suck the Lemon.

CHOCOLATE CHIP SHOOTER

- 1 part Swiss Chocolate Almond Liqueur
- 1 part Crème de Cacao (White)
- 1 part Irish Cream Liqueur
- Shot Glass

Shake with ice and strain

CHOCOLATE-COVERED CHERRY

- 1 part Coffee Liqueur
- 1 part Amaretto
- 1 part Crème de Cacao (White)
- splash Grenadine
- Shot Glass

Shake with ice and strain

CHOCOLATE HEAVEN

- 1 part Irish Cream Liqueur
- 1 part Coffee Liqueur
- 1 part Chocolate Liqueur
- splash Caramel Syrup
- Shot Glass

Shake with ice and strain

CHOCOLATE VALENTINE

- 1 part Vanilla-Flavored Vodka
- 1 part Crème de Cacao (Dark)
- 1 part Cherry Juice
- splash Cream
- splash Club Soda
- Shot Glass

Shake with ice and strain. *Note: Because this recipe includes many ingredients, it's easier to make in volume, about 6 shots.

CHRISTMAS CHEER

- 1 part Peppermint Schnapps
- 1 part Egg Nog
- Shot Glass

Shake with ice and strain

CHUNKY SNAKEBITE

- 1 part Tequila
- 1 part Salsa
- Shot Glass

Pour ingredients into glass neat (do not chill)

CINNAMON APPLE PIE

- 3 parts Sour Apple Schnapps
- 1 part Cinnamon Schnapps
- Shot Glass

Shake with ice and strain

CINNAMON ROLL

- 1 part Irish Cream Liqueur
- 1 part Cinnamon Schnapps
- Shot Glass

Shake with ice and strain

CITRON MY FACE

- 2 parts Citrus-Flavored Vodka
- 1 part Grand Marnier®
- 1 part Sour Mix
- Shot Glass

Shake with ice and strain

CITRON SOUR

- 1 part Citrus-Flavored Vodka
- 1 part Lime Juice
- Shot Glass

Shake with ice and strain

CLOSED CASKET

- 2 parts Jägermeister®
- 2 parts 151-Proof Rum
- 1 part Fire Water®
- 1 part Rumple Minze®
- Shot Glass

Shake with ice and strain

COBRA BITE

- 3 parts Yukon Jack®
- 1 part Lime Cordial
- 1 part Peppermint Schnapps
- Shot Glass

Shake with ice and strain

COCAINE

- 1 part Vodka
- 1 part Raspberry Liqueur
- 1 part Grapefruit Juice
- Shot Glass

Shake with ice and strain

COCKROACH

- 1 part Coffee Liqueur
- 1 part Drambuie®
- Shot Glass

Shake with ice and strain

COCKTEASER

- 1 part Triple Sec
- 1 part Peach Schnapps
- 1 part Melon Liqueur
- Shot Glass

Shake with ice and strain

COCO BONGO

- 1 part Crème de Cacao (White)
- 1 part Coconut-Flavored Liqueur
- 1 part Cream
- Shot Glass

Shake with ice and strain

COCONUT CREAM PIE

- 1 part Coconut-Flavored Rum
- Shot Glass
- top with Whipped Cream

Fill a shot glass with chilled Coconut-Flavored Rum and top it with Whipped Cream. Drink without using your hands.

COMA

- 1 part Grand Marnier®
- 1 part Coffee Liqueur
- 1 part Sambuca
- Shot Glass

Shake with ice and strain

COOL COUGAR

- 1 part Jack Daniel's®
- 1 part Peppermint Schnapps
- Shot Glass

Shake with ice and strain

COPPER CAMEL

- 1 part Irish Cream Liqueur
- 1 part Butterscotch Schnapps
- Shot Glass

Shake with ice and strain

COPPER COWBOY

- 1 part Butterscotch Schnapps
- 1 part Coffee Liqueur
- Shot Glass

Shake with ice and strain

CORDLESS SCREWDRIVER

- 1 part Vodka
- 1 Orange Wedge
- dash Sugar
- Shot Glass

Shake the Vodka with ice and strain into a shot glass. Dip the Orange Wedge in the Sugar, drink the shot, and suck on the Orange.

CORNHOLIO'S REVENGE

- 1 part Coconut-Flavored Rum
- 1 part Banana Liqueur
- 1 part Cherry Brandy
- Shot Glass

Shake with ice and strain

CORTISONE

- 1 part Coffee Liqueur
- 1 part Rum
- splash Vanilla Liqueur
- Shot Glass

Shake with ice and strain

COUGH DROP

- 1 part Crème de Menthe (White)
- 1 part Blackberry Liqueur
- Shot Glass

Shake with ice and strain

COUGH SYRUP

- 1 part Vodka
- 1 part Crème de Menthe (White)
- 1 part Blue Curaçao
- Shot Glass

Shake with ice and strain

COWBOY COCKSUCKER

- 1 part Butterscotch Schnapps
- 1 part Irish Cream Liqueur
- Shot Glass

Shake with ice and strain

COWGIRL

- 2 parts Butterscotch Schnapps
- 1 part Irish Cream Liqueur
- Shot Glass

Shake with ice and strain

CRACK HOUSE

- 1 part Blackberry Liqueur
- 1 part Cranberry Juice Cocktail
- Shot Glass

Shake with ice and strain

CRANAPPLE® BLAST

- 1 part Sour Apple Schnapps
- 1 part Cranberry Juice Cocktail
- 1 part Vodka
- Shot Glass

Shake with ice and strain

CRANBERRY ZAMBONI®

- 1 part Cranberry Liqueur
- 1 part Wild Spirit Liqueur
- Shot Glass

Shake with ice and strain

CRASH TEST DUMMY SHOTS

- 1 part Tequila
- 1 part Triple Sec
- 3 parts Margarita Mix
- Shot Glass

Shake with ice and strain

CRAZY COCO

- 1 part Coconut-Flavored Liqueur
- 1 part Irish Cream Liqueur
- Shot Glass

Shake with ice and strain

CRAZY NOGGIE

- 1 part Light Rum
- 1 part Vodka
- 1 part Southern Comfort®
- 1 part Amaretto
- Shot Glass

Shake with ice and strain

CREAM HASH

- 1 part Dark Rum
- 1 part Chocolate Liqueur
- Shot Glass

Shake with ice and strain

CREAM SODA SLAMMER

- 1 part Spiced Rum
- 1 part Lemon-Lime Soda
- Shot Glass

Pour ingredients into glass neat (do not chill)

CREAMY JONNY

- 1 part Irish Cream Liqueur
- 1 part Raspberry Liqueur
- 1 part Milk
- splash Grenadine
- Shot Glass

Shake with ice and strain

CREAMY NUTS

- 1 part Crème de Banana
- 1 part Frangelico®
- Shot Glass

Shake with ice and strain

CREAMY SNATCH

- 1 part Butterscotch Schnapps
- 1 part Coffee Liqueur
- 2 parts Half and Half
- Shot Glass

Shake with ice and strain

CRIMSON TIDE

- 1 part Vodka
- 1 part Coconut-Flavored Rum
- 1 part Raspberry Liqueur
- 1 part Southern Comfort®
- 1 part 151-Proof Rum
- 1 part Cranberry Juice Cocktail
- 1 part Lemon-Lime Soda
- Shot Glass

Shake with ice and strain. *Note: Because this recipe includes many ingredients, it's easier to make in volume, about 6 shots.

CRISPY CRUNCH

- 1 part Frangelico®
- 1 part Crème de Cacao (White)
- Shot Glass

Shake with ice and strain

CROCKET

- 2 parts Cherry Liqueur
- 1 part Grenadine
- 1 part Sour Mix
- Shot Glass

Shake with ice and strain

CROWBAR

- 1 part Crown Royal® Whiskey
- 1 part 151-Proof Rum
- 1 part Tequila
- Shot Glass

Shake with ice and strain

CRUZ AZUL

- 1 part 151-Proof Rum
- 1 part Citrus-Flavored Rum
- 1 part Citrus-Flavored Vodka
- 1 part Rumple Minze®
- 1 part Blue Curaçao
- Shot Glass

*Shake with ice and strain. *Note: Because this recipe includes many ingredients, it's easier to make in volume, about 6 shots.*

CRYSTAL VIRGIN

- 1 part Yukon Jack®
- 1 part Amaretto
- 2 parts Cranberry Juice Cocktail
- Shot Glass

Shake with ice and strain

CUCARACHA

- 1 part Vodka
- 1 part Coffee Liqueur
- 1 part Tequila
- Shot Glass

Shake with ice and strain

CUM IN A POND

- 1 part Blue Curaçao
- 1 part Vodka
- splash Irish Cream Liqueur
- Shot Glass

Shake all but Irish Cream with ice and strain into the glass.
Place a few drops of Irish Cream in the center of the drink.

CUM SHOT

- 1 part Butterscotch Schnapps
- 1 part Irish Cream Liqueur
- Shot Glass

Shake with ice and strain

CURLY TAIL TWIST

- splash 151-Proof Rum
- 1 part Jägermeister®
- 1 part Root Beer Schnapps
- Shot Glass

Shake with ice and strain

CURTAIN CALL

- 1 part Jägermeister®
- 1 part Melon Liqueur
- 1 part Jack Daniel's®
- Shot Glass

Shake with ice and strain

D.O.A.

- 1 part Crème de Cacao (White)
- 1 part Peach Schnapps
- 1 part Frangelico®
- Shot Glass

Shake with ice and strain

DADDY'S MILK

- 1 part Crème de Cacao (Dark)
- 1 part Crème de Cacao (White)
- 1 part Frangelico®
- splash Cream
- Shot Glass

Shake with ice and strain

DAKOTA

- 1 part Jim Beam®
- 1 part Tequila
- Shot Glass

Pour ingredients into glass neat (do not chill)

DALLAS STARS

- 1 part Crème de Menthe (White)
- 1 part Goldschläger®
- Shot Glass

Shake with ice and strain

DAMNED IF YOU DO

- 1 part Whiskey
- 1 part Cinnamon Schnapps
- Shot Glass

Pour ingredients into glass neat (do not chill)

DANGEROUS GRANDMA

- 1 part Coffee Liqueur
- ½ part Whiskey
- splash Amaretto
- Shot Glass

Pour ingredients into glass neat (do not chill)

DARK ANGEL

- 1 part Maraschino Liqueur
- 1 part Blackberry Liqueur
- 1 part Advocaat
- Shot Glass

Shake with ice and strain

DARK NIGHTMARE

- 2 parts Coffee Liqueur
- 1 part Goldschläger®
- 1 part Milk
- Shot Glass

Shake with ice and strain

D-DAY

- 1 part 151-Proof Rum
- 1 part Citrus-Flavored Vodka
- 1 part Crème de Banana
- 1 part Raspberry Liqueur
- 1 part Orange Juice
- Shot Glass

Shake with ice and strain. *Note: Because this recipe includes many ingredients, it's easier to make in volume, about 6 shots.

DEAD BIRD

- 1 part Jägermeister®
- 1 part Wild Turkey® Bourbon
- Shot Glass

Shake with ice and strain

DEAD END

- 1 part Amaretto
- 1 part Coffee Liqueur
- 1 part Grain Alcohol
- 1 part Irish Cream Liqueur
- Shot Glass

Shake with ice and strain

DEAD FROG

- 1 part Coffee Liqueur
- 1 part Irish Cream Liqueur
- 1 part Crème de Menthe (White)
- Shot Glass

Shake with ice and strain

DEAD GREEN FROG

- 1 part Rumple Minze®
- 1 part Coffee Liqueur
- 1 part Crème de Menthe (Green)
- 1 part Irish Cream Liqueur
- 1 part Vodka
- Shot Glass

Shake with ice and strain

DEAR SPERM

- 1 part Jägermeister®
- 1 part Irish Cream Liqueur
- Shot Glass

Shake with ice and strain

DEATH FROM WITHIN

- 1 part Spiced Rum
- 1 part Dark Rum
- 1 part Vodka
- Shot Glass

Shake with ice and strain

DEATH ROW

- 1 part Jack Daniel's®
- 1 part 151-Proof Rum
- Shot Glass

Shake with ice and strain

DEATH WISH

- 1 part Wild Turkey® 101
- 1 part Rumple Minze®
- 1 part Jägermeister®
- Shot Glass

Shake with ice and strain

DEEP BLUE SOMETHING

- 1 part Blue Curaçao
- 1 part Peach Schnapps
- 1 part Sour Mix
- 1 part Lemonade
- 1 part Pineapple Juice
- Shot Glass

Shake with ice and strain. *Note: Because this recipe includes many ingredients, it's easier to make in volume, about 6 shots.

THE DEMON KNIGHT

- 1 part Peppermint Schnapps
- 1 part Vodka
- 1 part Fruit Punch
- Shot Glass

Shake with ice and strain

DESERT SKIES

- 1 part Apricot Brandy
- 1 part Rum Crème Liqueur
- 1 part Coffee Liqueur
- Shot Glass

Shake with ice and strain

DETOX

- 1 part Peach Schnapps
- 1 part Vodka
- 1 part Cranberry Juice Cocktail
- Shot Glass

Shake with ice and strain

DEVASTATING BODY ROCKER

- 1 part Blackberry Brandy
- 1 part Gin
- Shot Glass

Shake with ice and strain

DEVIL'S KISS

- 1 part Dark Rum
- 1 part Coffee Liqueur
- 1 part Grand Marnier®
- Shot Glass

Shake with ice and strain

DEVIL'S MOUTHWASH

- 1 part Black Sambuca
- 1 part Southern Comfort®
- Shot Glass

Shake with ice and strain

DIAMOND CUTTER

- 1 part 151-Proof Rum
- 1 part Spiced Rum
- 1 part Grenadine
- Shot Glass

Shake with ice and strain

DIESEL FUEL

- 1 part Rum
- 1 part Jägermeister®
- Shot Glass

Shake with ice and strain

DIRTIEST ERNIE

- 1 part 151-Proof Rum
- 1 part Grain Alcohol
- 1 part Rumple Minze®
- Shot Glass

Shake with ice and strain

DIRTY DIAPER

- 1 part Vodka
- 1 part Amaretto
- 1 part Southern Comfort®
- 1 part Melon Liqueur
- 1 part Raspberry Liqueur
- 1 part Orange Juice
- Shot Glass

*Shake with ice and strain. *Note: Because this recipe includes many ingredients, it's easier to make in volume, about 6 shots.*

DIRTY GIRL SCOUT COOKIE

- 1 part Coffee Liqueur
- 1 part Irish Cream Liqueur
- 1 part Crème de Menthe (White)
- Shot Glass

Shake with ice and strain

DIRTY IRISH WHISKEY

- 1 part Irish Cream Liqueur
- 1 part Irish Whiskey
- Shot Glass

Shake with ice and strain

THE DIRTY LEPRECHAUN

- 1 part Jägermeister®
- 1 part Irish Cream Liqueur
- 1 part Midori®
- Shot Glass

Shake with ice and strain

DIRTY NAVEL

- 1 part Crème de Cacao (White)
- 1 part Triple Sec
- Shot Glass

Shake with ice and strain

DIRTY ROTTEN SCOUNDREL

- 1 part Vodka
- 1 part Melon Liqueur
- Shot Glass

Shake with ice and strain

DISNEY® ON ICE

- 1 part Peppermint Schnapps
- 1 part Grenadine
- 1 part 151-Proof Rum
- splash Lemon Juice
- Shot Glass

Shake with ice and strain

DIZZY DAMAGE

- 1 part Jägermeister®
- 1 part Rumple Minze®
- 1 part Goldschläger®
- Shot Glass

Shake with ice and strain

THE DOC'S MEDICINE

- 1 part Scotch
- 1 part Tequila
- Shot Glass

Shake with ice and strain

DOLT BOLT

- 1 part Grain Alcohol
- 1 part Rumple Minze®
- 1 part Goldschläger®
- Shot Glass

Shake with ice and strain

DOMINATOR

- 2 parts Crème de Menthe (White)
- 1 part Coffee
- 1 part Triple Sec
- Shot Glass

Shake with ice and strain

DON'T THRUST ME

- 1 part Goldschläger®
- 1 part Butterscotch Schnapps
- 1 part 151-Proof Rum
- Shot Glass

Shake with ice and strain

DOUBLE BERRY BLAST

- 1 part Blueberry Schnapps
- 1 part Strawberry Liqueur
- Shot Glass

Shake with ice and strain

DOUBLE CHOCOLATE

- 1 part Chocolate Liqueur
- 1 part Crème de Cacao (Dark)
- Shot Glass

Shake with ice and strain

DOUBLE GOLD

- 1 part Goldschläger®
- 1 part Gold Tequila
- Shot Glass

Shake with ice and strain

DOUBLE HOMICIDE

- 1 part Jägermeister®
- 1 part Goldschläger®
- 1 part Orange Juice
- Shot Glass

Shake with ice and strain

THE DOUBLE TEAM

- 1 part Amaretto
- 1 part Rum
- Shot Glass

Shake with ice and strain

DOUBLEMINT® BLOW JOB

- 1 part Coffee Liqueur
- 1 part Peppermint Schnapps
- 2 parts Cream
- Shot Glass

Shake with ice and strain

DOUCET DEVIL

- 1 part Amaretto
- 1 part Southern Comfort®
- 1 part Crème de Banana
- Shot Glass

Shake with ice and strain

DOWN THE STREET

- 1 part Vodka
- 1 part Grand Marnier®
- 1 part Raspberry Liqueur
- 1 part Orange Juice
- Shot Glass

Shake with ice and strain

DOWNINONE

- 2 parts Blavod® Black Vodka
- 1 part Triple Sec
- 1 part Gold Rum
- Shot Glass

Shake with ice and strain

DR. BANANA

- 1 part Tequila
- 1 part Crème de Banana
- Shot Glass

Shake with ice and strain

DRAGON'S BREATH

- 1 part Fire Water®
- 1 part 151-Proof Rum
- Shot Glass

Pour ingredients into glass neat (do not chill)

DRUNK IRISH MONK

- 1 part Irish Cream Liqueur
- 1 part Frangelico®
- 1 part Brandy
- Shot Glass

Shake with ice and strain

DUBLIN DOUBLER

- 1 part Irish Whiskey
- 1 part Irish Cream Liqueur
- Shot Glass

Shake with ice and strain

DUCK CALL SHOOTER

- 1 part 151-Proof Rum
- 1 part Coconut-Flavored Rum
- splash Cranberry Juice Cocktail
- splash Pineapple Juice
- Shot Glass

Shake with ice and strain

DUCK FUCK

- 2 parts Gin
- 1 part Vodka
- 1 part Beer
- Shot Glass

Shake with ice and strain

DUMB FUCK

- 1 part Cinnamon Schnapps
- 1 part Canadian Whiskey
- Shot Glass

Shake with ice and strain

EARTH TREMOR

- 1 part Gin
- 1 part Scotch
- 1 part Pernod®
- Shot Glass

Shake with ice and strain

EARTHQUAKE SHOOTER

- 1 part Sambuca
- 1 part Amaretto
- 1 part Southern Comfort®
- Shot Glass

Shake with ice and strain

EL DIABLILLO

- 3 parts Tequila Silver
- 1 part Crème de Cassis
- Shot Glass

Shake with ice and strain

ELECTRIC BANANA

- 1 part Tequila Silver
- 1 part Crème de Banana
- 1 part Lime Cordial
- Shot Glass

Shake with ice and strain

ELECTRIC KAMIKAZE

- 1 part Triple Sec
- 1 part Vodka
- 1 part Blue Curaçao
- 1 part Lime Juice
- Shot Glass

Shake with ice and strain

ELECTRIC SMURF®

- 1 part Coconut-Flavored Rum
- 1 part Blue Curaçao
- Shot Glass

Shake with ice and strain

ELVIS PRESLEY

- 1 part Vodka
- 1 part Frangelico®
- 1 part Crème de Banana
- splash Irish Cream Liqueur
- Shot Glass

Shake with ice and strain

EMBRYO

- 1 part Peppermint Schnapps
- splash Cream
- splash Grenadine
- Shot Glass

Place a few drops of Cream and a few drops of Grenadine in the center of a shot of Peppermint Schnapps

EMERALD ROCKET

- 1 part Vodka
- 1 part Coffee Liqueur
- 1 part Melon Liqueur
- 1 part Irish Cream Liqueur
- Shot Glass

Shake with ice and strain

THE END OF THE WORLD

- 1 part 151-Proof Rum
- 1 part Wild Turkey® 101
- 1 part Vodka
- Shot Glass

Pour ingredients into glass neat (do not chill)

EPIDURAL

- 1 part Grain Alcohol
- 1 part Vodka
- 1 part Coconut-Flavored Rum
- 1 part Coconut Crème
- Shot Glass

Shake with ice and strain

THE EQUALIZER

- 1 part Peach Schnapps
- 1 part Pineapple Juice
- 1 part Orange Juice
- Shot Glass

Shake with ice and strain

ERECT NIPPLE

- 1 part Tequila Silver
- 1 part Sambuca
- Shot Glass

Shake with ice and strain

EXPLOSIVE

- 2 parts Tequila Reposado
- 1 part Triple Sec
- Shot Glass

Shake with ice and strain

EXTENDED JAIL SENTENCE

- 1 part Jack Daniel's®
- 1 part Southern Comfort®
- 1 part Tequila
- splash Pineapple Juice
- Shot Glass

Shake with ice and strain

EYEBALL

- 1 part Irish Cream Liqueur
- splash Blue Curaçao
- splash Grenadine
- Shot Glass

Put a splash of Grenadine in the bottom of a shot glass, then top with Irish Cream Liqueur. Place a small splash of Blue Curaçao in the center for the iris.

FIG

- 1 part Coconut-Flavored Rum
- 1 part Pineapple Juice
- 1 part Cranberry Juice Cocktail
- Shot Glass

Shake with ice and strain

FINGER ME GOOD

- 1 part Butterscotch Schnapps
- 3 parts Crown Royal® Whiskey
- Shot Glass

Pour ingredients into glass neat (do not chill)

FIRE AND ICE

- 1 part Cinnamon Schnapps
- 1 part Irish Cream Liqueur
- Shot Glass

Shake with ice and strain

FIRE TRUCK

- 1 part Jägermeister®
- 1 part Ginger Ale
- Shot Glass

Pour ingredients into glass neat (do not chill)

FIREBALL

- 1 part Coffee Liqueur
- 1 part Ouzo
- Shot Glass

Shake with ice and strain

FIVE-STAR GENERAL

- 1 part Jägermeister®
- 1 part 151-Proof Rum
- 1 part Rumple Minze®
- 1 part Goldschläger®
- 1 part Tequila
- Shot Glass

*Shake with ice and strain. *Note: Because this recipe includes many ingredients, it's easier to make in volume, about 6 shots.*

FLAMETHROWER

- 1 part Vodka
- 2 parts Cinnamon Schnapps
- Shot Glass

Shake with ice and strain

FLAMING COCAINE

- 1 part Cinnamon Schnapps
- 1 part Vodka
- splash Cranberry Juice Cocktail
- Shot Glass

Shake with ice and strain

FLAMING SQUEEGEE

- 1 part Rum
- 1 part Vodka
- 1 part Lemon Juice
- 1 part Orange Juice
- Shot Glass

Shake with ice and strain

FLASH FIRE

- 1 part Cinnamon Schnapps
- 1 part Southern Comfort®
- 1 part Wild Turkey® 101
- Shot Glass

Pour ingredients into glass neat (do not chill)

FLAT TIRE

- 2 parts Tequila
- 1 part Black Sambuca
- Shot Glass

Shake with ice and strain

FLOOZE BOOZE

- 1 part Jägermeister®
- 1 part Root Beer Schnapps
- Shot Glass

Shake with ice and strain

FLÜGEL

- 1 part Cranberry-Flavored Vodka
- 1 part Red Bull® Energy Drink
- Shot Glass

Pour ingredients into glass neat (do not chill)

FLUKEMAN

- 1 part Irish Cream Liqueur
- 1 part Melon Liqueur
- Shot Glass

Pour ingredients into glass neat (do not chill)

FOG

- 3 parts Vodka
- 1 part Fresh Lime Juice
- Shot Glass

Shake with ice and strain

THE FOUR HORSEMEN

- 1 part Jägermeister®
- 1 part Tequila
- 1 part Sambuca
- 1 part Rum
- Shot Glass

Pour ingredients into glass neat (do not chill)

THE FOUR HORSEMEN #2

- 1 part Jack Daniel's®
- 1 part Sambuca
- 1 part Jägermeister®
- 1 part Rumple Minze®
- Shot Glass

Shake with ice and strain

FOXY LADY #2

- 1 part Amaretto
- 1 part Crème de Banana
- 1 part Cream
- Shot Glass

Shake with ice and strain

FREAKING SHOT

- 1 part Raspberry Liqueur
- 1 part Vodka
- 1 part Cranberry Juice Cocktail
- Shot Glass

Shake with ice and strain

FREDDY KRUEGER®

- 1 part Sambuca
- 1 part Jägermeister®
- 1 part Vodka
- Shot Glass

Shake with ice and strain

FREEBASE

- 1 part Coffee Liqueur
- 1 part Light Rum
- 1 part 151-Proof Rum
- Shot Glass

Shake with ice and strain

FREIGHT TRAIN

- 1 part Tequila
- 1 part Irish Cream Liqueur

- Shot Glass

Shake with ice and strain

FRENCH TOAST

- 1 part Irish Cream Liqueur
- 1 part Cinnamon Schnapps

- 1 part Butterscotch Schnapps
- Shot Glass

Shake with ice and strain

FRIGID ALASKAN NIPPLE

- 1 part Butterscotch Schnapps
- 1 part Rumple Minze®

- 2 parts Vodka
- Shot Glass

Shake with ice and strain

FROG IN A BLENDER

- 2 parts Tequila
- 1 part Sloe Gin
- splash Sweet Vermouth
- Shot Glass

Shake with ice and strain

FRUIT LOOP®

- 1 part Amaretto
- 1 part Blue Curaçao
- 1 part Grenadine
- 1 part Milk
- Shot Glass

Shake with ice and strain

FRUIT OF THE LOOM®

- 1 part Banana Liqueur
- 1 part Melon Liqueur
- 1 part Cherry Brandy
- 1 part Coconut-Flavored Rum
- Shot Glass

Shake with ice and strain

FRUIT SALAD

- 1 part Sour Apple Schnapps
- 1 part Cherry-Flavored Schnapps
- 1 part Grape-Flavored Schnapps
- splash Orange Juice
- Shot Glass

Shake with ice and strain

FRUIT TONGUE FUCK

- 1 part Citrus-Flavored Rum
- 1 part Light Rum
- 1 part Dark Rum
- 1 part Peach Schnapps
- Shot Glass

Shake with ice and strain

FRUITY FAIRY

- 1 part Peach Schnapps
- 1 part Grenadine
- 1 part Melon Liqueur
- Shot Glass

Shake with ice and strain

FRUITY PEBBLES®

- 1 part Vodka
- 1 part Blue Curaçao
- 1 part Milk
- splash Grenadine
- Shot Glass

Shake with ice and strain

FUCK ME RUNNING

- 1 part Jack Daniel's®
- 1 part Peach Schnapps
- 1 part Blackberry Brandy
- Shot Glass

Shake with ice and strain

FUCK ME UP

- 1 part Coffee Liqueur
- 1 part Irish Cream Liqueur
- 1 part Banana Liqueur
- Shot Glass

Shake with ice and strain

FUCKING HOT

- 1 part Pepper-Flavored Vodka
- 1 part Cinnamon Schnapps
- Shot Glass

Pour ingredients into glass neat (do not chill)

FUNKY CHICKEN

- 1 part Tequila
- 1 part Wild Turkey® Bourbon
- Shot Glass

Shake with ice and strain

FUZZY IRISHMAN

- 1 part Raspberry Liqueur
- 1 part Butterscotch Schnapps
- 1 part Irish Cream Liqueur
- Shot Glass

Pour ingredients into glass neat (do not chill)

FUZZY LOGIC

- 1 part Coffee Liqueur
- 1 part Peach Schnapps
- 2 parts Cream
- Shot Glass

Shake with ice and strain

FUZZY MELON SHOOTER

- 1 part Peach Schnapps
- 1 part Pineapple Juice
- 1 part Orange Juice
- 1 part Melon Liqueur
- splash Blue Curaçao
- Shot Glass

*Shake with ice and strain. *Note: Because this recipe includes many ingredients, it's easier to make in volume, about 6 shots.*

FUZZY MONKEY

- 1 part Vodka
- 1 part Peach Schnapps
- 1 part Crème de Banana
- 1 part Orange Juice
- Shot Glass

Shake with ice and strain

FUZZY MONKEY #2

- 3 parts Crème de Banana
- 2 parts Orange Juice
- 1 part Peach Schnapps
- Shot Glass

Shake with ice and strain

FUZZY NUTTED BANANA

- 1 part Peach Schnapps
- 1 part Amaretto
- 1 part Banana Liqueur
- 1 part Orange Juice
- splash Grenadine
- Shot Glass

Shake with ice and strain. *Note: Because this recipe includes many ingredients, it's easier to make in volume, about 6 shots.

FUZZY PIRATE

- 1 part Dark Rum
- 1 part Peach Schnapps
- splash Triple Sec
- Shot Glass

Shake with ice and strain

FUZZY RUSSIAN

- 1 part Vodka
- 1 part Peach Schnapps
- Shot Glass

Shake with ice and strain

FUZZY SMURF®

- 1 part Blue Curaçao
- 1 part Peach Schnapps
- Shot Glass

Shake with ice and strain

G SPOT

- 1 part Southern Comfort®
- 1 part Raspberry Liqueur
- 1 part Orange Juice
- Shot Glass

Shake with ice and strain

G. T. O.

- 1 part Vodka
- 1 part Rum
- 1 part Gin
- 1 part Southern Comfort®
- 1 part Amaretto
- 1 part Grenadine
- 4 parts Orange Juice
- Shot Glass

*Shake with ice and strain. *Note: Because this recipe includes many ingredients, it's easier to make in volume, about 6 shots.*

GALACTIC ALE

- 2 parts Vodka
- 2 parts Blue Curaçao
- 1 part Lime Juice
- splash Blackberry Liqueur
- Shot Glass

Shake with ice and strain

GASOLINE

- 1 part Southern Comfort®
- 1 part Tequila
- Shot Glass

Shake with ice and strain

GATOR CUM

- 1 part Vodka
- 1 part Crème de Cacao (Dark)
- 1 part Frangelico®
- Shot Glass

Shake with ice and strain

GATOR TAIL

- 1 part Melon Liqueur
- 1 part Rum
- 1 part Pineapple Juice
- 1 part Coconut-Flavored Rum
- Shot Glass

Shake with ice and strain

GEIGER COUNTER

- 1 part 151-Proof Rum
- 1 part Jägermeister®
- Shot Glass

Pour ingredients into glass neat (do not chill)

GENTLE BULL SHOT

- 1 part Coffee
- 1 part Tequila Reposado
- splash Cream
- Shot Glass

Shake with ice and strain

GERMAN BURRITO

- 1 part Tequila
- 1 part Jägermeister®
- Shot Glass

Shake with ice and strain

GERMAN DEATH

- 1 part Jägermeister®
- 1 parts Rumple Minze®
- Shot Glass

Shake with ice and strain

GERMAN FRUIT CUP

- 1 part Rum
- 1 part Blackberry Liqueur
- 1 part Blue Curaçao
- 1 part Grenadine
- 1 part Honey
- Shot Glass

Shake with ice and strain. *Note: Because this recipe includes many ingredients, it's easier to make in volume, about 6 shots.

GESTAPO

- 1 part Rumple Minze®
- 1 part Jägermeister®
- Shot Glass

Shake with ice and strain

GETAWAY CAR

- 3 parts Peach Schnapps
- 1 part Citrus-Flavored Vodka
- Shot Glass

Shake with ice and strain

GHETTO BLASTER

- 1 part Coffee Liqueur
- 1 part Sambuca
- 1 part Tequila
- 1 part Rye Whiskey
- Shot Glass

Shake with ice and strain

GHOSTBUSTER

- 1 part Vodka
- 1 part Melon Liqueur
- 1 part Pineapple Juice
- 1 part Orange Juice
- Shot Glass

Shake with ice and strain

GILA MONSTER

- 1 part Jägermeister®
- 1 part Tequila
- 1 part Orange Juice
- Shot Glass

Shake with ice and strain

GILLIGAN

- 1 part Coconut-Flavored Rum
- 1 part Watermelon Schnapps
- Shot Glass

Shake with ice and strain

GIN AND BEAR IT

- 2 parts Gin
- 1 part Beer
- Shot Glass

Pour ingredients into glass neat (do not chill)

GINGERBREAD MAN

- 1 part Goldschläger®
- 1 part Irish Cream Liqueur
- 1 part Butterscotch Schnapps
- 1 part Vodka
- Shot Glass

Shake with ice and strain

THE GIRL MOM WARNED YOU ABOUT

- 1 part Grenadine
- 1 part Triple Sec
- 1 part Rum
- 1 part Melon Liqueur
- 1 part Blue Curaçao
- Shot Glass

*Shake with ice and strain. *Note: Because this recipe includes many ingredients, it's easier to make in volume, about 6 shots.*

GIRL SCOUT COOKIE

- 1 part Coffee Liqueur
- 1 part Milk
- 1 part Rumple Minze®
- Shot Glass

Shake with ice and strain

GLADIATOR'S STINGER

- 3 parts Brandy
- 2 parts Crème de Menthe (White)
- 1 part Sambuca
- Shot Glass

Shake with ice and strain

GLITTERBOX

- 1 part Black Sambuca
- 1 part Coffee Liqueur
- Shot Glass

Shake with ice and strain

GODHEAD

- 1 part Rum
- 1 part Vodka
- 1 part Raspberry Liqueur
- splash Lime Juice
- splash 151-Proof Rum
- Shot Glass

Shake with ice and strain

GODZILLA®

- 2 parts Tequila Silver
- 1 part Orange Bitters

- Shot Glass

Shake with ice and strain

GOLD BARON

- 3 parts Rumple Minze®
- 1 part Goldschläger®

- Shot Glass

Shake with ice and strain

GOLD FEVER

- 1 part Goldschläger®
- 1 part Gold Tequila

- Shot Glass

Shake with ice and strain

GOLDDIGGER

- 1 part Jack Daniel's®
- 1 part Goldschläger®
- Shot Glass

Pour ingredients into glass neat (do not chill)

GOLDEN COMFORT

- 1 part Goldschläger®
- 1 part Southern Comfort®
- 1 part Jägermeister®
- Shot Glass

Shake with ice and strain

GOLDEN RUSSIAN

- 1 part Vodka
- 1 part Galliano®
- Shot Glass

Shake with ice and strain

GOLDEN SENSATION

- 2 parts Amaretto
- 2 parts Coffee Liqueur
- 1 part Crème de Banana
- 1 part Crème de Cacao (Dark)
- 1 part Goldschläger®
- Shot Glass

Shake with ice and strain. *Note: Because this recipe includes many ingredients, it's easier to make in volume, about 6 shots.

GOOD AND PLENTY

- 1 part Sambuca
- 1 part Tequila
- Shot Glass

Shake with ice and strain

GOODY TWO SHOES

- 2 parts Passion Fruit Liqueur
- 1 part Pineapple Juice
- 1 part Blue Curaçao
- Shot Glass

Shake with ice and strain

GORILLA FART

- 1 part Rum
- 1 part Wild Turkey® Bourbon
- Shot Glass

Shake with ice and strain

GRAB MY COCONUTS

- 1 part Dark Rum
- 1 part Coconut-Flavored Liqueur
- 2 parts Pineapple Juice
- Shot Glass

Shake with ice and strain

THE GRADUATE

- 3 parts Southern Comfort®
- 2 parts Pineapple Juice
- 1 part Amaretto
- Shot Glass

Shake with ice and strain

GRANDMA'S CANDY

Shake with ice and strain

GRANDPA IS ALIVE

- 2 parts Amaretto
- 1 part Vodka
- Shot Glass

Shake with ice and strain

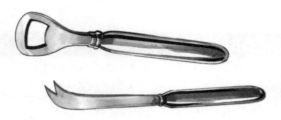

GRAPE KOOL-AID®

- 1 part Blue Curaçao
- 1 part Southern Comfort®
- 1 part Raspberry Liqueur
- 1 part Pineapple Juice
- 1 part Sour Mix
- 2 parts Cranberry Juice Cocktail
- Shot Glass

Shake with ice and strain. *Note: Because this recipe includes many ingredients, it's easier to make in volume, about 6 shots.

GRAPEVINE SPECIAL

- 1 part Brandy
- 1 part Apricot Brandy
- 1 part Banana Liqueur
- 1 part Cherry Liqueur
- 1 part Grand Marnier®
- Shot Glass

Shake with ice and strain. *Note: Because this recipe includes many ingredients, it's easier to make in volume, about 6 shots.

GRASSHOPPER SHOT

- 1 part Brandy
- 1 part Blue Curaçao
- Shot Glass

Shake with ice and strain

GRAVE DIGGER

- 1 part 151-Proof Rum
- 1 part Jim Beam®
- Shot Glass

Shake with ice and strain

GRAZYSURFER

- 1 part Dark Rum
- 1 part Goldschläger®
- 1 part Sambuca
- Shot Glass

Pour ingredients into glass neat (do not chill)

GREEK FIRE

- 3 parts Brandy
- 1 part Ouzo
- Shot Glass

Shake with ice and strain

GREEK LIGHTNING

- 1 part Ouzo
- 1 part Vodka
- 1 part Raspberry Liqueur
- Shot Glass

Shake with ice and strain

GREEK REVOLUTION

- 1 part Grenadine
- 1 part Ouzo
- Shot Glass

Shake with ice and strain

THE GREEK WAY

- 2 parts Ouzo
- 1 part Metaxa®
- Shot Glass

Shake with ice and strain

GREEN AFTERMATH

- 1 part Peppermint Schnapps
- 1 part Mountain Dew®
- Shot Glass

Pour ingredients into glass neat (do not chill)

GREEN APPLE KAMIKAZI

- 1 part Melon Liqueur
- 1 part Vodka
- 1 part Sour Mix
- splash Lime Juice
- Shot Glass

Shake with ice and strain

GREEN APPLE TOFFEE

- 1 part Vodka
- 1 part Butterscotch Schnapps
- 1 part Sour Apple Schnapps
- Shot Glass

Shake with ice and strain

GREEN BOOGER

- 1 part Irish Cream Liqueur
- 1 part Crème de Menthe (White)
- splash Lime Juice
- Shot Glass

Shake with ice and strain

GREEN COOKIE MONSTER®

- 2 parts Gin
- 1 part Melon Liqueur
- 1 part Rum
- Shot Glass

Shake with ice and strain

GREEN FLY SHOOTER

- 1 part Crème de Menthe (Green)
- 1 part Melon Liqueur
- Shot Glass

Shake with ice and strain

GREEN GECKO

- 1 part Crème de Menthe (White)
- 1 part Triple Sec
- splash Limoncello
- Shot Glass

Shake with ice and strain

GREEN GUMMY BEAR

- 1 part Orange-Flavored Vodka
- 1 part Melon Liqueur
- splash Lemon-Lime Soda
- Shot Glass

Shake with ice and strain

GREEN JOLLY RANCHER®

- 1 part Melon Liqueur
- 1 part Southern Comfort®
- splash Sour Mix
- Shot Glass

Shake with ice and strain

GREEN LIZARD ON THE BEACH

- 2 parts Crème de Banana
- 1 part Blue Curaçao
- splash Orange Juice
- Shot Glass

Shake with ice and strain

GREEN MOTHERFUCKER

- 1 part 151-Proof Rum
- 1 part Crème de Menthe (Green)
- Shot Glass

Shake with ice and strain

GREEN SNEAKER

- 2 parts Vodka
- 1 part Melon Liqueur
- 1 part Cointreau®
- splash Cream
- Shot Glass

Shake with ice and strain

GREEN THING

- 1 part Coconut-Flavored Rum
- 1 part Melon Liqueur
- 2 parts Pineapple Juice
- Shot Glass

Shake with ice and strain

GREEN VOODOO

- 1 part Melon Liqueur
- 1 part Malibu® Rum
- 1 part Lemon-Lime Soda
- splash Triple Sec
- splash Sour Mix
- Shot Glass

Shake with ice and strain

GRENADE

- 1 part Vodka
- 1 part Triple Sec
- 1 part Grenadine
- Shot Glass

Shake with ice and strain

GREYHOUND

- 1 part Cointreau®
- 1 part Drambuie®
- Shot Glass

Shake with ice and strain

GROSS ONE

- 1 part Vodka
- 1 part Gin
- 1 part Jack Daniel's®
- 1 part Amaretto
- 1 part Sambuca
- Shot Glass

Shake with ice and strain. *Note: Because this recipe includes many ingredients, it's easier to make in volume, about 6 shots.

GROUND ZERO

- 1 part Peppermint Schnapps
- 1 part Vodka
- 1 part Coffee Liqueur
- Shot Glass

Shake with ice and strain

GUMBALL HUMMER

- 1 part Raspberry Liqueur
- 1 part Banana Liqueur
- 1 part Grapefruit Juice
- Shot Glass

Shake with ice and strain

HAGGIS

- 1 part Bourbon
- 1 part Cognac
- 1 part Southern Comfort®
- Shot Glass

Shake with ice and strain

HAIL CAESAR

- 1 part Melon Liqueur
- 1 part Crème de Banana
- 1 part Sour Mix
- Shot Glass

Shake with ice and strain

HALLOWEEN SHOOTER

- 1 part Licor 43®
- 1 part Sambuca
- Shot Glass

Shake with ice and strain

HANGIN' AROUND

- 1 part Tequila Silver
- 1 part Triple Sec
- 1 part Grenadine
- Shot Glass

Shake with ice and strain

HAPPY CAMPER

- 1 part Amaretto
- 1 part Frangelico®
- 1 part Coffee Liqueur
- Shot Glass

Shake with ice and strain

HAPPY IRISH

- 1 part Crème de Menthe (White)
- 1 part Sambuca
- Shot Glass

Shake with ice and strain

HAPPY JUICE

- 1 part Lemon Juice
- 1 part Vodka
- Shot Glass

Shake with ice and strain

HAPPY TOOTH

- 1 part Coffee Liqueur
- 1 part Sambuca
- Shot Glass

Shake with ice and strain

HARLEY DAVIDSON®

- 1 part Yukon Jack®
- 1 part Jack Daniel's®
- Shot Glass

Shake with ice and strain

HARLEY OIL

- 2 parts Jägermeister®
- 1 part Coffee Liqueur
- Shot Glass

Shake with ice and strain

HARSH

- 1 part Tequila
- 1 part Jägermeister®
- Shot Glass

Shake with ice and strain

HAWAIIAN PUNCH® FROM HELL

- 1 part Vodka
- 1 part Southern Comfort®
- 1 part Amaretto
- splash Orange Juice
- splash Lemon-Lime Soda
- splash Grenadine
- Shot Glass

*Shake with ice and strain. *Note: Because this recipe includes many ingredients, it's easier to make in volume, about 6 shots.*

HAWOO-WOO

- 1 part Vodka
- 1 part Peach Schnapps
- 1 part Cranberry Juice Cocktail
- 1 part Pineapple Juice
- Shot Glass

Shake with ice and strain

HEAD IN THE SAND

- 1 part Crème de Menthe (White)
- 1 part Brandy
- 1 part Tequila Silver
- 1 part Grenadine
- Shot Glass

Shake with ice and strain

HEAD RUSH

- 1 part Peach Schnapps
- 1 part Pear Liqueur
- 1 part Sambuca
- Shot Glass

Shake with ice and strain

HEAVENLY ORGASM

- 2 parts Frangelico®
- 1 part Amaretto
- 1 part Irish Cream Liqueur
- Shot Glass

Shake with ice and strain

HEILIG

- 1 part Vodka
- 1 part Blueberry Schnapps
- 1 part Cranberry Juice Cocktail
- Shot Glass

Shake with ice and strain

HELICOPTER

- 1 part Green Chartreuse®
- 1 part 151-Proof Rum
- Shot Glass

Pour ingredients into glass neat (do not chill)

HELL'S EYE

- 1 part Canadian Whiskey
- 2 parts Coffee Liqueur
- 1 part Milk
- Shot Glass

Shake with ice and strain

HELL-RAISER

- 1 part Melon Liqueur
- 1 part Black Sambuca
- 1 part Strawberry Liqueur
- Shot Glass

Shake with ice and strain

HEMORRHAGING BRAIN

- 2 parts Strawberry Liqueur
- 1 part Irish Cream Liqueur
- splash Grenadine
- Shot Glass

Shake all but Grenadine with ice and strain into the glass. Place a few drops of Grenadine in the center of the drink.

HERMAN'S SPECIAL

- 1 part Vodka
- 1 part Brandy
- 3 parts Peach Schnapps
- splash Raspberry Liqueur
- Shot Glass

Shake with ice and strain

HEROIN

- 1 part Black Sambuca
- 1 part Grand Marnier®
- Shot Glass

Shake with ice and strain

HIDE THE BANANA

- 1 part Amaretto
- 1 part Melon Liqueur
- 1 part Citrus-Flavored Vodka
- Shot Glass

Shake with ice and strain

HIT AND RUN

- 1 part Anisette
- 1 part Gin
- Shot Glass

Shake with ice and strain

HOLE-IN-ONE SHOOTER

- 3 parts Melon Liqueur
- 1 part Apple Brandy
- splash Half and Half
- Shot Glass

Shake with ice and strain

HONEY BEAR

- 1 part Cream
- 1 part Coffee Liqueur
- 1 part Frangelico®
- 1 part Honey
- Shot Glass

Shake with ice and strain

HONEY-DEW-ME

- 1 part Bärenjäger®
- 1 part Melon Liqueur
- 2 parts Orange Juice
- Shot Glass

Shake with ice and strain

HONEYSUCKLE SHOOTER

- 2 parts Light Rum
- 1 part Simple Syrup
- 1 part Sour Mix
- Shot Glass

Shake with ice and strain

HONOLULU ACTION

- 1 part Grenadine
- 1 part Melon Liqueur
- 1 part Blue Curaçao
- 1 part Irish Cream Liqueur
- 1 part Tequila
- 1 part Vodka
- 1 part 151-Proof Rum
- top with Whipped Cream
- Shot Glass

Shake with ice and strain. *Note: Because this recipe includes many ingredients, it's easier to make in volume, about 6 shots.

HONOLULU HAMMER SHOOTER

- 2 parts Vodka
- 1 part Amaretto
- 1 part Pineapple Juice
- Shot Glass

Shake with ice and strain

HOOTER

- 1 part Citrus-Flavored Vodka
- 1 part Amaretto
- 1 part Orange Juice
- 1 part Grenadine
- Shot Glass

Shake with ice and strain

HORNET

- 2 parts Sloe Gin
- 1 part Peppermint Schnapps
- Shot Glass

Shake with ice and strain

HORNY BASTARD

- 1 part Vodka
- 1 part Caramel Liqueur
- splash Grenadine
- Shot Glass

Shake with ice and strain

HORNY BULL

- 1 part Tequila
- 1 part Rum
- Shot Glass

Shake with ice and strain

HORNY GIRL SCOUT

- 1 part Coffee Liqueur
- 1 part Peppermint Schnapps
- Shot Glass

Shake with ice and strain

HORNY MONKEY

- 1 part Banana Liqueur
- 1 part Black Sambuca
- Shot Glass

Shake with ice and strain

HORNY SOUTHERNER

- 2 parts Southern Comfort®
- 2 parts Melon Liqueur
- 1 part Sour Mix
- 1 part Lemon-Lime Soda
- Shot Glass

Shake with ice and strain

HORSEMEN OF THE APOCALYPSE

- 1 part Jack Daniel's®
- 1 part Jim Beam®
- 1 part Tequila
- 1 part Spiced Rum
- Shot Glass

Pour ingredients into glass neat (do not chill)

HOT AFTERNOON

- 1 part Peach Schnapps
- 1 part Coffee Liqueur
- Shot Glass

Shake with ice and strain

HOT APPLE PIE

- 1 part Irish Cream Liqueur
- 1 part Goldschläger®
- Shot Glass

Shake with ice and strain

HOT BEACH SHOOTER

- 1 part Hot Coffee
- 1 part Peach Schnapps
- 1 part Coconut-Flavored Rum
- Shot Glass

Pour ingredients into glass neat (do not chill)

HOT BOMB

- 3 parts Tequila
- 1 part Cinnamon Schnapps
- Shot Glass

Shake with ice and strain

HOT BROWN LIZARD

- 1 part Cinnamon Schnapps
- 1 part Melon Liqueur
- Shot Glass

Pour ingredients into glass neat (do not chill)

HOT DAMN

- 1 part Whiskey
- 1 part Orange Juice
- 1 part Rum
- 1 part Vodka
- Shot Glass

Shake with ice and strain

HOT DOCTOR

- 1 part Hot Damn!® Cinnamon Schnapps.
- 1 part Dr. McGillicuddy's® Mentholmint Schnapps
- Shot Glass

Shake with ice and strain

HOT FUCK

- 1 part Hot Damn!® Cinnamon Schnapps
- 1 part Jägermeister®
- Shot Glass

Shake with ice and strain

HOT FUSION

- 1 part Melon Liqueur
- 1 part Absolut® Peppar Vodka
- Shot Glass

Shake with ice and strain

HOT GEORGIA PEACH

- 1 part Hot Damn!® Cinnamon Schnapps
- 1 part Peach Schnapps
- Shot Glass

Shake with ice and strain

HOT JOSÉ

- 1 part Hot Damn!® Cinnamon Schnapps
- 1 part Tequila
- Shot Glass

Shake with ice and strain

HOT PEACH PIE

- 1 part 151-Proof Rum
- 1 part Peach Schnapps
- Shot Glass

Shake with ice and strain

HOT STUFF

- 1 part Amaretto
- 1 part Hot Coffee
- Shot Glass

Pour ingredients into glass neat (do not chill)

HOT TAMALE

- 3 parts Goldschläger®
- 1 part Tequila Silver
- Shot Glass

Shake with ice and strain

HOT TO TROT

- 1 part Cinnamon Schnapps
- 1 part Tequila
- splash Lime Juice
- Shot Glass

Shake with ice and strain

HOT WET PUSSY

- 1 part 151-Proof Rum
- 1 part Melon Liqueur
- 1 part Peach Schnapps
- 1 part Lemon-Lime Soda
- 2 parts Pineapple Juice
- Shot Glass

Shake with ice and strain. *Note: Because this recipe includes many ingredients, it's easier to make in volume, about 6 shots.

HOWLING COYOTE

- 1 part Chambord®
- 3 parts Tequila
- Shot Glass

Shake with ice and strain

HUNTING PARTY

- 1 part Tequila Reposado
- 1 part Jack Daniel's®
- 1 part Jim Beam®
- 1 part Whiskey
- 1 part Wild Turkey® Bourbon
- Shot Glass

*Shake with ice and strain. *Note: Because this recipe includes many ingredients, it's easier to make in volume, about 6 shots.*

HYPER MONKEY

- 1 part Banana Liqueur
- 1 part Coffee Liqueur
- Shot Glass

Shake with ice and strain

I LOVE ROSA

- 1 part Jack Daniel's®
- 1 part Amaretto
- 1 part Cola
- Shot Glass

Pour ingredients into glass neat (do not chill)

ICE BLUE KAMIKAZE

- 1 part Rumple Minze®
- 1 part Vodka
- 1 part Lemon-Lime Soda
- Shot Glass

Pour ingredients into glass neat (do not chill)

ICE BOLTS

- 1 part Coffee Liqueur
- 1 part Tonic Water
- Shot Glass

Pour ingredients into glass neat (do not chill)

ICE CREAM SHOT

- 1 part Vanilla Liqueur
- 1 part Irish Cream Liqueur
- Shot Glass

Shake with ice and strain

ICEBERG SHOOTER

- 1 part Crème de Menthe (White)
- 1 part Citrus-Flavored Vodka
- Shot Glass

Shake with ice and strain

ICED BLUES

- 1 part Blackberry Liqueur
- 1 part Blue Curaçao
- Shot Glass

Shake with ice and strain

ICY AFTER EIGHT

- 2 parts Vodka
- 1 part Crème de Menthe (Green)
- 1 part Chocolate Syrup
- Shot Glass

Shake with ice and strain

IGUANA

- 1 part Vodka
- 1 part Tequila
- 1 part Coffee Liqueur
- Shot Glass

Shake with ice and strain

ILLUSION

- 1 part Coconut-Flavored Rum
- 1 part Melon Liqueur
- 1 part Vodka
- 1 part Cointreau®
- splash Pineapple Juice
- Shot Glass

Shake with ice and strain

IMMACULATE INGESTION

- 1 part Coffee Liqueur
- 1 part Peppermint Schnapps
- 1 part Vodka
- Shot Glass

Shake with ice and strain

IN THE NAVY

- 1 part Crème de Cacao (White)
- 1 part Crème de Menthe (White)
- Shot Glass

Shake with ice and strain

INK SPOT

- 3 parts Blackberry Liqueur
- 1 part Crème de Menthe (White)
- Shot Glass

Shake with ice and strain

INTERNATIONAL INCIDENT

- 1 part Vodka
- 1 part Coffee Liqueur
- 1 part Amaretto
- 1 part Frangelico®
- 2 parts Irish Cream Liqueur
- Shot Glass

Shake with ice and strain

INTO THE BLUE

- 1 part Blue Curaçao
- 1 part Pineapple Juice
- 1 part Coffee Liqueur
- Shot Glass

Shake with ice and strain

IRISH BROGUE

- 3 parts Whiskey
- 1 part Irish Mist®

- Shot Glass

Shake with ice and strain

IRISH BULLDOG

- 1 part Irish Cream Liqueur
- 1 part Vodka

- Shot Glass

Shake with ice and strain

IRISH HAMMER

- 1 part Jack Daniel's®
- 1 part Irish Mist®

- 1 part Irish Cream Liqueur
- Shot Glass

Shake with ice and strain

IRISH KISS

- 1 part Irish Cream Liqueur
- 1 part Rumple Minze®

- Shot Glass

Shake with ice and strain

IRISH KISS SHOT

- 1 part Whiskey
- 1 part Irish Mist®

- Shot Glass

Shake with ice and strain

IRISH MELON BALL

- 1 part Irish Whiskey
- 1 part Melon Liqueur

- Shot Glass

Shake with ice and strain

IRISH PIRATE

- 1 part Spiced Rum
- 1 part Irish Mist®

- Shot Glass

Shake with ice and strain

IRISH POTATO FAMINE

- 1 part Vodka
- 1 part Irish Whiskey

- 1 part Irish Cream Liqueur
- Shot Glass

Shake with ice and strain

IRISH QUAALUDE

- 1 part Crème de Cacao (White)
- 1 part Frangelico®

- 1 part Citrus-Flavored Vodka
- Shot Glass

Shake with ice and strain

IRISH SETTER

- 2 parts Irish Mist®
- 2 parts Frangelico®
- 1 part Brandy
- 1 part Crème de Menthe (White)
- Shot Glass

Shake with ice and strain

IRISH SLAMMER

- 3 parts Crème de Banana
- 1 part Whiskey
- Shot Glass

Shake with ice and strain

IRON CROSS

- 1 part Crème de Menthe (White)
- 1 part Apricot Brandy
- Shot Glass

Shake with ice and strain

ITALIAN ECSTASY

- 1 part Grappa
- 1 part Frangelico®
- 1 part Cream
- 1 part Espresso
- Shot Glass

Shake with ice and strain

ITALIAN ORGASM

- 1 part Vodka
- 1 part Amaretto
- 1 part Irish Cream Liqueur
- 1 part Frangelico®
- Shot Glass

Shake with ice and strain

ITALIAN RUSSIAN

- 1 part Vodka
- 1 part Sambuca
- Shot Glass

Shake with ice and strain

ITALIAN SPEAR

- 1 part Crème de Menthe (White)
- 1 part Amaretto
- Shot Glass

Shake with ice and strain

ITALIAN STALLION

- 2 parts Sambuca
- 1 part Amaretto
- 1 part Frangelico®
- Shot Glass

Shake with ice and strain

ITALIAN STALLION SHOOTER

- 1 part Galliano®
- 1 part Cream
- 1 part Crème de Banana
- Shot Glass

Shake with ice and strain

JACK AND JILL

- 1 part Jack Daniel's®
- 1 part Root Beer Schnapps
- Shot Glass

Shake with ice and strain

JACK IN THE BOX

- 1 part Coffee Liqueur
- 1 part Jack Daniel's®
- 1 part Cream de Banana
- Shot Glass

Shake with ice and strain

JACKASS

- 2 parts Cinnamon Schnapps
- 1 part Yukon Jack®
- Shot Glass

Shake with ice and strain

JACKHAMMER

- 1 part Jack Daniel's®
- 1 part Tequila
- Shot Glass

Pour ingredients into glass neat (do not chill)

JACKHAMMER#2

- 1 part Jack Daniel's®
- 1 part Tequila
- Shot Glass

Shake with ice and strain

JACKSON 5

- 1 part Jim Beam®
- 1 part Jack Daniel's®
- 1 part Rye Whiskey
- 1 part Tequila
- 1 part Jägermeister®
- Shot Glass

Shake with ice and strain. *Note: Because this recipe includes many ingredients, it's easier to make in volume, about 6 shots.

JÄGER® BABY

- 1 part Irish Cream Liqueur
- 1 part Jägermeister®
- Shot Glass

Pour ingredients into glass neat (do not chill)

JÄGER® BARREL

- 1 part Jägermeister®
- 1 part Root Beer Schnapps
- 1 part Cola
- Shot Glass

Shake with ice and strain

JÄGER® MINT

- 1 part Jägermeister®
- 1 part Peppermint Schnapps
- Shot Glass

Shake with ice and strain

JÄGER® OATMEAL COOKIE

- 1 part Jägermeister®
- 1 part Coffee Liqueur
- 1 part Irish Cream Liqueur
- 1 part Butterscotch Schnapps
- Shot Glass

Shake with ice and strain

JÄGER® SHAKE

- 1 part Jägermeister®
- 1 part Crème de Cacao (White)
- splash Half and Half
- Shot Glass

Shake with ice and strain

JÄGERITA

- 1 part Jägermeister®
- 1 part Tequila
- 1 part Lime Juice
- Shot Glass

Shake with ice and strain

JÄGERSHOCK

- 1 part After Shock® Cinnamon Schnapps
- 1 part Jägermeister®
- Shot Glass

Shake with ice and strain

JAMAICA DUST

- 1 part Southern Comfort®
- 1 part Tia Maria®
- 1 part Pineapple Juice
- Shot Glass

Shake with ice and strain

JAMAICAN BOBSLED

- 1 part Vodka
- 1 part Banana Liqueur
- Shot Glass

Shake with ice and strain

JAMAICAN DUSTBUSTER®

- 1 part Rum
- 1 part Coffee Liqueur
- 2 parts Pineapple Juice
- Shot Glass

Shake with ice and strain

JAMAICAN LEMON DROP

- 1 part Dark Rum
- 1 part Triple Sec
- 1 part Lemonade
- Shot Glass

Shake with ice and strain

JAMAICAN QUAALUDE

- 1 part Coconut-Flavored Rum
- 1 part Frangelico®
- 1 part Irish Cream Liqueur
- 1 part Milk
- Shot Glass

Shake with ice and strain

JAMAICAN WIND

- 1 part Coffee Liqueur
- 3 parts Dark Rum
- Shot Glass

Shake with ice and strain

JAMBALAYA

- 1 part Peach Schnapps
- 1 part Southern Comfort®
- 1 part Sour Mix
- splash Grenadine
- Shot Glass

Shake with ice and strain

JAMBOREE

- 1 part Vodka
- 1 part Wild Berry Schnapps
- 1 part Cranberry Juice Cocktail
- Shot Glass

Shake with ice and strain

JEALOUS QUEEN

- 1 part Triple Sec
- 2 parts Vodka
- dash Bitters
- dash Salt
- Shot Glass

Shake with ice and strain

JEDI® MIND PROBE

- 1 part Irish Cream Liqueur
- 1 part Butterscotch Schnapps
- 1 part Jägermeister®
- Shot Glass

Pour ingredients into glass neat (do not chill)

JELL-O® SHOTS

- 1 package instant Jell-O® (see flavor combinations)
- 1 part Hot Water
- 1 part Liqueur (see flavor combinations)
- Shot Glass

Basic Recipe: Dissolve Jell-O® in hot water. Add Liqueur. Pour into small paper cups and chill. Serve after the Jell-O® has set.

Flavor Combinations

	Jell-O® Flavor	Liqueur
Cape Cods	Cranberry	Vodka
Gimlets	Lime	Gin
Lemonheads	Lemon	Vodka
Coco Blue	Blue Raspberry	Coconut Rum
Coco Islands	Island Pineapple	Coconut Rum
Margaritas	Lime	Tequila
Melon Sours	Lime	Melon Liqueur

JELLY BEAN

- 1 part Blackberry Brandy
- 1 part Peppermint Schnapps
- Shot Glass

Shake with ice and strain

JELLY BEAN #2

- 1 part Coffee Liqueur
- 1 part Anisette
- 1 part 151-Proof Rum
- Shot Glass

Shake with ice and strain

JELLY FISH

- 1 part Crème de Cacao (White)
- 1 part Amaretto
- 1 part Irish Cream Liqueur
- 2 splashes Grenadine
- Shot Glass

Shake all but Grenadine with ice and strain into the glass. Place a few drops of Grenadine in the center of the drink.

JET FUEL

- 1 part Grand Marnier®
- 1 part Southern Comfort®
- Shot Glass

Shake with ice and strain

JIVE-AID

- 1 part Vodka
- 1 part Sloe Gin
- 1 part Cherry Liqueur
- 1 part Watermelon Schnapps
- splash Lemon-Lime Soda
- splash Sour Mix
- Shot Glass

Shake with ice and strain

JOGGER

- 1 part Citrus-Flavored Vodka
- 1 part Vodka
- 1 part Orange Juice
- 1 part Galliano®
- Shot Glass

Shake with ice and strain

JOHNNY ON THE BEACH

- 3 parts Vodka
- 2 parts Melon Liqueur
- 2 parts Blackberry Liqueur
- 1 part Pineapple Juice
- 1 part Orange Juice
- 1 part Grapefruit Juice
- 1 part Cranberry Juice Cocktail
- Shot Glass

Shake with ice and strain. *Note: Because this recipe includes many ingredients, it's easier to make in volume, about 6 shots.

JONNY APPLESEED

- 1 part Vodka
- 1 part Raspberry Liqueur
- 1 part Melon Liqueur
- 1 part Peach Schnapps
- 1 part Pineapple Juice
- Shot Glass

Shake with ice and strain. *Note: Because this recipe includes many ingredients, it's easier to make in volume, about 6 shots.

JONNY G SPOT

- 1 part Vodka
- 1 part Blue Curaçao
- 1 part Orange Juice
- Shot Glass

Shake with ice and strain

JOSÉ FLAME-O

- 1 part Tequila
- 1 part Fire Water®
- Shot Glass

Pour ingredients into glass neat (do not chill)

JOSÉ PACHE SOMBRERO

- 1 part Jack Daniel's®
- 1 part Brandy
- 1 part Tequila
- Shot Glass

Pour ingredients into glass neat (do not chill)

JUDGMENT DAY

- 1 part Coffee Liqueur
- 1 part Jägermeister®
- 1 part Rumple Minze®
- splash 151-Proof Rum
- splash Grain Alcohol
- Shot Glass

Shake with ice and strain. *Note: Because this recipe includes many ingredients, it's easier to make in volume, about 6 shots.

JUICY FRUIT®

- 2 parts Raspberry Liqueur
- 1 part Triple Sec
- 1 part Melon Liqueur
- Shot Glass

Shake with ice and strain

JUICY LIPS

- 1 part Vodka
- 1 part Crème de Banana
- 1 part Pineapple Juice
- Shot Glass

Shake with ice and strain

JUICY PUSSY

- 1 part Irish Cream Liqueur
- 1 part Peach Schnapps
- 1 part Pineapple Juice
- Shot Glass

Shake with ice and strain

JUICY VOLKHEIMER

- 1 part Vodka
- 1 part Coconut-Flavored Rum
- Shot Glass

Shake with ice and strain

JUNIOR MINT®

- 1 part Peppermint Schnapps
- 1 part Crème de Cacao (Dark)
- Shot Glass

Shake with ice and strain

JUST SHOOT ME

- 1 part Jim Beam®
- 1 part Jack Daniel's®
- 1 part Johnnie Walker® Red Label
- 1 part Tequila
- 1 part Jägermeister®
- 1 part 151-Proof Rum
- Shot Glass

Shake with ice and strain. *Note: Because this recipe includes many ingredients, it's easier to make in volume, about 6 shots.

KAISERMEISTER

- 1 part Jägermeister®
- 1 part Root Beer Schnapps
- Shot Glass

Shake with ice and strain

KALABREEZE

- 1 part Cherry Brandy
- 1 part Apricot Brandy
- 1 part Triple Sec
- Shot Glass

Shake with ice and strain

KAMIHUZI

- 1 part Tequila
- 1 part Triple Sec
- 1 part Sour Mix
- Shot Glass

Shake with ice and strain

KAMIKAZE

- 1 part Vodka
- 1 part Triple Sec
- 1 part Lime Juice
- Shot Glass

Shake with ice and strain

KARE BEAR

- 1 part Amaretto
- 1 part Blue Curaçao
- 1 part Banana Liqueur
- Shot Glass

Shake with ice and strain

KE LARGO

- 1 part KeKe Beach® Key Lime Cream Liqueur
- 1 part Melon Liqueur
- Shot Glass

Shake with ice and strain

KEITH JACKSON

- 1 part Amaretto
- 1 part Southern Comfort®
- 1 part Peach Schnapps
- 1 part Sour Mix
- 1 part Lemon-Lime Soda
- Shot Glass

Shake with ice and strain

KEREMIKI

- 1 part 151-Proof Rum
- 1 part Goldschläger®
- 1 part Rumple Minze®
- Shot Glass

Shake with ice and strain

KERMIT'S BELLY BUTTON

- 1 part Peach Schnapps
- 1 part Blue Curaçao
- 1 part Orange Juice
- Shot Glass

Shake with ice and strain

KEY LIME PIE

- 2 parts Licor 43®
- 2 parts Half and Half
- 1 part Lime Juice
- Shot Glass

Shake with ice and strain

KEY LIME SHOOTER

- 2 parts Licor 43®
- 1 part Light Rum
- 1 part Sour Mix
- splash Sweetened Lime Juice
- splash Half and Half
- Shot Glass

Shake with ice and strain

KEY WEST SHOOTER

- 1 part Vodka
- 1 part Melon Liqueur
- 1 part Orange Juice
- 1 part Pineapple Juice
- Shot Glass

Shake with ice and strain

KICK ME IN THE JIMMY

- 1 part Jägermeister®
- 1 part Jack Daniel's®
- 1 part Tequila
- 1 part Fire Water®
- Shot Glass

Shake with ice and strain

KICKSTAND

- 1 part Amaretto
- 1 part Southern Comfort®
- 1 part Coffee Liqueur
- 1 part Irish Cream Liqueur
- Shot Glass

Shake with ice and strain

KILLER BEE

- 1 part Jägermeister®
- 1 part Bärenjäger®
- Shot Glass

Shake with ice and strain

KILLER CRAWDAD

- 1 part Goldschläger®
- 1 part Cherry Brandy
- Shot Glass

Shake with ice and strain

KILLER KOOL-AID®

- 2 parts Vodka
- 1 part Amaretto
- 1 part Melon Liqueur
- 1 part Cranberry Juice Cocktail
- Shot Glass

Shake with ice and strain

KILLER OREOS®

- 1 part Jägermeister®
- 1 part Coffee Liqueur
- 1 part Irish Cream Liqueur
- Shot Glass

Shake with ice and strain

KILLER SNIFF

- 1 part Sambuca
- 1 part Blue Curaçao
- Shot Glass

Shake with ice and strain

KILLING SPREE

- 1 part Passion Fruit Liqueur
- 1 part Advocaat
- Shot Glass

Shake with ice and strain

KIMBER KRUSH

- 1 part Vanilla-Flavored Vodka
- 1 part Rumple Minze®
- 1 part Irish Cream Liqueur
- 1 part Raspberry Liqueur
- Shot Glass

Shake with ice and strain

KING'S RANSOM

- 1 part Goldschläger®
- 1 part Crown Royal® Whiskey
- Shot Glass

Shake with ice and strain

KISH WACKER

- 1 part Irish Cream Liqueur
- 1 part Crème de Cacao (Dark)
- 1 part Vodka
- 1 part Coffee Liqueur
- Shot Glass

Shake with ice and strain

KITTY

- 1 part Crème de Banana
- 1 part Triple Sec
- 1 part Jim Beam®
- 1 part Lemon Juice
- Shot Glass

Shake with ice and strain

KIWIKI

- 1 part Vodka
- 1 part Kiwi Schnapps
- 1 part Triple Sec
- Shot Glass

Shake with ice and strain

KLINGON® DISRUPTER

- 1 part Jim Beam®
- 1 part Mescal
- 1 part Cinnamon Schnapps
- Shot Glass

Shake with ice and strain

KLONDYKE

- 1 part Irish Cream Liqueur
- 1 part Jägermeister®
- Shot Glass

Shake with ice and strain

KOOL-AID®

- 1 part Vodka
- 1 part Amaretto
- 1 part Melon Liqueur
- 1 part Raspberry Liqueur
- Shot Glass

Shake with ice and strain

KRAZY KAT

- 1 part Coffee Liqueur
- 1 part Coconut-Flavored Liqueur
- 1 part Crème de Banana
- Shot Glass

Shake with ice and strain

KREMLIN SHOOTER

- 1 part Vodka
- splash Grenadine
- Shot Glass

Shake with ice and strain

KRIAURA

- 1 part Wild Berry Schnapps
- 1 part Lemon-Lime Soda
- 1 part Cranberry Juice Cocktail
- Shot Glass

Shake with ice and strain

KRIS KRINGLE

- 1 part Crème de Noyaux
- 1 part Root Beer Schnapps
- 1 part Half and Half
- Shot Glass

Shake with ice and strain

KURANT SHOOTER

- 1 part Melon Liqueur
- 1 part Currant-Flavored Vodka
- 2 parts Pineapple Juice
- Shot Glass

Shake with ice and strain

KURANT STINGER

- 1 part Bärenjäger®
- 1 part Currant-Flavored Vodka
- Shot Glass

Shake with ice and strain

LA PUSSY

- 1 part Light Rum
- 1 part Cointreau®
- 1 part Brandy
- 1 part Sour Apple Schnapps
- Shot Glass

Shake with ice and strain

THE LADY IN RED

- 1 part Peppermint Schnapps
- 1 part Peach Schnapps
- 1 part Vodka
- 1 part Grenadine
- Shot Glass

Shake with ice and strain

LADY KILLER SHOOTER

- 1 part Coffee
- 1 part Melon Liqueur
- 1 part Frangelico®
- Shot Glass

Shake with ice and strain

LAND ROVER®

- 1 part Spiced Rum
- 1 part Coffee Liqueur
- 1 part Irish Cream Liqueur
- Shot Glass

Shake with ice and strain

LANDMINE

- 1 part 151-Proof Rum
- 1 part Jägermeister®
- Shot Glass

Shake with ice and strain

LASER BEAM

- 1 part Amaretto
- 1 part Grand Marnier®
- 1 part Melon Liqueur
- 1 part Pineapple Juice
- 1 part Southern Comfort®
- Shot Glass

Shake with ice and strain. *Note: Because this recipe includes many ingredients, it's easier to make in volume, about 6 shots.

THE LAST STOP

- 1 part Maraschino Liqueur
- 1 part Blackberry Liqueur
- splash Absinthe
- Shot Glass

Shake with ice and strain

LAY DOWN AND SHUT UP!

- 1 part Jägermeister®
- 1 part Cinnamon Schnapps
- 1 part Coffee Liqueur
- splash Cream
- Shot Glass

Shake with ice and strain

LAZER BEAM

- 1 part Amaretto
- 1 part Peach Schnapps
- 1 part Orange Juice
- Shot Glass

Shake with ice and strain

LEATHER WHIP

- 1 part Tequila
- 1 part Triple Sec
- 1 part Jack Daniel's®
- 1 part Peach Schnapps
- Shot Glass

Shake with ice and strain

LEMON DROP SHOOTER

- 1 part Vodka
- 1 Lemon Wedge
- dash Sugar
- Shot Glass

Shake the Vodka with ice and strain into a shot glass. Pour the Sugar onto the Lemon Wedge. Drink the shot and bite down on the Lemon Wedge.

LEMON MERINGUE

- 1 part Vodka
- 1 part Lemon Juice
- Shot Glass

Shake with ice and strain. Top with Whipped Cream.

LEPRECHAUN SHOOTER

- 1 part Blue Curaçao
- 1 part Peach Schnapps
- 1 part Orange Juice
- Shot Glass

Shake with ice and strain

LEPRECHAUN'S GOLD

- 1 part Goldschläger®
- 1 part Irish Cream Liqueur
- Shot Glass

Shake with ice and strain

LETHAL INJECTION

- 1 part Rum
- 1 part Coconut-Flavored Rum
- 1 part Dark Rum
- 1 part Amaretto
- 1 part Orange Juice
- 1 part Pineapple Juice
- Shot Glass

Shake with ice and strain

LEVITE PEPPER SLAMMER

- 1 part Southern Comfort®
- 2 parts Dr Pepper®
- Shot Glass

Build in the glass with no ice

LEWINSKY BLOW JOB

- 1 part Amaretto
- 2 parts Cola
- splash 151-Proof Rum
- Shot Glass

Shake with ice and strain. Top with whipped cream and drink without using your hands.

LIFE PRESERVER

- 1 part Blue Curaçao
- 1 part Vodka
- 1 piece Cheerios® cereal
- Shot Glass

Shake the Vodka and Blue Curaçao with ice and strain. Float the Cheerio in the center of the shot.

LIGHT GREEN PANTIES

- 1 part Crème de Menthe (Green)
- 1 part Vodka
- 1 part Irish Cream Liqueur
- splash Grenadine
- Shot Glass

Shake all but Grenadine with ice and strain into the glass. Place a few drops of Grenadine in the center of the drink.

LIGHT-HEADED

- 1 part Blue Curaçao
- 1 part Coconut-Flavored Liqueur
- 1 part Strawberry Liqueur
- Shot Glass

Shake with ice and strain

LIME LIZARD

- 1 part Vodka
- 1 part Rum
- 1 part Lime Juice
- 1 part Grenadine
- Shot Glass

Shake with ice and strain

LIP LOCK

- 1 part Dark Rum
- 1 part Coconut-Flavored Rum
- 1 part Grenadine
- 1 part Pineapple Juice
- 1 part Orange Juice
- Shot Glass

*Shake with ice and strain.
*Note: Because this recipe
includes many ingredients,
it's easier to make in volume,
about 6 shots.*

LIPSTICK LESBIAN

- 1 part Raspberry-Flavored Vodka
- 1 part Watermelon Schnapps
- 1 part Cranberry Juice Cocktail
- 1 part Sour Mix
- Shot Glass

Shake with ice and strain

LIQUID ASPHALT

- 1 part Sambuca
- 1 part Jägermeister®
- Shot Glass

Shake with ice and strain

LIQUID CANDY CANE

- 1 part Vodka
- 2 parts Cherry Liqueur
- 2 parts Peppermint Schnapps
- Shot Glass

Shake with ice and strain

LIQUID COCAINE

- 1 part Grand Marnier®
- 1 part Southern Comfort®
- 1 part Vodka
- 1 part Amaretto
- 1 part Pineapple Juice
- Shot Glass

*Shake with ice and strain. *Note: Because this recipe includes many ingredients, it's easier to make in volume, about 6 shots.*

LIQUID CRACK

- 1 part Jägermeister®
- 1 part Rumple Minze®
- 1 part 151-Proof Rum
- 1 part Goldschläger®
- Shot Glass

Shake with ice and strain

LIQUID HEROIN

- 1 part Vodka
- 1 part Rumple Minze®
- 1 part Jägermeister®
- Shot Glass

Shake with ice and strain

LIQUID MENTOS®

- 1 part Blue Curaçao
- 1 part Peach Schnapps
- 1 part Banana Liqueur
- Shot Glass

Shake with ice and strain

LIQUID NITROGEN

- 1 part Sambuca
- 1 part Ouzo
- Shot Glass

Shake with ice and strain

LIQUID QUAALUDE

- 1 part Jägermeister®
- 3 parts Irish Cream Liqueur
- Shot Glass

Shake with ice and strain

LIQUID ROCHER®

- 2 parts Crème de Cacao (White)
- 1 part Frangelico®
- 1 part Vanilla Liqueur
- Shot Glass

Shake with ice and strain

LIQUID SCREW

- 1 part Coconut-Flavored Rum
- 1 part Peach Schnapps
- 1 part Vodka
- 1 part Lemon-Lime Soda
- Shot Glass

Shake with ice and strain

LIQUID VALIUM®

- 1 part Jack Daniel's®
- 1 part Amaretto
- 1 part Tequila
- 1 part Triple Sec
- Shot Glass

Shake with ice and strain

LIT CITY

- 1 part Jägermeister®
- 1 part Butterscotch Schnapps
- 1 part Irish Cream Liqueur
- 1 part Goldschläger®
- Shot Glass

Shake with ice and strain

LITTLE BITCH

- 1 part Southern Comfort®
- 1 part Amaretto
- 1 part Cranberry Juice Cocktail
- 1 part Orange Juice
- Shot Glass

Shake with ice and strain

A LITTLE GREEN MAN FROM MARS

- 1 Green Maraschino Cherry
- 1 part Jägermeister®
- 1 part Rumple Minze®
- Shot Glass

Remove stem from the Green Maraschino Cherry and drop the cherry in the glass. Pour equal parts Jägermeister and Rumple Minze.

A LITTLE NERVOUS

- 1 part Vodka
- 1 part Peach Schnapps
- 1 part Blackberry Liqueur
- Shot Glass

Shake with ice and strain

A LITTLE PIECE OF HELL

- 1 part Cinnamon Schnapps
- 1 part Simple Syrup
- Shot Glass

Shake with ice and strain

LOBOTOMY

- 1 part Amaretto
- 1 part Raspberry Liqueur
- 1 part Pineapple Juice
- Shot Glass

Shake with ice and strain

LONDON PUMMEL

- 1 part Gin
- 1 part Tonic Water
- splash Lime Juice
- Shot Glass

Build in a shot glass

LONG ISLAND SHOOTER

- 1 part Tequila Silver
- 1 part Vodka
- 1 part Light Rum
- 1 part Gin
- 1 part Triple Sec
- 1 part Cola
- 1 part Sour Mix
- Shot Glass

Shake with ice and strain. *Note: Because this recipe includes many ingredients, it's easier to make in volume, about 6 shots.

LOVE IN THE SNOW

- 1 part Crème de Cacao (White)
- 1 part Amaretto
- 1 part Pisang Ambon® Liqueur
- Shot Glass

Shake with ice and strain

LOVE IS IN THE AIR

- 1 part Amaretto
- 1 part Coconut-Flavored Liqueur
- 1 part Crème de Banana
- Shot Glass

Shake with ice and strain

LOVE SHACK SHOOTER

- 2 parts Dark Rum
- 1 part Lemon-Lime Soda
- 1 part Orange Juice
- splash Grenadine
- Shot Glass

Shake with ice and strain

LUNA ROSSA

- 1 part Peach Schnapps
- 1 part Campari®
- 1 part Limoncello
- Shot Glass

Shake with ice and strain

M&M®

- 1 part Amaretto
- 1 part Coffee Liqueur
- Shot Glass

Shake with ice and strain

M.O. SHOOTER

- 1 part Cream
- 1 part Amaretto
- Shot Glass

Shake with ice and strain

M.V.P.'S STRAWBERRY BOMB

- 1 part Tequila Rose®
- 1 part Vodka
- 1 part Strawberry Liqueur
- Shot Glass

Shake with ice and strain

MAD COW

- 1 part Coffee Liqueur
- 1 part Cream
- 1 part 151-Proof Rum
- Shot Glass

Shake with ice and strain

MAD HATTER

- 1 part Vodka
- 1 part Peach Schnapps
- 1 part Lemonade
- 1 part Cola
- Shot Glass

Shake with ice and strain

MAD MELON SHOOTER

- 1 part Watermelon Schnapps
- 1 part Vodka
- Shot Glass

Shake with ice and strain

MAD SCIENTIST

- 1 part Blueberry Schnapps
- 1 part Raspberry Liqueur
- splash Irish Cream Liqueur
- Shot Glass

Shake with ice and strain

MADMAN'S RETURN

- 1 part Triple Sec
- 1 part Goldschläger®
- 1 part Cachaça
- 1 part Gin
- Shot Glass

Shake with ice and strain

MAGE'S FIRE

- 2 parts Vodka
- 1 part Cinnamon Schnapps
- 1 part Blue Curaçao
- Shot Glass

Shake with ice and strain

MAGIC POTION

- 1 part Coffee Liqueur
- 1 part Amaretto
- 1 part Crème de Cacao (Dark)
- Shot Glass

Shake with ice and strain

MAIDEN'S PRAYER SHOOTER

- 1 part Gin
- 1 part Lillet
- 1 part Calvados Apple Brandy
- Shot Glass

Shake with ice and strain

MASCONIVICH SHOOTER

- 1 part Brandy
- 1 part Triple Sec
- 1 part Cognac
- Shot Glass

Shake with ice and strain

MATTIKAZE

- 1 part Vodka
- 1 part Lime Juice
- 1 part Triple Sec
- 1 part Peach Schnapps
- Shot Glass

Shake with ice and strain

MAX FACTOR®

- 1 part Raspberry Liqueur
- 1 part Cranberry Juice Cocktail
- 1 part Triple Sec
- Shot Glass

Shake with ice and strain

MEAN MACHINE

- 1 part Crème de Menthe (White)
- 1 part Triple Sec
- Shot Glass

Shake with ice and strain

MEAT AND POTATOES

- 1 part Potato Vodka
- 1 Pepperoni Slice
- Shot Glass

Shake the Vodka with ice and strain into a shot glass. Garnish with a slice of Pepperoni.

MELARETTO

- 1 part Melon Liqueur
- 1 part Amaretto
- Shot Glass

Shake with ice and strain

MELON BALL SHOOTER

- 2 parts Melon Liqueur
- 1 part Vodka
- 1 part Orange Juice
- Shot Glass

Shake with ice and strain

MELON CHEER

- 1 part Melon Liqueur
- 1 part Strawberry Liqueur
- 1 part Sour Mix
- Shot Glass

Shake with ice and strain

MELON KAMIKAZE

- 1 part Vodka
- 1 part Melon Liqueur
- 1 part Sour Mix
- Shot Glass

Shake with ice and strain

MELONOMA

- 2 parts Vodka
- 1 part Melon Liqueur
- Shot Glass

Shake with ice and strain

MEMORY LOSS

- 1 part Vodka
- 1 part Raspberry Liqueur
- 1 part Banana Liqueur
- 1 part Cranberry Juice Cocktail
- 1 part Orange Juice
- Shot Glass

Shake with ice and strain. *Note: Because this recipe includes many ingredients, it's easier to make in volume, about 6 shots.

MENSTRUAL MINT

- 1 part Gin
- 1 part Grenadine
- 1 part Tequila
- Shot Glass

Shake with ice and strain

MERRY KAY

- 2 parts Jim Beam®
- 1 part Blue Curaçao
- Shot Glass

Shake with ice and strain

MEXICAN APPLE

- 1 part Apple Liqueur
- 1 part Tequila Silver
- Shot Glass

Shake with ice and strain

MEXICAN CHERRY BOMB

- 1 part Coffee Liqueur
- 1 part Cream
- 1 part Grenadine
- Shot Glass

Shake with ice and strain

MEXICAN GLOW WORM

- 1 part Melon Liqueur
- 1 part Gold Tequila
- Shot Glass

Shake with ice and strain

MEXICAN INCA

- 1 part Tequila Silver
- 1 part Coffee
- 1 part Grenadine
- Shot Glass

Shake with ice and strain

MEXICAN KAMIKAZE

- 2 parts Tequila
- 1 part Vodka
- 1 part Lemon Juice
- 1 part Lime Juice
- Shot Glass

Shake with ice and strain

MEXICAN KILLER

- 1 part Gold Tequila
- 1 part Peach Schnapps
- 1 part Sweetened Lime Juice
- Shot Glass

Shake with ice and strain

MEXICAN MELON

- 1 part Tequila Silver
- 1 part Melon Liqueur
- Shot Glass

Shake with ice and strain

MEXICAN MOUNTIE

- 1 part Tequila
- 1 part Yukon Jack®
- Shot Glass

Shake with ice and strain

MEXICAN MOUTHWASH

- 1 part Tequila
- 1 part Rumple Minze®
- Shot Glass

Shake with ice and strain

MEXICAN PEBBLE

- 1 part Blue Curaçao
- 1 part Gold Tequila
- 1 part Raspberry Liqueur
- 1 part Lemon-Lime Soda
- Shot Glass

Shake with ice and strain

MEXICAN SHAKE

- 1 part Tequila
- 1 part Coffee Liqueur
- 1 part Cola
- 1 part Cream
- Shot Glass

Shake with ice and strain

MEXICAN SNOWSHOE

- 1 part Peppermint Schnapps
- 1 part Tequila
- Shot Glass

Shake with ice and strain

MEXICAN STAND-OFF

- 1 part Vodka
- 1 part Tequila
- 1 part Passoã®
- Shot Glass

Shake with ice and strain

MEXICAN THANKSGIVING

- 1 part Tequila
- 1 part Wild Turkey® Bourbon
- Shot Glass

Shake with ice and strain

MEXICAN WATER

- 1 part Crown Royal® Whiskey
- 1 part Tequila Reposado
- 1 part Vodka
- Shot Glass

Shake with ice and strain

MIDNIGHT MATINEE

- 1 part Peach Schnapps
- 1 part Passion Fruit Liqueur
- 1 part Lemon Juice
- Shot Glass

Shake with ice and strain

MILANO SHOOTER

- 1 part Crème de Menthe (White)
- 1 part Fernet-Branca®
- 1 part Sambuca
- Shot Glass

Shake with ice and strain

MILD JIZZ

- 1 part Vodka
- 1 part Melon Liqueur
- 1 part Coconut-Flavored Rum
- 1 part Lemon-Lime Soda
- Shot Glass

Shake with ice and strain

MILKY NOOKY

- 1 part Peppermint Schnapps
- 1 part Irish Cream Liqueur
- 1 part Jägermeister®
- Shot Glass

Shake with ice and strain

MILKY WAY®

- 1 part Amaretto
- 1 part Crème de Cacao (Dark)
- 1 part Cream
- Shot Glass

Shake with ice and strain

MILKY WAY® #2

- 3 parts Irish Cream Liqueur
- 2 parts Root Beer Schnapps
- 1 part Goldschläger®
- Shot Glass

Shake with ice and strain

MIND COLLAPSE

- 1 part Crème de Menthe (White)
- 1 part Whiskey
- Shot Glass

Shake with ice and strain

MIND GAME

- 1 part Pernod®
- 1 part Blue Curaçao
- 2 parts Milk
- Shot Glass

Shake with ice and strain

MIND PROBE

- 1 part 151-Proof Rum
- 1 part Sambuca
- 1 part Jägermeister®
- Shot Glass

Shake with ice and strain

MINI MARGARITA

- 1 part Tequila Silver
- 1 part Triple Sec
- 1 part Sour Mix
- Shot Glass

Shake with ice and strain

MINT CHOCOLATE

- 2 parts Crème de Menthe (Green)
- 1 part Coffee Liqueur
- 1 part Irish Cream Liqueur
- Shot Glass

Shake with ice and strain

MINT DESIRE

- 1 part Rumple Minze®
- 1 part Coconut Cream
- 2 parts Cream
- Shot Glass

Shake with ice and strain

MINT JULEP SHOT

- 1 part Crème de Menthe (Green)
- 2 parts Bourbon
- Shot Glass

Shake with ice and strain

MINTARITA

- 1 part Crème de Menthe (White)
- 1 part Tequila Silver
- Shot Glass

Shake with ice and strain

MISCONAVITCH

- 1 part Cointreau®
- 3 parts Grand Marnier®
- Shot Glass

Shake with ice and strain

MISDEMEANOR

- 1 part Butterscotch Schnapps
- 1 part Crown Royal® Whiskey
- Shot Glass

Shake with ice and strain

MISTY BLUE CUMMING

- 1 part Vodka
- 1 part Sloe Gin
- 1 part Blue Curaçao
- 1 part Peach Schnapps
- Shot Glass

Shake with ice and strain

MONGOLIAN CLUSTERFUCK

- 1 part Jägermeister®
- 1 part Goldschläger®
- 1 part Rumple Minze®
- Shot Glass

Shake with ice and strain

MONKEY BRAIN

- 3 parts Coffee Liqueur
- 1 part Advocaat
- splash Grenadine
- Shot Glass

Shake all but Grenadine with ice and strain into the glass. Place a few drops of Grenadine in the center of the drink.

MONKEY POOPSHOOTER

- 1 part Vodka
- 1 part Crème de Banana
- 1 part Pineapple Juice
- 1 part Orange Juice
- 1 part Lime Cordial
- Shot Glass

Shake with ice and strain. *Note: Because this recipe includes many ingredients, it's easier to make in volume, about 6 shots.

MONKEY PUSSY

- 1 part Irish Cream Liqueur
- 1 part Banana Liqueur
- 1 part Crown Royal® Whiskey
- 1 part Raspberry Liqueur
- Shot Glass

Shake with ice and strain

MONSOON

- 1 part Currant-Flavored Vodka
- 1 part Amaretto
- 1 part Coffee Liqueur
- 1 part Frangelico®
- Shot Glass

Shake with ice and strain

MONTANA STUMP PULLER

- 1 part Crème de Cacao (White)
- 2 parts Canadian Whiskey
- Shot Glass

Shake with ice and strain

MOOSE FART

- 1 part Vodka
- 1 part Bourbon
- 1 part Coffee Liqueur
- 1 part Irish Cream Liqueur
- Shot Glass

Shake with ice and strain

MORANGUITO

- 1 part Absinthe
- 1 part Tequila
- 1 part Grenadine
- Shot Glass

Shake with ice and strain

MORGAN'S WENCH

- 1 part Spiced Rum
- 1 part Amaretto
- 1 part Crème de Cacao (Dark)
- Shot Glass

Shake with ice and strain

MORNING WOOD

- 1 part Vodka
- 1 part Peach Schnapps
- 1 part Orange Juice
- 1 part Sour Mix
- 1 part Raspberry Liqueur
- Shot Glass

Shake with ice and strain. *Note: Because this recipe includes many ingredients, it's easier to make in volume, about 6 shots.

MOTHER LOAD

- 1 part Vodka
- 1 part Blackberry Liqueur
- 1 part Coconut-Flavored Rum
- Shot Glass

Shake with ice and strain

MOTHER PUCKER SHOOTER

- 1 part Vodka
- 1 part Sour Apple Schnapps
- splash Lemon-Lime Soda
- splash Club Soda
- Shot Glass

Shake with ice and strain

MOUTHWASH

- 1 part Crème de Menthe (White)
- 1 part Vodka
- 1 part Blue Curaçao
- Shot Glass

Shake with ice and strain

MOUTHWATERING

- 1 part Amaretto
- 1 part Melon Liqueur

- Shot Glass

Shake with ice and strain

MR. BEAN

- 1 part Anisette
- 1 part Blackberry Liqueur

- Shot Glass

Shake with ice and strain

MR. G

- 1 part Licor 43®
- 1 part Vodka

- 2 parts Grenadine
- Shot Glass

Shake with ice and strain

MUD SLIDE SHOOTER

- 1 part Vodka
- 1 part Coffee Liqueur
- 1 part Irish Cream Liqueur
- Shot Glass

Shake with ice and strain

MUDDY WATER

- 1 part Vodka
- 1 part Coffee Liqueur
- 1 part Irish Cream Liqueur
- Shot Glass

Shake with ice and strain

MUDGUPPY

- 1 part Amaretto
- 1 part Irish Cream Liqueur
- 2 parts Bourbon
- Shot Glass

Shake with ice and strain

MUFF DIVE

- 1 part Vodka
- 1 part Peach Schnapps
- 1 part Cranberry Juice Cocktail
- Shot Glass

Shake with ice and strain

MUSSOLINI

- 1 part Goldschläger®
- 1 part Jägermeister®
- 1 part Sambuca
- Shot Glass

Shake with ice and strain

MUTATED MOTHER'S MILK

- 1 part Jägermeister®
- 1 part Irish Cream Liqueur
- 1 part Peppermint Schnapps
- Shot Glass

Shake with ice and strain

MY JOHNSON IS TEN INCHES LONG

- 2 parts Malibu® Rum
- 2 parts Raspberry Liqueur
- 2 parts Melon Liqueur
- 1 part Sour Mix
- 1 part Cranberry Juice Cocktail
- Shot Glass

Shake with ice and strain

NALGAS DE ORO

- 1 part Raspberry Liqueur
- 1 part Vanilla Liqueur
- 1 part 151-Proof Rum
- 1 part Grand Marnier®
- Shot Glass

Shake with ice and strain

NASTY STEWARDESS

- 1 part Licor 43®
- 2 parts Tonic Water
- 2 parts Orange Bitters
- Shot Glass

Build in the glass with no ice

NATURAL DISASTER

- 1 part Cinnamon Schnapps
- 1 part Peppermint Schnapps
- Shot Glass

Shake with ice and strain

NAUGHTY ANGEL

- 3 parts Chocolate Liqueur
- 1 part 151-Proof Rum
- Shot Glass

Shake with ice and strain

NAVY SEAL

- 1 part Crown Royal® Whiskey
- 1 part Rum
- Shot Glass

Shake with ice and strain

NEON BULLFROG

- 1 part Vodka
- 1 part Blue Curaçao
- 1 part Melon Liqueur
- 1 part Sour Mix
- Shot Glass

Shake with ice and strain

NEON CACTUS

- 1 part Cactus Juice Schnapps
- 1 part Margarita Mix
- Shot Glass

Shake with ice and strain

NEON LIZARD

- 1 part Blue Curaçao
- 1 part Melon Liqueur

- Shot Glass

Shake with ice and strain

NERD

- 1 part Cream
- 1 part Black Sambuca

- 1 part Strawberry Liqueur
- Shot Glass

Shake with ice and strain

NERO'S DELIGHT

- 1 part Vodka
- 1 part Sambuca

- Shot Glass

Shake with ice and strain

NEURONIUM

- 1 part Crème de Menthe (White)
- 1 part Vodka
- splash Grenadine
- Shot Glass

Shake all but Grenadine with ice and strain into the glass. Place a few drops of Grenadine in the center of the drink.

NEVER A SEVEN

- 2 parts Jack Daniel's®
- 1 part Tequila
- 1 part Rum
- 1 part Goldschläger®
- 1 part Hot Sauce
- Shot Glass

Shake with ice and strain

NEW ENGLAND KAMIKAZE

- 2 parts Grand Marnier®
- 1 part Sour Mix
- Shot Glass

Shake with ice and strain

NEW YORK SLAMMER

- 1 part Amaretto
- 1 part Orange Juice
- 1 part Southern Comfort®
- 1 part Triple Sec
- 1 part Sloe Gin
- Shot Glass

Shake with ice and strain

A NIGHT AT NAUGHTY NIKKI'S

- 1 part Vodka
- 2 parts Lemon-Lime Soda
- Skittles
- Shot Glass

Place the Skittles, or other fruity chewy candy, in the bottom of a shot glass, then pour Lemon-Lime Soda and Vodka.

NIGHT FLIGHT SHOOTER

- 1 part Amaretto
- 1 part Peach Schnapps
- 1 part Blackberry Liqueur
- Shot Glass

Shake with ice and strain

NINJA

- 3 parts Frangelico®
- 1 part Melon Liqueur
- Shot Glass

Shake with ice and strain

NITRO

- 1 part Sambuca
- 1 part Goldschläger®
- 1 part Brandy
- Shot Glass

Shake with ice and strain

NO NAME

- 1 part Amaretto
- 1 part Whiskey
- 1 part Sour Mix
- Shot Glass

Shake with ice and strain

NORWEGIAN PASTRY

- 1 part Crème de Cacao (Dark)
- 1 part Coffee
- 1 part Aquavit
- 1 part Vanilla Liqueur
- Shot Glass

Shake with ice and strain

NUCLEAR ACCELERATOR

- 1 part Citrus-Flavored Vodka
- 1 part Crème de Menthe (White)
- Shot Glass

Shake with ice and strain

NUCLEAR HOLOCAUST

- 1 part Blue Curaçao
- 1 part Peach Schnapps
- 1 part Crème de Banana
- 1 part Dark Rum
- Shot Glass

Shake with ice and strain

NUCLEAR KAMIKAZE

- 3 parts Vodka
- 1 part Lime Juice
- 1 part Triple Sec

- 2 parts Melon Liqueur
- Shot Glass

Shake with ice and strain

NUCLEAR WASTE

- 2 parts Vodka
- 1 part Melon Liqueur
- 1 part Triple Sec
- splash Lime Juice
- Shot Glass

Shake with ice and strain

NUTS 'N' HOLLY

- 1 part Drambuie®
- 1 part Irish Cream Liqueur
- 1 part Frangelico®
- 1 part Amaretto
- Shot Glass

Shake with ice and strain

NUTTY ARUBAN

- 1 part Frangelico®
- 1 part Ponche Kuba®
- Shot Glass

Shake with ice and strain

NUTTY JAMAICAN

- 1 part Dark Rum
- 1 part Frangelico®
- Shot Glass

Shake with ice and strain

NUTTY MEXICAN

- 1 part Tequila Silver
- 1 part Frangelico®

- Shot Glass

Shake with ice and strain

NUTTY ORANGE

- 1 part Amaretto
- 1 part Triple Sec

- Shot Glass

Shake with ice and strain

NUTTY PROFESSOR

- 1 part Grand Marnier®
- 1 part Frangelico®

- 1 part Irish Cream Liqueur
- Shot Glass

Shake with ice and strain

NYMPHOMANIAC

- 3 parts Spiced Rum
- 1 part Peach Schnapps
- 1 part Coconut-Flavored Rum
- Shot Glass

Shake with ice and strain

OATMEAL COOKIE

- 2 parts Cinnamon Schnapps
- 1 part Irish Cream Liqueur
- 1 part Coffee Liqueur
- 1 part Frangelico®
- 1 part Cream
- Shot Glass

Shake with ice and strain

OBLY GOOH

- 2 parts Crème de Menthe (White)
- 1 part Brandy
- Shot Glass

Shake with ice and strain

AN OFFER YOU CAN'T REFUSE

- 1 part Amaretto
- 1 part Sambuca

- Shot Glass

Shake with ice and strain

OIL SLICK

- 1 part Jägermeister®
- 1 part Rumple Minze®

- Shot Glass

Pour ingredients into glass neat (do not chill)

OLD CRUSTY

- 1 part 151-Proof Rum
- 1 part Wild Turkey® Bourbon

- Shot Glass

Shake with ice and strain

OPEN GRAVE

- 1 part Jägermeister®
- 1 part Rumple Minze®
- 1 part Irish Cream Liqueur
- Shot Glass

Shake with ice and strain

OPERA HOUSE SPECIAL

- 1 part Tequila
- 1 part Gin
- 1 part Light Rum
- 1 part Vodka
- 1 part Pineapple Juice
- 1 part Orange Juice
- 1 part Sour Mix
- Shot Glass

Shake with ice and strain. *Note: Because this recipe includes many ingredients, it's easier to make in volume, about 6 shots.

ORAL SEX

- 1 part Amaretto
- 1 part Irish Cream Liqueur
- Shot Glass

Shake with ice and strain

ORANGE CRISIS

- 2 parts Light Rum
- 2 parts Peach Schnapps
- 1 part Triple Sec
- 1 part Apricot Brandy
- 1 part Cream
- splash Grenadine
- Shot Glass

*Shake with ice and strain. *Note: Because this recipe includes many ingredients, it's easier to make in volume, about 6 shots.*

ORANGE CRUSH SHOOTER

- 1 part Vodka
- 1 part Triple Sec
- 1 part Club Soda
- Shot Glass

Stir gently with ice and strain

ORANGE MONK

- 3 parts Frangelico®
- 1 part Grand Marnier®
- Shot Glass

Pour ingredients into glass neat (do not chill)

ORGASM #1

- 1 part Amaretto
- 1 part Coffee Liqueur
- 1 part Light Cream
- Shot Glass

Shake with ice and strain

ORGASM #2

- 1 part Vodka
- 1 part Amaretto
- 1 part Coffee Liqueur
- 1 part Irish Cream Liqueur
- Shot Glass

Shake with ice and strain

ORGASM #3

- 3 parts Southern Comfort®
- 2 parts Pineapple Juice
- 1 part Amaretto
- Shot Glass

Shake with ice and strain

OTTER POP

- 2 parts Light Rum
- 2 parts Blue Curaçao
- 1 part Sour Mix
- 1 part Lemon-Lime Soda
- Shot Glass

Shake with ice and strain

PADDINGTON BEAR SURPRISE

- 1 part Bacardi® Limón Rum
- 1 part Coffee Liqueur
- 2 splashes Orange Marmalade
- dash Brown Sugar
- Shot Glass

Combine all ingredients in a blender with no ice. Blend until smooth.

PADDY'S DAY SPECIAL

- 1 part Crème de Menthe (Green)
- 1 part Triple Sec
- 1 part Melon Liqueur
- Shot Glass

Build in the glass with no ice

PAINT BOX

- 1 part Banana Liqueur
- 1 part Blue Curaçao
- 1 part Cherry Liqueur
- Shot Glass

Shake with ice and strain

PAINTBALL

- 1 part Banana Liqueur
- 1 part Blue Curaçao
- 1 part Irish Cream Liqueur
- 1 part Southern Comfort®
- 1 part Triple Sec
- Shot Glass

Shake with ice and strain. *Note: Because this recipe includes many ingredients, it's easier to make in volume, about 6 shots.

PAMOYO

- 1 part Gin
- 1 part Lemon-Lime Soda
- 1 part Grape Juice (Red)
- Shot Glass

Shake with ice and strain

PANCAKE

- 1 part Cinnamon Schnapps
- 1 part Irish Cream Liqueur
- 1 part Cream
- Shot Glass

Shake with ice and strain

PANCHO VILLA SHOOTER

- 1 part Tequila Silver
- 1 part Amaretto
- 1 part 151-Proof Rum
- Shot Glass

Shake with ice and strain

PANTS ON FIRE

- 1 part Vodka
- 1 part Strawberry Liqueur
- 1 part Banana Liqueur
- 1 part Grapefruit Juice
- 1 part Orange Juice
- Shot Glass

Shake with ice and strain. *Note: Because this recipe includes many ingredients, it's easier to make in volume, about 6 shots.

PANTY BURNER SHOOTER

- 1 part Advocaat
- 1 part Coffee
- 1 part Frangelico®
- Shot Glass

Shake with ice and strain

PANTY QUIVER

- 1 part Jägermeister®
- 1 part Blackberry Brandy
- Shot Glass

Shake with ice and strain

PANTY RAID

- 2 parts Citrus-Flavored Vodka
- 1 part Chambord®
- splash Lemon-Lime Soda
- splash Pineapple Juice
- Shot Glass

Shake with ice and strain

PARALYZER SHOOTER

- 1 part Vodka
- 1 part Coffee Liqueur
- 1 part Cola
- 1 part Milk
- Shot Glass

Shake with ice and strain

PARANOIA

- 2 parts Amaretto
- 1 part Orange Juice
- Shot Glass

Shake with ice and strain

PARTY ANIMAL

- 1 part Parfait Amour
- 1 part Coconut-Flavored Liqueur
- 1 part Orange Juice
- Shot Glass

Shake with ice and strain

PASSION KILLER SHOOTER

- 1 part Tequila Silver
- 1 part Melon Liqueur
- 1 part Passion Fruit Liqueur
- Shot Glass

Shake with ice and strain

PASSION SLAM

- 1 part Passion Fruit Liqueur
- 1 part Kiwi Schnapps
- 1 part Lime Juice
- Shot Glass

Shake with ice and strain

PASSOUT

- 1 part Amaretto
- 1 part Licor 43®
- 1 part Southern Comfort®
- 1 part Triple Sec
- 1 part Jack Daniel's®
- Shot Glass

Shake with ice and strain. *Note: Because this recipe includes many ingredients, it's easier to make in volume, about 6 shots.

PB&J

- 1 part Vodka
- 1 part Raspberry Liqueur
- 1 part Frangelico®
- Shot Glass

Shake with ice and strain

PEACH DEATH

- 1 part Vodka
- 1 part Peach Schnapps
- 1 part Amaretto
- Shot Glass

Shake with ice and strain

PEACH FUZZ

- 1 part Peach Schnapps
- 1 part Cranberry Juice Cocktail
- Shot Glass

Shake with ice and strain

PEACH NEHI

- 1 part Vodka
- 1 part Peach Schnapps
- 1 part Cherry Liqueur
- 1 part Sour Mix
- 1 part Pineapple Juice
- 1 part Lemon-Lime Soda
- Shot Glass

Shake with ice and strain. *Note: Because this recipe includes many ingredients, it's easier to make in volume, about 6 shots.

PEACHES AND CREAM SHOT

- 3 parts Peach Schnapps
- 2 parts Cream
- 1 part 151-Proof Rum
- Shot Glass

Shake with ice and strain

PEARL DIVER

- 1 part Melon Liqueur
- 1 part Pineapple Juice
- 1 part Coconut-Flavored Rum
- Shot Glass

Shake with ice and strain

PEARL HARBOR

- 1 part Vodka
- 1 part Melon Liqueur
- 1 part Orange Juice
- Shot Glass

Shake with ice and strain

PEARL NECKLACE

- 1 part Tequila Rose®
- 1 part Irish Cream Liqueur
- Shot Glass

Shake with ice and strain

PECKER HEAD

- 1 part Southern Comfort®
- 1 part Amaretto
- 1 part Pineapple
- Shot Glass

Shake with ice and strain

PECKER WRECKER

- 1 part Blackberry Brandy
- 1 part Crème de Noyaux
- 1 part 151-Proof Rum
- 1 part Pineapple Juice
- 1 part Cranberry Juice Cocktail
- Shot Glass

Shake with ice and strain. *Note: Because this recipe includes many ingredients, it's easier to make in volume, about 6 shots.

PEDRA

- 1 part Tequila
- 1 part Vodka
- 1 part Dark Rum
- 1 part Irish Cream Liqueur
- 1 part Grenadine
- 1 part Absinthe
- Shot Glass

Shake with ice and strain. *Note: Because this recipe includes many ingredients, it's easier to make in volume, about 6 shots.

PEE GEE

- 1 part Cinnamon Schnapps
- 1 part Orange Juice
- 1 part Vodka
- Shot Glass

Shake with ice and strain

PENTHOUSE

- 1 part Tequila
- 1 part Bacardi® Limón Rum
- 1 part Lime Juice
- Shot Glass

Shake with ice and strain

PEPPERMINT

- 3 parts Pepper-Flavored Vodka
- 1 part Crème de Menthe (White)
- Shot Glass

Shake with ice and strain

PEPPERMINT BONBON

- 4 parts Peppermint Schnapps
- 1 part Chocolate Syrup
- Shot Glass

Shake with ice and strain

PEPPERMINT PATTIE®

- 1 part Coffee Liqueur
- 1 part Peppermint Schnapps
- 1 part Half and Half
- Shot Glass

Shake with ice and strain

PEPPERMINT ROSE

- 1 part Peppermint Schnapps
- 1 part Tequila Rose®
- Shot Glass

Shake with ice and strain

PESCHINO

- 1 part Peach Schnapps
- 1 part Strawberry Liqueur
- Shot Glass

Shake with ice and strain

PETRONIUS

- 2 parts Jim Beam®
- 1 part Vanilla Liqueur
- 1 part Peppermint Liqueur
- Shot Glass

Shake with ice and strain

PEZ®

- 1 part Spiced Rum
- 1 part Raspberry Liqueur
- 1 part Sour Mix
- Shot Glass

Shake with ice and strain

PHOTON TORPEDO

- 1 part After Shock® Cinnamon Schnapps
- 1 part Vodka
- Shot Glass

Shake with ice and strain

A PIECE OF ASS

- 1 part Amaretto
- 1 part Southern Comfort®
- Shot Glass

Shake with ice and strain

PIERCED FUZZY NAVEL

- 2 parts Peach Schnapps
- 1 part Vodka
- 1 part Orange Juice
- Shot Glass

Shake with ice and strain

PIERCED NIPPLE

- 1 part Sambuca
- 1 part Irish Cream Liqueur
- Shot Glass

Shake with ice and strain

PIGSKIN SHOT

- 1 part Vodka
- 1 part Melon Liqueur
- 1 part Sour Mix
- Shot Glass

Shake with ice and strain

PIÑA CRANA KAZI

- 2 parts Vodka
- 1 part Triple Sec
- 1 part Pineapple Juice
- Shot Glass

Shake with ice and strain

PINEAPPLE BOMB

- 1 part Southern Comfort®
- 1 part Triple Sec
- 1 part Pineapple Juice
- Shot Glass

Shake with ice and strain

PINEAPPLE UPSIDE-DOWN CAKE

- 1 part Irish Cream Liqueur
- 1 part Vodka
- 1 part Butterscotch Schnapps
- 1 part Pineapple Juice
- Shot Glass

Shake with ice and strain

PINEBERRY

- 1 part Cranberry-Flavored Vodka
- 1 part Pineapple-Flavored Vodka
- Shot Glass

Shake with ice and strain

PINK BELLY

- 1 part Jim Beam®
- 1 part Amaretto
- 1 part Sloe Gin
- 1 part Irish Cream Liqueur
- 1 part Lemon-Lime Soda
- Shot Glass

Shake with ice and strain. *Note: Because this recipe includes many ingredients, it's easier to make in volume, about 6 shots.

PINK CADILLAC

- 2 parts Vodka
- 1 part Cherry Juice
- 1 part Lemonade
- 1 part Orange Juice
- Shot Glass

Shake with ice and strain

PINK COD SHOOTER

- 1 part Tequila Reposado
- 1 part Sour Mix
- Shot Glass

Shake with ice and strain

PINK COTTON CANDY

- 1 part Vodka
- 1 part Amaretto
- splash Grenadine
- Shot Glass

Shake with ice and strain

PINK DANGER

- 1 part Butterscotch Schnapps
- 2 parts Vodka
- 3 parts Fruit Punch
- Shot Glass

Shake with ice and strain

PINK FLOYD

- 1 part Vodka
- 1 part Peach Schnapps
- 1 part Cranberry Juice Cocktail
- 1 part Grapefruit Juice
- Shot Glass

Shake with ice and strain

PINK LEMONADE SHOOTER

- 1 part Vodka
- 1 part Sour Mix
- 1 part Cranberry Juice Cocktail
- Shot Glass

Shake with ice and strain

PINK NIPPLE SHOOTER

- 3 parts Currant-Flavored Vodka
- 1 part Sambuca
- Shot Glass

Shake with ice and strain

PINK RANGER

- 2 parts Vodka
- 1 part Coconut-Flavored Rum
- 1 part Peach Schnapps
- 1 part Cranberry Juice Cocktail
- 1 part Pineapple Juice
- Shot Glass

Shake with ice and strain. *Note: Because this recipe includes many ingredients, it's easier to make in volume, about 6 shots.

PINKEYE

- 1 part Vodka
- 1 part Cranberry Juice Cocktail
- 1 part Sour Mix
- Shot Glass

Shake with ice and strain

PINKY

- 3 parts Rumple Minze®
- 1 part Fire Water®
- Shot Glass

Shake with ice and strain

PISSED OFF MEXICAN

- 1 part Cinnamon Schnapps
- 1 part Tequila Silver
- Shot Glass

Shake with ice and strain

PISTOL SHOT

- 1 part Triple Sec
- 1 part Apricot Brandy
- 1 part Cherry Brandy
- Shot Glass

Shake with ice and strain

PIT BULL AND CRANK SHOOTER

- 1 part Rum
- 1 part Tequila
- 1 part Seagram's® Crown 7 Whiskey
- 1 part Jägermeister®
- 1 part Peppermint Schnapps
- Shot Glass

Shake with ice and strain* Note: Because this recipe includes many ingredients, it's easier to make in volume, about 6 shots.

PIXY STIX®

- 2 parts Southern Comfort®
- 1 part Amaretto
- Shot Glass

Shake with ice and strain

PLEADING INSANITY

- 1 part Tequila Silver
- 1 part Vodka
- 1 part Dark Rum
- Shot Glass

Shake with ice and strain

POCO LOCO BOOM

- 1 part Vodka
- 1 part Tia Maria®
- 1 part Coconut Cream
- Shot Glass

Shake with ice and strain

POINT-BLANK

- 1 part Brandy
- 1 part Crème de Banana
- 1 part Apricot Brandy
- 1 part Cherry Brandy
- Shot Glass

Shake with ice and strain

POISON APPLE

- 1 part Apple Brandy
- 1 part Vodka
- Shot Glass

Shake with ice and strain

POISON IVY

- 1 part Cinnamon Schnapps
- 1 part Coffee Liqueur
- Shot Glass

Shake with ice and strain

POISON MILK

- 1 part Jägermeister®
- 1 part Irish Cream Liqueur
- Shot Glass

Shake with ice and strain

POLAR BEAR SHOT

- 1 part Crème de Cacao (White)
- 1 part Peppermint Schnapps
- Shot Glass

Shake with ice and strain

POOP SHOOT

- 2 parts Sambuca
- 1 part Fruit Punch
- Shot Glass

Shake with ice and strain

POPPER

- 1 part Vodka
- 3 parts Lemon-Lime Soda

- Shot Glass

Build in the glass with no ice

PORTO COVO

- 1 part Vodka
- 1 part Absinthe
- 1 part Banana Liqueur

- 1 part Coconut-Flavored Liqueur
- Shot Glass

Shake with ice and strain

POUCE COUPE PUDDLE

- 2 parts Irish Cream Liqueur
- 1 part Crème de Menthe (White)

- 1 part Peach Schnapps
- Shot Glass

Shake with ice and strain

POWER DRILL

- 1 part Vodka
- 1 part Orange Juice
- 1 part Beer
- Shot Glass

Build in the glass with no ice

POWER SHOT

- 2 parts Vodka
- 1 part Absolut® Peppar Vodka
- dash Wasabi
- Shot Glass

Build in the glass with no ice

PRESTONE

- 1 part Melon Liqueur
- 2 parts Citrus-Flavored Vodka
- 2 parts Lemon-Lime Soda
- Shot Glass

Shake with ice and strain

PROTEIN SMOOTHIE

- 1 part Scotch
- 1 part Cream
- 1 part Clamato® Juice
- Shot Glass

Shake with ice and strain

PROZAC®

- 1 part Crown Royal® Whiskey
- 1 part Melon Liqueur
- 1 part Lemon-Lime Soda
- Shot Glass

Shake with ice and strain

PUCKER SUCKER

- 1 part Sour Apple Schnapps
- 1 part Coffee Liqueur
- 1 part Orange Juice
- Shot Glass

Shake with ice and strain

PUERTO RICAN MONKEY FUCK

- 2 parts Coffee Liqueur
- 2 parts Crème de Banana
- 1 part 151-Proof Rum
- Shot Glass

Shake with ice and strain

PUKE

- 1 part Jack Daniel's®
- 1 part Jim Beam®
- 1 part Yukon Jack®
- 1 part Vodka
- 1 part Tequila
- Shot Glass

Shake with ice and strain

PUMPKIN PIE

- 2 parts Coffee Liqueur
- 1 part Irish Cream Liqueur
- 1 part Goldschläger®
- Shot Glass

Shake with ice and strain

PUPPY'S NOSE

- 1 part Peppermint Schnapps
- 1 part Tia Maria®
- 1 part Irish Cream Liqueur
- Shot Glass

Build in the glass with no ice

PURPLE ALASKAN

- 1 part Amaretto
- 1 part Jack Daniel's®
- 1 part Orange Juice
- 1 part Southern Comfort®
- 1 part Raspberry Liqueur
- Shot Glass

*Shake with ice and strain. *Note: Because this recipe includes many ingredients, it's easier to make in volume, about 6 shots.*

PURPLE ELASTIC THUNDER FUCK

- 1 part Vodka
- 1 part Crown Royal® Whiskey
- 1 part Southern Comfort®
- 1 part Amaretto
- 1 part Raspberry Liqueur
- 1 part Pineapple Juice
- 1 part Cranberry Juice Cocktail
- Shot Glass

Shake with ice and strain. *Note: Because this recipe includes many ingredients, it's easier to make in volume, about 6 shots.

PURPLE HAZE #1

- 1 part Citrus-Flavored Vodka
- 1 part Raspberry Liqueur
- 1 part Lemon-Lime Soda
- Shot Glass

Shake with ice and strain

PURPLE HAZE #2

- 1 part Amaretto
- 1 part Root Beer Schnapps
- 1 part Milk
- 1 part Grape Soda
- Shot Glass

Shake with ice and strain

PURPLE HELMETED WARRIOR

- 1 part Gin
- 1 part Southern Comfort®
- 1 part Peach Schnapps
- 1 part Blue Curaçao
- 1 part Lime Juice
- 1 part Grenadine
- 1 part Lemon-Lime Soda
- Shot Glass

*Shake with ice and strain. *Note: Because this recipe includes many ingredients, it's easier to make in volume, about 6 shots.*

PURPLE NIPPLE

- 3 parts Melon Liqueur
- 1 part Jägermeister®
- 2 parts Cranberry Juice Cocktail
- 1 part Orange Juice
- Shot Glass

Shake with ice and strain

PURPLE PANTHER

- 3 parts Sour Apple-Flavored Vodka
- 1 part Blue Curaçao
- Shot Glass

Shake with ice and strain

PURPLE PENIS

- 2 parts Vodka
- 1 part Blue Curaçao
- 1 part Raspberry Liqueur
- Shot Glass

Shake with ice and strain

PURPLE RAIN SHOOTER

- 3 parts Cranberry-Flavored Vodka
- 1 part Blue Curaçao
- Shot Glass

Shake with ice and strain

PURPLE VIPER

- 1 part Sloe Gin
- 1 part Vodka
- 2 parts Raspberry Liqueur
- Shot Glass

Shake with ice and strain

PURPLE WIND

- 1 part Raspberry Liqueur
- 2 parts Sake
- Shot Glass

Shake with ice and strain

PUSSY IN FIGHT

- 1 part Gin
- 1 part Frangelico®
- Shot Glass

Shake with ice and strain

PUSSY JUICE

- 1 part Goldschläger®
- 1 part Vodka
- 1 part Vegetable Juice Blend
- Shot Glass

Shake with ice and strain

QUAALUDE

- 1 part Vodka
- 1 part Coffee Liqueur
- 1 part Irish Cream Liqueur
- 1 part Amaretto
- 1 part Frangelico®
- Shot Glass

*Shake with ice and strain. *Note: Because this recipe includes many ingredients, it's easier to make in volume, about 6 shots.*

QUICK FUCK

- 1 part Coffee Liqueur
- 1 part Melon Liqueur
- 1 part Irish Cream Liqueur
- Shot Glass

Shake with ice and strain

QUICK SILVER

- 1 part Anisette
- 1 part Triple Sec
- 1 part Tequila
- Shot Glass

Shake with ice and strain

QUICKSAND SHOOTER

- 1 part Black Sambuca
- 3 parts Orange Juice
- Shot Glass

Shake with ice and strain

RABBIT PUNCH

- 1 part Campari®
- 1 part Crème de Cacao (Dark)
- 1 part Coconut-Flavored Rum
- 2 parts Irish Cream Liqueur
- Shot Glass

Shake with ice and strain

RAGING INDIAN

- 1 part Vodka
- 1 part Coffee Liqueur
- 1 part Orange Juice
- 1 part Mango Nectar
- Shot Glass

Shake with ice and strain

RAIJA

- 1 part Vanilla Liqueur
- 1 part Coffee Liqueur
- 1 part Orange Juice
- 1 part Mango Juice
- Shot Glass

Shake with ice and strain

RAMBO SHOT

- 1 part Jägermeister®
- 1 part Rumple Minze®
- Shot Glass

Shake with ice and strain

RASPBERRY BERET

- 1 part Vodka
- 1 part Raspberry Liqueur
- 1 part Cream
- Shot Glass

Shake with ice and strain

RAT SHOOTER

- 3 parts Green Chartreuse®
- 1 part Rumple Minze®
- Shot Glass

Build in the glass with no ice

RAY OF LIGHT

- 1 part Crème de Cacao (White)
- 1 part Galliano®
- 1 part Grand Marnier®
- Shot Glass

Shake with ice and strain

RAZOR BLADE

- 1 part Jägermeister®
- 1 part 151-Proof Rum
- Shot Glass

Shake with ice and strain

READY SET GO

- 1 part Crème de Banana
- 1 part Melon Liqueur
- 1 part Strawberry Liqueur
- Shot Glass

Shake with ice and strain

A REAL STRONG DIRTY ROTTEN SCOUNDREL

- 1 part Cranberry-Flavored Vodka
- ½ part Melon Liqueur
- Shot Glass

Shake with ice and strain

REBEL JESTER

- 2 parts Kiwi Schnapps
- 1 part Goldschläger®
- Shot Glass

Shake with ice and strain

REBOOT

- 1 part Crème de Menthe (Green)
- 1 part Cachaça
- 2 parts Absolut® Peppar Vodka
- Shot Glass

Shake with ice and strain

RED BARON SHOOTER

- 2 parts Crown Royal® Whiskey
- 1 part Amaretto
- 1 part Cranberry Juice Cocktail
- Shot Glass

Shake with ice and strain

RED BEARD

- 2 parts Spiced Rum
- 2 parts Coconut-Flavored Rum
- 1 part Grenadine
- 1 part Lemon-Lime Soda
- Shot Glass

Shake with ice and strain

RED DEATH

- 1 part Vodka
- 1 part Fire Water®
- 1 part Yukon Jack®
- 1 part 151-Proof Rum
- Shot Glass

Shake with ice and strain

RED DEVIL SHOOTER

- 1 part Vodka
- 1 part Southern Comfort®
- 1 part Amaretto
- 1 part Triple Sec
- 1 part Grenadine
- 1 part Orange Juice
- 1 part Sour Mix
- Shot Glass

*Shake with ice and strain. *Note: Because this recipe includes many ingredients, it's easier to make in volume, about 6 shots.*

RED DRAGON'S BREATH

- 1 part Cinnamon Schnapps
- 1 part Whiskey
- Shot Glass

Shake with ice and strain

RED-EYED HELL

- 1 part Triple Sec
- 1 part Vodka
- 1 part 151-Proof Rum
- 2 parts Vegetable Juice Blend
- Shot Glass

Build in the glass with no ice

RED FROG ROADKILL

- 1 part Raspberry Liqueur
- 1 part Amaretto
- 1 part Jim Beam®
- 2 parts Cranberry Juice Cocktail
- Shot Glass

Shake with ice and strain

RED-HEADED PRINCESS

- 1 part Jägermeister®
- 1 part Peach Schnapps
- 2 parts Cranberry Juice Cocktail
- Shot Glass

Shake with ice and strain

RED-HEADED VAMP

- 1 part Raspberry Liqueur
- 1 part Jägermeister®
- 1 part Cranberry Juice Cocktail
- Shot Glass

Shake with ice and strain

RED-LINE

- 1 part Tequila Silver
- 1 part Sambuca
- splash Crème de Cassis
- Shot Glass

Shake with ice and strain

RED LOBSTER

- 1 part Amaretto
- 1 part Southern Comfort®
- 1 part Cranberry Juice Cocktail
- Shot Glass

Shake with ice and strain

RED MONSTER

- 1 part Tequila
- 1 part Orange Juice
- Shot Glass

Shake with ice and strain

RED MOSQUITO

- 1 part Vodka
- 1 part Hot Damn!® Cinnamon Schnapps
- Shot Glass

Shake with ice and strain

RED ROYAL SHOT

- 1 part Crown Royal® Whiskey
- 1 part Amaretto
- Shot Glass

Shake with ice and strain

RED SNAPPER SHOOTER

- 2 parts Canadian Whiskey
- 1 part Amaretto
- Shot Glass

Shake with ice and strain

REDNECK KILLER

- 1 part Jack Daniel's®
- 1 part Jim Beam®
- 1 part Wild Turkey® 101
- Shot Glass

Build in the glass with no ice

REGULATOR

- 1 part Crown Royal® Whiskey
- 1 part Melon Liqueur
- 3 parts Cranberry Juice Cocktail
- Shot Glass

Shake with ice and strain

REPUBLICA DAS BANANAS

- 1 part Tequila Silver
- 1 part Rum
- 1 part Crème de Banana
- Shot Glass

Shake with ice and strain

RETRIBUTION

- 1 part Rumple Minze®
- 1 part Tequila
- 1 part Jägermeister®
- 1 part Fire Water®
- Shot Glass

Shake with ice and strain

ROADKILL SHOT

- 1 part Tequila
- 1 part Hot Damn!® Cinnamon Schnapps
- 1 part Whiskey
- Shot Glass

Shake with ice and strain

ROADRUNNER PUNCH

- 1 part Coconut-Flavored Rum
- 1 part Blue Curaçao
- 1 part Peach Schnapps
- 1 part Fruit Punch
- Shot Glass

Shake with ice and strain

ROASTED TOASTED ALMOND SHOOTER

- 1 part Amaretto
- 1 part Coffee Liqueur
- 1 part Cream
- 1 part Vodka
- Shot Glass

Shake with ice and strain

ROBOT

- 2 parts Jack Daniel's®
- 1 part Vodka
- 1 part Grenadine
- Shot Glass

Shake with ice and strain

ROCKET FUEL

- 2 parts 151-Proof Rum
- 1 part Vodka
- 1 part Blue Curaçao
- Shot Glass

Shake with ice and strain

ROCKET POP

- 2 parts Bacardi® Limón Rum
- 1 part Lemon-Lime Soda
- 1 part Cranberry Juice Cocktail
- 1 part Sour Mix
- Shot Glass

Shake with ice and strain

ROCKY MOUNTAIN

- 2 parts Southern Comfort®
- 2 parts Amaretto
- 1 part Lime Juice
- Shot Glass

Shake with ice and strain

ROCKY MOUNTAIN BEAR FUCKER

- 1 part Tequila
- 1 part Jack Daniel's®
- 1 part Southern Comfort®
- Shot Glass

Shake with ice and strain

ROMULAN ALE SHOOTER

- 1 part Vodka
- 1 part Tropical Punch Schnapps
- 1 part Cactus Juice Schnapps
- Shot Glass

Shake with ice and strain

ROOMMATE KILLER

- 1 part Jägermeister®
- 1 part Rumple Minze®
- Shot Glass

Shake with ice and strain

ROOSTER PISS

- 1 part Jack Daniel's®
- 1 part Cinnamon Schnapps
- Shot Glass

Shake with ice and strain

ROOSTER TAIL

- 1 part Tequila
- 1 part Orange Juice
- dash Salt
- Shot Glass

Shake with ice and strain

ROSSO DI SERA

- 1 part Vodka
- 1 part Strawberry Liqueur
- 1 part Triple Sec
- Shot Glass

Shake with ice and strain

ROSY CHEEKS

- 1 part Strawberry Liqueur
- 1 part Melon Liqueur
- 1 part Sour Mix
- Shot Glass

Shake with ice and strain

ROTT GUT

- 1 part Cinnamon Schnapps
- 1 part Vodka
- Shot Glass

Shake with ice and strain

ROTTEN APPLE

- 1 part Jägermeister®
- 1 part Sour Apple Schnapps
- Shot Glass

Shake with ice and strain

ROTTEN PUSSY

- 2 parts Midori®
- 1 part Amaretto
- 1 part Southern Comfort®
- 1 part Coconut-Flavored Rum
- 1 part Sour Mix
- 1 part Pineapple Juice
- Shot Glass

Shake with ice and strain

ROYAL

- 1 part Vodka
- 1 part Crème de Banana
- 1 part Blue Curaçao
- 1 part Lemon Juice
- Shot Glass

Shake with ice and strain

ROYAL APPLE

- 1 part Crown Royal® Whiskey
- 2 parts Cranberry Juice Cocktail
- 1 part Sour Apple Schnapps
- Shot Glass

Shake with ice and strain

ROYAL BITCH

- 1 part Frangelico®
- 1 part Crown Royal® Whiskey
- Shot Glass

Shake with ice and strain

ROYAL FLUSH

- 1 part Crown Royal® Whiskey
- 1 part Peach Schnapps
- 2 parts Cranberry Juice Cocktail
- 2 parts Orange Juice
- splash Club Soda
- Shot Glass

Shake all but Club Soda with ice and strain into the glass. Top with Club Soda.

ROYAL FUCK

- 1 part Crown Royal® Whiskey
- 1 part Chambord®
- 1 part Peach Schnapps
- 1 part Cranberry Juice Cocktail
- 1 part Pineapple-Flavored Vodka
- Shot Glass

Shake with ice and strain

ROYAL SCANDAL

- 1 part Crown Royal® Whiskey
- 1 part Southern Comfort®
- 1 part Amaretto
- 1 part Sour Mix
- 1 part Pineapple Juice
- Shot Glass

*Shake with ice and strain. *Note: Because this recipe includes many ingredients, it's easier to make in volume, about 6 shots.*

ROYAL SHOCK

- 1 part After Shock® Cinnamon Schnapps.
- 2 parts Crown Royal® Whiskey
- Shot Glass

Build in the glass with no ice

ROYAL SICILIAN KISS

- 2 parts Amaretto
- 1 part Crown Royal® Whiskey
- 1 part Southern Comfort®
- Shot Glass

Shake with ice and strain

RUBBER BISCUIT

- 1 part Crown Royal® Whiskey
- 1 part Butterscotch Schnapps
- Shot Glass

Shake with ice and strain

RUBY RED

- 2 parts Vodka
- 2 parts Cranberry Juice Cocktail
- 1 part Sour Mix
- Shot Glass

Shake with ice and strain

RUG BURN

- 1 part Irish Cream Liqueur
- 1 part Coffee Liqueur
- 1 part Irish Whiskey
- Shot Glass

Shake with ice and strain

RUM BUBBLEGUM

- 1 part Crème de Banana
- 1 part Irish Cream Liqueur
- 1 part Light Rum
- Shot Glass

Shake with ice and strain

RUMKA

- 1 part Vodka
- 1 part Spiced Rum
- Shot Glass

Shake with ice and strain

RUMRUNNER SHOOTER

- 1 part Dark Rum
- 1 part Spiced Rum
- 1 part Coconut-Flavored Rum
- 1 part Crème de Banana
- 1 part Blackberry Liqueur
- 1 part Grenadine
- 1 part Sour Mix
- 1 part Orange Juice
- Shot Glass

Shake with ice and strain. *Note: Because this recipe includes many ingredients, it's easier to make in volume, about 6 shots.

RUSSIAN BALLET

- 3 parts Vodka
- 1 part Crème de Cassis
- Shot Glass

Shake with ice and strain

RUSSIAN KAMIKAZE

- 2 parts Vodka
- 1 part Raspberry Liqueur
- Shot Glass

Shake with ice and strain

RUSSIAN QUAALUDE SHOOTER

- 1 part Vodka
- 1 part Frangelico®
- 1 part Irish Cream Liqueur
- 1 part Coffee Liqueur
- 1 part Cream
- Shot Glass

*Shake with ice and strain. *Note: Because this recipe includes many ingredients, it's easier to make in volume, about 6 shots.*

RUSSIAN ROULETTE

- 1 part Vodka
- 1 part Galliano®
- 1 part 151-Proof Rum
- Shot Glass

Shake with ice and strain

RUSSIAN TONGUE

- 1 part Goldschläger®
- 1 part Rumple Minze®
- 1 part Vodka
- Shot Glass

Shake with ice and strain

RUSTED THROAT

- 1 part Light Rum
- 1 part Orange Juice
- 1 part Passion Fruit Nectar
- 1 part 151-Proof Rum
- Shot Glass

Shake with ice and strain

RUSTY HALO

- 1 part Vodka
- 1 part Amaretto
- 1 part Banana Liqueur
- 1 part Melon Liqueur
- Shot Glass

Shake with ice and strain

RUSTY NAVEL

- 1 part Tequila
- 1 part Amaretto
- Shot Glass

Shake with ice and strain

RHYTHM AND BLUES

- 1 part Jack Daniel's®
- 1 part Blueberry Schnapps
- Shot Glass

Shake with ice and strain

S.H.I.T.

- 1 part Sambuca
- 2 parts Crème Liqueur
- 2 parts Irish Mist®
- 1 part Tequila
- Shot Glass

Shake with ice and strain

SAIKKOSEN SPECIAL

- 1 part Cointreau®
- 2 parts Crème de Cassis
- 2 parts Tia Maria®
- Shot Glass

Shake with ice and strain

SAMBUCA SLIDE

- 2 parts Sambuca
- 1 part Vodka
- 1 part Light Cream
- Shot Glass

Shake with ice and strain

SAMBUCA SURPRISE

- 1 part Crème de Cacao (White)
- 1 part Sambuca
- 1 part Crème de Menthe (White)
- Shot Glass

Shake with ice and strain

SAMMY SLAMMER

- 2 parts Southern Comfort®
- 1 part Vanilla Liqueur
- 1 part Peach Schnapps
- Shot Glass

Shake with ice and strain

A SAMPLE

- 1 part Grain Alcohol
- 1 part Gatorade®
- Shot Glass

Shake with ice and strain

SAND BAG

- 1 part Tequila
- 1 part Jägermeister®
- dash Salt
- Shot Glass

Shake with ice and strain

SANDBLASTER

- 1 part Light Rum
- 1 part Fresh Lime Juice
- 2 parts Cola
- Shot Glass

Stir gently with ice and strain

SANDY BEACH

- 1 part Irish Cream Liqueur
- 1 part Butterscotch Schnapps
- 1 part Amaretto
- 1 part Cream
- Shot Glass

Shake with ice and strain

SARATOGA TRUNK

- 1 part Tequila Silver
- 1 part Tia Maria®
- 1 part Goldschläger®
- Shot Glass

Shake with ice and strain

SATAN'S MOUTHWASH

- 1 part Jack Daniel's®
- 1 part Sambuca
- Shot Glass

Shake with ice and strain

SATURNUS

- 1 part Crème de Banana
- 1 part Gin
- 1 part Dry Vermouth
- 2 parts Orange Juice
- Shot Glass

Shake with ice and strain

SCARLET O'HARA SHOOTER

- 2 parts Southern Comfort®
- 1 part Sour Mix
- 1 part Grenadine
- Shot Glass

Shake with ice and strain

SCHWIMMER

- 2 parts Sambuca
- 1 part Coffee Liqueur
- 1 part Irish Cream Liqueur
- 1 part Butterscotch Schnapps
- 1 part Jägermeister®
- Shot Glass

Shake with ice and strain. *Note: Because this recipe includes many ingredients, it's easier to make in volume, about 6 shots.

SCOOBY SHOOTER

- 2 parts Coconut-Flavored Rum
- 2 parts Peach Schnapps
- 2 parts Melon Liqueur
- 1 part Vodka
- 1 part Orange Juice
- 1 part Pineapple Juice
- Shot Glass

Shake with ice and strain. *Note: Because this recipe includes many ingredients, it's easier to make in volume, about 6 shots.

SCORPION SHOOTER

- 2 parts Vodka
- 1 part Blackberry Liqueur
- Shot Glass

Shake with ice and strain

SCORPION SUICIDE

- 2 parts Cherry Brandy
- 1 part Whiskey
- 1 part Pernod®
- Shot Glass

Shake with ice and strain

SCREAMER

- 1 part Gin
- 1 part Rum
- 1 part Tequila
- 1 part Triple Sec
- 1 part Vodka
- Shot Glass

*Shake with ice and strain. *Note: Because this recipe includes many ingredients, it's easier to make in volume, about 6 shots.*

SCREAMING BLUE MESSIAH

- 1 part Goldschläger®
- 1 part Blue Curaçao
- Shot Glass

Shake with ice and strain

SCREAMING BLUE VIKING

- 1 part Yukon Jack®
- 1 part Rumple Minze®
- 1 part Blue Curaçao
- Shot Glass

Shake with ice and strain

SCREAMING GREEN MONSTER

- 1 part Coconut-Flavored Rum
- 1 part Midori®
- 1 part 151-Proof Rum
- 1 part Pineapple Juice
- 1 part Lemon-Lime Soda
- Shot Glass

Shake with ice and strain. *Note: Because this recipe includes many ingredients, it's easier to make in volume, about 6 shots.

SCREAMING MOOSE

- 1 part Jägermeister®
- 1 part Coffee Liqueur
- 1 part Irish Cream Liqueur
- Shot Glass

Shake with ice and strain

SCREAMING ORGASM

- 1 part Cream
- 1 part Vodka
- 1 part Amaretto
- 1 part Crème de Banana
- Shot Glass

Shake with ice and strain

SCREAMING PEACH

- 1 part Peach Schnapps
- 1 part Melon Liqueur
- 1 part Grenadine
- 2 parts Pineapple Juice
- Shot Glass

Shake with ice and strain

SCREAMING PURPLE JESUS

- 1 part Vodka
- 1 part Grape Juice (Red)

- Shot Glass

Shake with ice and strain

SCREAMING YODA®

- 1 part Melon Liqueur
- 1 part Jägermeister®

- 1 part Orange Juice
- Shot Glass

Shake with ice and strain

SCREW 'N' MAIL

- 1 part Crème de Banana
- 1 part Cherry Brandy

- 1 part Chocolate Mint Liqueur
- Shot Glass

Shake with ice and strain

SECOND CHILDHOOD

- 1 part Crème de Menthe (White)
- 1 part Vodka
- Shot Glass

Shake with ice and strain

SECRET HEART

- 1 part Crème de Cacao (White)
- 1 part Amaretto
- 1 part Strawberry Liqueur
- Shot Glass

Shake with ice and strain

SEEING STARS

- 1 part Crème de Menthe (White)
- 1 part Coffee
- 1 part Crème de Banana
- Shot Glass

Shake with ice and strain

SEÑOR FREAK

- 1 part Tequila Reposado
- 1 part Light Rum
- 1 part Vodka
- 1 part Lemon-Lime Soda
- Shot Glass

Shake with ice and strain

SENSEI ON THE ROCKS

- 1 part Coffee Liqueur
- 1 part Coconut-Flavored Rum
- 1 part Jack Daniel's®
- Shot Glass

Shake with ice and strain

SEVEN TWENTY-SEVEN

- 1 part Vodka
- 1 part Coconut-Flavored Liqueur
- Shot Glass

Shake with ice and strain

SHOTS & SHOOTERS | **425**

SEX IN THE PARKING LOT

- 1 part Raspberry Liqueur
- 1 part Vodka
- 1 part Sour Apple Schnapps
- Shot Glass

Shake with ice and strain

SEX MACHINE

- 1 part Coffee Liqueur
- 1 part Irish Cream Liqueur
- 1 part Milk
- Shot Glass

Shake with ice and strain

SEX ON ACID

- 2 parts Jägermeister®
- 1 part Melon Liqueur
- 1 part Blackberry Liqueur
- 1 part Pineapple Juice
- 1 part Cranberry Juice Cocktail
- Shot Glass

*Shake with ice and strain. *Note: Because this recipe includes many ingredients, it's easier to make in volume, about 6 shots.*

SEX ON A POOL TABLE

- 1 part Peach Schnapps
- 1 part Vodka
- 1 part Pineapple Juice
- 1 part Sour Mix
- 1 part Melon Liqueur
- Shot Glass

Shake with ice and strain. *Note: Because this recipe includes many ingredients, it's easier to make in volume, about 6 shots.

SEX ON THE BEACH SHOOTER

- 1 part Vodka
- 1 part Peach Schnapps
- 1 part Orange Juice
- Shot Glass

Shake with ice and strain

SEX ON THE LAKE

- 2 parts Crème de Banana
- 2 parts Crème de Cacao (Dark)
- 1 part Light Rum
- 1 part Cream
- Shot Glass

Shake with ice and strain

SEX UNDER THE MOONLIGHT

- 2 parts Vodka
- 1 part Coffee
- 1 part Port
- 1 part Cream
- Shot Glass

Shake with ice and strain

SEX UP AGAINST THE WALL

- 2 parts Currant-Flavored Vodka
- 1 part Pineapple Juice
- 1 part Sour Mix
- Shot Glass

Shake with ice and strain

SEX WITH AN ALLIGATOR

- 1 part Jägermeister®
- 1 part Melon Liqueur
- 1 part Raspberry Liqueur
- 1 part Pineapple Juice
- Shot Glass

Shake with ice and strain

SEXUAL STIMULATION

- 2 parts Rum
- 1 part Crème de Menthe (Green)
- 1 part Crème de Banana
- 1 part Passion Fruit Nectar
- Shot Glass

Shake with ice and strain

SEXY ALLIGATOR

- 2 parts Coconut-Flavored Rum
- 2 parts Melon Liqueur
- 1 part Jägermeister®
- 1 part Raspberry Liqueur
- 1 part Pineapple Juice
- Shot Glass

*Shake with ice and strain. *Note: Because this recipe includes many ingredients, it's easier to make in volume, about 6 shots.*

SHAG LATER

- 2 parts After Shock® Cinnamon Schnapps
- 1 part Canadian Whiskey
- 1 part Root Beer
- splash Chocolate Syrup
- Shot Glass

Shake with ice and strain

SHAKE THAT ASS

- 1 part Blue Curaçao
- 1 part Banana Liqueur
- 1 part Sour Mix
- 1 part Orange Juice
- Shot Glass

Shake with ice and strain

SHAMPOO

- 1 part Irish Cream Liqueur
- 1 part Butterscotch Schnapps
- Shot Glass

Shake with ice and strain

SHAPE SHIFTER

- 1 part Crème de Menthe (Green)
- 1 part Orange Juice
- dash Wasabi
- Shot Glass

Build in the glass with no ice

SHARK BITE SHOOTER

- 1 part Dark Rum
- 1 part Grenadine
- 2 parts Orange Juice
- Shot Glass

Shake with ice and strain

SHAZAM SHOOTER

- 1 part Sour Apple Schnapps
- 1 part Raspberry Liqueur
- 1 part Cranberry Juice Cocktail
- Shot Glass

Shake with ice and strain

SHIPWRECK SHOOTER

- 2 parts Rum
- 1 part Crème de Banana
- 1 part Strawberry Liqueur
- 1 part Sour Mix
- Shot Glass

Shake with ice and strain

SHIT KICKER

- 1 part Rye Whiskey
- 1 part Crème de Menthe (Green)
- 1 part Grenadine
- Shot Glass

Shake with ice and strain

SHIT STAIN

- 1 part Crème de Cacao (Dark)
- 1 part Jägermeister®
- 1 part Vodka
- Shot Glass

Shake with ice and strain

SHOGUN SHOOTER

- 3 parts Citrus-Flavored Vodka
- 1 part Melon Liqueur
- Shot Glass

Shake with ice and strain

SHORT VODKA

- 1 part Triple Sec
- 1 part Orange-Flavored Vodka
- Shot Glass

Shake with ice and strain

SHOT FROM HELL

- 1 part Jägermeister®
- 2 parts Peppermint Schnapps
- Shot Glass

Shake with ice and strain

SHOT IN THE BACK

- 3 parts Vodka
- 1 part Goldschläger®
- dash Wasabi
- Shot Glass

Pour ingredients into glass neat (do not chill)

SHOTGUN

- 1 part Jim Beam®
- 1 part Jack Daniel's®
- 1 part Wild Turkey® Bourbon
- Shot Glass

Shake with ice and strain

SHOT-O-HAPPINESS

- 2 parts Goldschläger®
- 2 parts Raspberry Liqueur
- 1 part Pineapple Juice
- 1 part Sour Mix
- 1 part Lemon-Lime Soda
- Shot Glass

Shake with ice and strain

SHREWSBURY SLAMMER

- 1 part Southern Comfort®
- 1 part Peach Schnapps
- 2 parts Apple Cider
- Shot Glass

Shake with ice and strain

SIBERIAN GOLD

- 2 part Vodka
- 2 part Goldschläger®
- 1 part Blue Curaçao
- Shot Glass

Shake with ice and strain

SIBERIAN TOOLKIT

- 4 parts Vodka
- 1 part Whiskey
- Shot Glass

Shake with ice and strain

SIBERIAN WALRUS

- 2 parts Blue Curaçao
- 1 part Light Rum
- 1 part Vodka
- 1 part Jack Daniel's®
- 1 part Kirschwasser
- 1 part Orange Juice
- Shot Glass

Shake with ice and strain. *Note: Because this recipe includes many ingredients, it's easier to make in volume, about 6 shots.

SICILIAN SUNSET

- 1 part Southern Comfort®
- 1 part Amaretto
- 1 part Grenadine
- 2 parts Orange Juice
- Shot Glass

Shake with ice and strain

SILK PANTIES

- 1 part Peach Schnapps
- 3 parts Vodka
- Shot Glass

Shake with ice and strain

SILVER BULLET SHOOTER

- 2 parts Peppermint Schnapps
- 1 part Vodka
- Shot Glass

Shake with ice and strain

SILVER DEVIL

- 1 part Tequila
- 1 part Peppermint Schnapps
- Shot Glass

Shake with ice and strain

SILVER NIPPLE

- 4 parts Sambuca
- 1 part Vodka
- Shot Glass

Shake with ice and strain

SILVER SPIDER

- 1 part Vodka
- 1 part Rum
- 1 part Triple Sec
- 1 part Crème de Cacao (White)
- Shot Glass

Shake with ice and strain

SILVER WILSON

- 1 part Kiwi Schnapps
- 1 part Passion Fruit Liqueur
- 1 part Sour Mix
- Shot Glass

Shake with ice and strain

SIMPLE GREEN

- 1 part Blue Curaçao
- 1 part Galliano®
- 1 part Jägermeister®
- Shot Glass

Shake with ice and strain

SIMPSON BRONCO

- 4 parts Sambuca
- 1 part Grenadine
- 1 part Orange Juice
- Shot Glass

Shake with ice and strain

SINGLES NIGHT

- 1 part Coffee Liqueur
- 1 part Crème de Banana
- 1 part Cointreau®
- 1 part Irish Cream Liqueur
- Shot Glass

Shake with ice and strain

SING-SING

- 1 part Blue Curaçao
- 1 part Cream
- 1 part Crème de Banana
- 1 part Frangelico®
- Shot Glass

Shake with ice and strain

SIT DOWN AND SHUT UP

- 1 part Blackberry Liqueur
- 1 part Peppermint Liqueur
- 1 part Southern Comfort®
- Shot Glass

Shake with ice and strain

SIT ON MY FACE SAMMY

- 1 part Crown Royal® Whiskey
- 1 part Frangelico®
- 1 part Irish Cream Liqueur
- Shot Glass

Shake with ice and strain

SIVITRI

- 1 part Lychee Liqueur
- 1 part Absinthe
- Shot Glass

Shake with ice and strain

SKANDIA ICEBERG

- 1 part Crème de Menthe (White)
- 1 part Vodka
- Shot Glass

Shake with ice and strain

SKID MARK

- 1 part Coffee Liqueur
- 1 part Jägermeister®
- 1 part Rumple Minze®
- Shot Glass

Shake with ice and strain

SKITTLES®

- 1 part Vodka
- 1 part Southern Comfort®
- 1 part Melon Liqueur

- 1 part Pineapple Juice
- 1 part Sour Mix
- Shot Glass

Shake with ice and strain

SKULL

- 1 part Coffee Liqueur
- 1 part Irish Cream Liqueur

- 1 part Whiskey
- Shot Glass

Shake with ice and strain

SKY PILOT

- 1 part Vodka
- 1 part Irish Cream Liqueur

- 1 part Peppermint Schnapps
- Shot Glass

Shake with ice and strain

SLAM DUNK SHOOTER

- 2 parts Tequila Reposado
- 1 part Lime Cordial
- 1 part Club Soda
- Shot Glass

Shake all but Club Soda with ice and strain into the glass. Top with Club Soda.

SLAMMER

- 1 part Vodka
- 1 part Lemon-Lime Soda
- Shot Glass

Build in the glass with no ice

SLAP SHOT

- 2 parts Southern Comfort®
- 1 part Peppermint Schnapps
- Shot Glass

Shake with ice and strain

SLICE OF APPLE PIE

- 3 parts Vodka
- 1 part Apple Juice
- Shot Glass

Shake with ice and strain

SLICK AND SLEEZY

- 1 part Salsa
- 5 parts Vodka
- Shot Glass

Build in the glass with no ice

SLICKSTER

- 2 parts Southern Comfort®
- 1 part Peach Schnapps
- 1 part Lemon-Lime Soda
- Shot Glass

Stir gently with ice and strain

SLIPPERY CRICKET

- 1 part Vodka
- 1 part Blue Hawaiian Schnapps
- 1 part Tropical Punch Schnapps
- Shot Glass

Shake with ice and strain

SLIPPERY NIPPLE

- 1 part Coffee Liqueur
- 1 part Irish Cream Liqueur
- 1 part Peppermint Schnapps
- Shot Glass

Shake with ice and strain

SLIPPERY SADDLE

- 1 part Vodka
- 1 part Licor 43®
- 1 part Orange Juice
- Shot Glass

Shake with ice and strain

SLOE SOUTHERN FUCK

- 1 part Sloe Gin
- 1 part Southern Comfort®
- 1 part Sour Mix
- 1 part Lemon-Lime Soda
- Shot Glass

Build in the glass with no ice

SLOPPY BAGINA

- 1 part Vodka
- 1 part Irish Cream Liqueur
- 2 parts 151-Proof Rum
- splash Lime Juice
- Shot Glass

Shake with ice and strain

SMALL BOMB

- 1 part Vodka
- 1 part Triple Sec
- 1 part Grenadine
- Shot Glass

Shake with ice and strain

SMARTIE®

- 1 part Grape-Flavored Schnapps
- 1 part Melon Liqueur
- Shot Glass

Shake with ice and strain

SMASHING PUMPKIN

- 1 part Coffee Liqueur
- 1 part Irish Cream Liqueur
- 1 part Goldschläger®
- Shot Glass

Shake with ice and strain

SMERALDO

- 3 parts Gin
- 3 parts Fruit Punch
- 2 parts Blue Curaçao
- 1 part Cointreau®
- 1 part Peach Nectar
- Shot Glass

Shake with ice and strain

SMILES

- 1 part Crème de Menthe (White)
- 1 part Amaretto
- 1 part Whiskey
- 1 part Lemon-Lime Soda
- Shot Glass

Build in the glass with no ice

SMOOTH AND SWEET

- 2 parts Amaretto
- 2 parts Blackberry Liqueur
- 1 part Pineapple Juice
- Shot Glass

Shake with ice and strain

SMOOTH DOG

- 3 parts Amaretto
- 1 part Lemon-Lime Soda
- Shot Glass

Build in the glass with no ice

SMOOTHIE

- 1 part Crown Royal® Whiskey
- 1 part Amaretto
- 1 part Triple Sec
- 1 part Sour Mix
- 1 part Lemon-Lime Soda
- Shot Glass

Shake with ice and strain

SMURF® FART

- 1 part Blue Curaçao
- 2 parts Blueberry Schnapps
- 1 part Cream
- Shot Glass

Shake with ice and strain

SMURF® PEE

- 1 part 151-Proof Rum
- 1 part Blue Curaçao
- 1 part Jägermeister®
- 1 part Rumple Minze®
- Shot Glass

Shake with ice and strain

SNAKEBITE

- 1 part Tequila
- 1 part Southern Comfort®

- Shot Glass

Shake with ice and strain

SNEEKER

- 1 part Raspberry Liqueur
- 1 part Coconut-Flavored Rum
- 1 part 151-Proof Rum
- 1 part Midori®

- 1 part Cranberry Juice Cocktail
- 1 part Lemon-Lime Soda
- Shot Glass

Shake with ice and strain. *Note: Because this recipe includes many ingredients, it's easier to make in volume, about 6 shots.

SNICKERS®

- 1 part Crème de Cacao (Dark)
- 1 part Frangelico®
- Shot Glass

Shake with ice and strain

SNOOPY® DOG

- 2 parts Vodka
- 1 part Grenadine
- 1 part Amaretto
- 1 part Crème de Banana
- Shot Glass

Shake with ice and strain

SNOT ROCKET

- 1 part Apple Brandy
- 1 part Sour Apple Schnapps
- 1 part Vodka
- Shot Glass

Shake with ice and strain

SNOTTY TODDY

- 1 part Midori®
- 1 part 151-Proof Rum
- 1 part Orange Juice
- Shot Glass

Shake with ice and strain

SNOW DROP SHOOTER

- 1 part Crème de Cacao (White)
- 1 part Vodka
- 1 part Triple Sec
- Shot Glass

Shake with ice and strain

SNOW MELTER

- 1 part Sambuca
- 1 part Crème de Cacao (White)
- 1 part Rum
- Shot Glass

Shake with ice and strain

SNOW SNAKE JUICE

- 1 part Bourbon
- 1 part Peppermint Schnapps
- Shot Glass

Pour ingredients into glass neat (do not chill)

SNOWBALL

- 1 part Jack Daniel's®
- 1 part Rumple Minze®
- Shot Glass

Shake with ice and strain

SNOWSHOE

- 1 part Vodka
- 1 part Peppermint Schnapps
- Shot Glass

Shake with ice and strain

SOCO AND LIME

- 1 part Southern Comfort®
- splash Lime Juice
- Shot Glass

Shake with ice and strain

SOCO PEACH AND LIME

- 2 parts Peach Schnapps
- 2 parts Southern Comfort®
- 1 part Lime Juice
- Shot Glass

Shake with ice and strain

SOCO SLAMMER

- 1 part Southern Comfort®
- 2 parts Cola
- Shot Glass

Build in the glass with no ice

SOLAR FLARE

- 1 part Vodka
- 1 part Triple Sec
- Shot Glass

Shake with ice and strain

SOLARIS

- 1 part Spiced Rum
- 1 part Grenadine
- dash Sugar
- Shot Glass

Shake with ice and strain

SOLO SHOT

- 1 part Peach Schnapps
- 3 parts Cranberry Juice Cocktail
- 1 part Raspberry Liqueur
- Shot Glass

Shake with ice and strain

SON OF A PEACH

- 1 part Vodka
- 1 part Peach Schnapps
- 1 part Honey
- Shot Glass

Shake with ice and strain

SONGBIRD

- 1 part Tequila Silver
- 1 part Vodka
- 1 part Crème de Banana
- Shot Glass

Shake with ice and strain

SOOTHER

- 2 parts Amaretto
- 2 parts Melon Liqueur
- 1 part Vodka
- 1 part Sour Mix
- Shot Glass

Shake with ice and strain

SOUL TAKER

- 1 part Vodka
- 1 part Tequila
- 1 part Amaretto
- Shot Glass

Shake with ice and strain

SOUR GRAPES

- 1 part Vodka
- 1 part Raspberry Liqueur
- 1 part Sour Mix
- Shot Glass

Shake with ice and strain

SOUR JACK

- 1 part Jack Daniel's®
- 1 part Raspberry Liqueur
- Shot Glass

Shake with ice and strain

SOURBALL

- 1 part Vodka
- 1 part Lemonade
- 1 part Orange Juice
- Shot Glass

Shake with ice and strain

SOUTHERN BEAMY BRAIN DAMAGE

- 1 part Southern Comfort®
- 1 part Jim Beam®
- 1 part Tia Maria®
- splash Grenadine
- Shot Glass

Shake all but Grenadine with ice and strain into the glass. Place a few drops of Grenadine in the center of the drink.

SOUTHERN BITCH

- 1 part Southern Comfort®
- 1 part Amaretto
- 1 part Peach Schnapps
- 1 part Pineapple Juice
- 1 part Orange Juice
- Shot Glass

*Shake with ice and strain. *Note: Because this recipe includes many ingredients, it's easier to make in volume, about 6 shots.*

SOUTHERN BONDAGE

- 1 part Southern Comfort®
- 1 part Amaretto
- 1 part Peach Schnapps
- 1 part Triple Sec
- 1 part Cranberry Juice Cocktail
- 1 part Sour Mix
- Shot Glass

*Shake with ice and strain. *Note: Because this recipe includes many ingredients, it's easier to make in volume, about 6 shots.*

SOUTHERN CHASE

- 1 part Galliano®
- 1 part Southern Comfort®
- 1 part Jim Beam®
- Shot Glass

Shake with ice and strain

SOUTHERN COMFORT® KAMIKAZE

- 3 parts Southern Comfort®
- 2 parts Triple Sec
- 1 part Lime Juice
- Shot Glass

Shake with ice and strain

SOUTHERN COMFORT® PINK

- 1 part Light Rum
- 1 part Southern Comfort®
- 1 part Grapefruit Juice
- 1 part Grenadine
- Shot Glass

Shake with ice and strain

SOUTHERN FRUITY PASSION

- 1 part Southern Comfort®
- 1 part Triple Sec
- 1 part Grenadine
- Shot Glass

Shake with ice and strain

SOUTHERN IRELAND

- 1 part Irish Cream Liqueur
- 1 part Southern Comfort®
- Shot Glass

Shake with ice and strain

SOUTHERN PEACH

- 2 parts Peach Schnapps
- 1 part Southern Comfort®
- Shot Glass

Shake with ice and strain

SOUTHERN PINK FLAMINGO

- 1 part Southern Comfort®
- 1 part Coconut-Flavored Rum
- 1 part Pineapple Juice
- splash Grenadine
- splash Lemon Juice
- Shot Glass

Shake with ice and strain

SOUTHERN PRIDE

- 2 parts Southern Comfort®
- 1 part Peach Schnapps
- Shot Glass

Shake with ice and strain

SOUTHERN SLAMMER

- 1 part Peach Schnapps
- 1 part Vanilla Liqueur
- 1 part Southern Comfort®
- Shot Glass

Shake with ice and strain

SOUTHERN SMILE

- 1 part Southern Comfort®
- 1 part Amaretto
- 1 part Cranberry Juice Cocktail
- Shot Glass

Shake with ice and strain

SOUTHPAW

- 1 part Brandy
- 1 part Orange Juice
- 1 part Lemon-Lime Soda
- Shot Glass

Build in the glass with no ice

SPACE ODYSSEY

- 1 part 151-Proof Rum
- 1 part Coconut-Flavored Rum
- 1 part Pineapple Juice
- Shot Glass

Shake with ice and strain

SPANISH MOSS SHOOTER

- 2 parts Coffee Liqueur
- 1 part Crème de Menthe (Green)
- 1 part Tequila Silver
- Shot Glass

Shake with ice and strain

SPARATO MILANO

- 2 parts Sambuca
- 1 part Amaretto
- 1 part Cherry Brandy
- Shot Glass

Shake with ice and strain

SPARKPLUG

- 1 part 151-Proof Rum
- 1 part Rumple Minze®
- Shot Glass

Pour ingredients into glass neat (do not chill)

SPEEDY GONZALES® SHOOTER

- 1 part Amaretto
- 1 part Irish Cream Liqueur
- Shot Glass

Shake with ice and strain

SPERM

- 1 part Tequila
- 1 part Vodka
- splash Cream
- Shot Glass

Shake all but Cream with ice and strain into the glass. Place a few drops of Cream in the center of the drink.

SPERM BANK SHOOTER

- 1 part Tequila Reposado
- splash Irish Cream Liqueur
- Shot Glass

Pour the Tequila into the shot glass. Place a few drops of Irish Cream Liqueur in the center of the drink.

SPERM WHALE

- 3 parts Rye Whiskey
- 3 parts Southern Comfort®
- 1 part Cream
- Shot Glass

Shake with ice and strain

SPICE CAKE

- 1 part Irish Cream Liqueur
- 1 part Amaretto
- 1 part Cinnamon Schnapps
- Shot Glass

Shake with ice and strain

SPICED APPLE

- 1 part Apple Brandy
- 1 part Goldschläger®
- 2 parts Spiced Rum
- Shot Glass

Shake with ice and strain

SPICED JOLLY ROGER

- 1 part Goldschläger®
- 1 part Spiced Rum
- Shot Glass

Shake with ice and strain

SPINDLE

- 1 part Amaretto
- 1 part Crown Royal® Whiskey
- 1 part Peach Schnapps
- Shot Glass

Shake with ice and strain

SPIRITWALKER

- 1 part Jägermeister®
- 1 part Rumple Minze®
- 1 part 151-Proof Rum
- 1 part Fire Water®
- Shot Glass

Shake with ice and strain

SPITFIRE

- 1 part Jack Daniel's®
- 1 part Rum
- 1 part Vodka
- Shot Glass

Shake with ice and strain

SPRAWLING DUBINSKY

- 1 part Johnnie Walker® Red Label
- 1 part Johnnie Walker® Black Label
- 1 part Citrus-Flavored Vodka
- splash Amaretto
- Shot Glass

Shake with ice and strain

SPY CATCHER

- 2 parts Whiskey
- 1 part Sambuca
- Shot Glass

Shake with ice and strain

SQUIRREL'S FANTASY

- 2 parts Amaretto
- 1 part Frangelico®
- 1 part Club Soda
- Shot Glass

Build in the glass with no ice

SQUISHED SMURF®

- 2 parts Peach Schnapps
- 1 part Irish Cream Liqueur
- 1 part Blue Curaçao
- splash Grenadine
- Shot Glass

Build in the glass with no ice

SQUISHY

- 1 part Raspberry Liqueur
- 1 part Amaretto
- 1 part Vodka
- Shot Glass

Shake with ice and strain

SR-71

- 1 part Amaretto
- 1 part Irish Cream Liqueur

- Shot Glass

Shake with ice and strain

ST. CLEMENT'S SHOOTER

- 1 part Triple Sec
- 1 part Mandarine Napoléon® Liqueur

- Shot Glass

Shake with ice and strain

ST. DELIAH

- 1 part Crème de Banana
- 1 part Raspberry Liqueur

- Shot Glass

Shake with ice and strain

STABILIZER

- 1 part 151-Proof Rum
- 1 part Rumple Minze®
- Shot Glass

Shake with ice and strain

STAINED BLUE DRESS

- 1 part Vodka
- 1 part Blue Curaçao
- splash Irish Cream Liqueur
- Shot Glass

Shake all but Irish Cream with ice and strain into the glass. Place a few drops of Irish Cream in the center of the drink.

STAR WARS® II

- 2 parts Southern Comfort®
- 1 part Orange Juice
- Shot Glass

Shake with ice and strain

STARBURST SHOOTER

- 2 parts Dark Rum
- 1 part Pineapple Juice
- 1 part Vermouth
- Shot Glass

Shake with ice and strain

STARDUST

- 1 part Citrus-Flavored Vodka
- 1 part Peach Schnapps
- 1 part Blue Curaçao
- 1 part Sour Mix
- 1 part Pineapple Juice
- 1 part Grenadine
- Shot Glass

Shake with ice and strain. *Note: Because this recipe includes many ingredients, it's easier to make in volume, about 6 shots.

START ME UP

- 2 parts Vodka
- 1 part Tequila
- 1 part Currant-Flavored Vodka
- 1 part Dark Rum
- Shot Glass

Shake with ice and strain

STEEL SHOOTER

- 2 parts Cinnamon Schnapps
- 2 parts Vanilla Liqueur
- 1 part Whiskey
- Shot Glass

Shake with ice and strain

STEVIE RAY VAUGHAN

- 1 part Jack Daniel's®
- 1 part Southern Comfort®
- 1 part Triple Sec
- 1 part Sour Mix
- 4 parts Orange Juice
- Shot Glass

Shake with ice and strain

STEVIE WONDER

- 1 part Coffee Liqueur
- 1 part Crème de Cacao (Dark)
- 1 part Amaretto
- 1 part Galliano®
- Shot Glass

Shake with ice and strain

STIFF DICK

- 1 part Butterscotch Schnapps
- 1 part Irish Cream Liqueur
- Shot Glass

Shake with ice and strain

STILETTO SHOOTER

- 1 part Coffee Liqueur
- 1 part Peppermint Schnapps
- 1 part Tequila
- Shot Glass

Shake with ice and strain

STINKY WEASEL

- 1 part Tequila
- 1 part 151-Proof Rum
- 1 part Lemon Juice
- 2 dashes Sugar
- Shot Glass

Shake with ice and strain

STOP LIGHTS

- 3 parts Vodka
- splash Midori®
- splash Orange Juice
- splash Cranberry Juice Cocktail
- Shot Glass

Shake Vodka with ice and strain equal parts into three shot glasses. Top the first glass with Melon Liqueur, the second with Orange Juice, and the third one with Cranberry Juice. Drink all three shots rapidly and in order.

STORMTROOPER®

- 1 part Peppermint Schnapps
- 1 part Jägermeister®
- Shot Glass

Shake with ice and strain

STRAIGHT JACKET

- 2 parts Cinnamon Schnapps
- 1 part Passoã®
- 1 part Orange Juice
- Shot Glass

Shake with ice and strain

STRANDED IN TIJUANA

- 1 part Sloe Gin
- 1 part Tequila Reposado
- 1 part 151-Proof Rum
- Shot Glass

Shake with ice and strain

STRAWBERRY BLISS BOMB

- 1 part Crème de Cacao (White)
- 1 part Strawberry Liqueur
- 1 part Coconut-Flavored Liqueur
- Shot Glass

Shake with ice and strain

STRAWBERRY LEMON DROP

- 1 part Vodka
- 1 part Strawberry Liqueur
- fill with Lemonade
- Shot Glass

Build over ice and stir

STRAWBERRY LIPS

- 1 part Strawberry Liqueur
- 1 part Coconut-Flavored Liqueur
- 1 part Cream
- Shot Glass

Shake with ice and strain

STROKE

- 3 parts Banana Liqueur
- 1 part Irish Cream Liqueur
- splash Grenadine
- Shot Glass

Shake all but Grenadine with ice and strain into the glass. Place a few drops of Grenadine in the center of the drink.

STRONG BAD

- 1 part Southern Comfort®
- 1 part Vanilla-Flavored Vodka
- 1 part Tonic Water
- Shot Glass

Build in the glass with no ice

STUMBLE FUCK

- 1 part Jägermeister®
- 1 part Rumple Minze®
- 1 part Cinnamon Schnapps
- Shot Glass

Shake with ice and strain

STUMPFUCKER

- 1 part Jägermeister®
- 1 part Rumple Minze®
- 1 part 151-Proof Rum
- Shot Glass

Shake with ice and strain

SUBLIME

- 1 part Amaretto
- 1 part Crème de Cacao (White)
- 1 part Banana Liqueur
- Shot Glass

Shake with ice and strain

SUICIDE STOP LIGHT

- 1 part Midori®
- 1 part Vodka
- 1 part After Shock® Cinnamon Schnapps
- splash Orange Juice
- Shot Glass

Fill the first of three shot glasses with Midori®, the second one with 1 part Vodka and 1 part Orange Juice, and the last one with After Shock. Drink all three rapidly and in order.

SUN SCORCHER

- 3 parts Butterscotch Schnapps
- 1 part Vodka
- Shot Glass

Shake with ice and strain

SUNNY MEXICO

- 1 part Galliano®
- 1 part Tequila

- Shot Glass

Shake with ice and strain

SUNSET AT THE BEACH

- 2 parts Cranberry-Flavored Vodka
- 1 part Melon Liqueur

- 1 part Raspberry Liqueur
- 2 parts Pineapple Juice
- Shot Glass

Shake with ice and strain

SUPER DAVE

- 1 part Spiced Rum
- 1 part Coconut-Flavored Rum
- 1 part Pineapple Juice

- 1 part Cola
- Shot Glass

Shake with ice and strain

SUPERMODEL

- 3 parts Bacardi® Limón Rum
- 1 part Melon Liqueur
- 1 part Blue Curaçao
- Shot Glass

Shake with ice and strain

SURFER ON ACID

- 1 part Jägermeister®
- 1 part Coconut-Flavored Rum
- 1 part Pineapple Juice
- Shot Glass

Shake with ice and strain

SUSU

- 2 parts Vodka
- 1 part Irish Cream Liqueur
- 1 part Crème de Cacao (Dark)
- 1 part Coffee Liqueur
- 1 part Grenadine
- 2 parts Milk
- Shot Glass

Shake with ice and strain. *Note: Because this recipe includes many ingredients, it's easier to make in volume, about 6 shots.

SWAMP THING

- 1 part Coffee Liqueur
- 1 part Crème de Menthe (White)
- 1 part Irish Cream Liqueur
- Shot Glass

Shake with ice and strain

SWAN SONG

- 1 part Southern Comfort®
- 1 part Whiskey
- 1 part Amaretto
- 1 part Dark Rum
- 1 part Orange Juice
- 1 part Cranberry Juice Cocktail
- 1 part Lime Juice
- Shot Glass

Shake with ice and strain. *Note: Because this recipe includes many ingredients, it's easier to make in volume, about 6 shots.

SWEDISH COLOR

- 1 part Banana Liqueur
- 1 part Blue Curaçao
- 1 part Vodka
- Shot Glass

Shake with ice and strain

SWEET AND SOUR PUSSY

- 1 part Raspberry Liqueur
- 1 part Cherry Whiskey
- Shot Glass

Shake with ice and strain

SWEET INDULGENCE

- 1 part Crème de Cacao (Dark)
- 1 part Cherry Brandy
- 1 part Cream
- Shot Glass

Shake with ice and strain

SWEET JESUS

- 1 part 151-Proof Rum
- 1 part Southern Comfort®
- Shot Glass

Shake with ice and strain

SWEET LIPS

- 1 part 151-Proof Rum
- 1 part Whiskey
- 1 part Tequila Reposado
- Shot Glass

Shake with ice and strain

SWEET PICKLE

- 1 part Vodka
- 1 part Rumple Minze®
- 1 part Melon Liqueur
- Shot Glass

Shake with ice and strain

SWEET PIGEON

- 1 part Citrus-Flavored Vodka
- 2 parts Crème de Cacao (White)
- 1 part Blue Curaçao
- 2 parts Cream
- Shot Glass

Shake with ice and strain

SWEET SHIT

- 1 part Vodka
- 1 part Amaretto
- 1 part Irish Cream Liqueur
- 1 part Coffee Liqueur
- 2 parts Chocolate Syrup
- Shot Glass

Shake with ice and strain. *Note: Because this recipe includes many ingredients, it's easier to make in volume, about 6 shots.

SWEET STING

- 1 part Goldschläger®
- 1 part Cream
- Shot Glass

Shake with ice and strain

SWEET TART

- 1 part Raspberry Liqueur
- 1 part Sour Mix
- 1 part Southern Comfort®
- Shot Glass

Shake with ice and strain

SWEET TITS

- 1 part Strawberry Liqueur
- 1 part Apricot Brandy
- 1 part Pineapple Juice
- Shot Glass

Shake with ice and strain

SWELL SEX

- 1 part Vodka
- 1 part Coconut-Flavored Rum
- 1 part Melon Liqueur
- 1 part Cream
- 1 part Pineapple Juice
- Shot Glass

Shake with ice and strain

SWIFT KICK IN THE BALLS

- 1 part Rum
- 1 part Vodka
- 1 part Lemon Juice
- Shot Glass

Shake with ice and strain

SWISS PEACH

- 1 part Peach Schnapps
- 1 part Crème de Cacao (White)
- Shot Glass

Shake with ice and strain

T.G.V.

- 1 part Tequila
- 1 part Gin
- 1 part Vodka
- Shot Glass

Build in the glass with no ice

T.K.O.

- 1 part Tequila
- 1 part Coffee Liqueur
- 1 part Ouzo
- Shot Glass

Shake with ice and strain

TABLAZO

- 1 part Vodka
- 1 part Ginger Ale
- Shot Glass

Build in the glass with no ice

TAINTED HEART

- 1 part Cinnamon Schnapps
- 1 part Chocolate Liqueur
- Shot Glass

Shake with ice and strain

TAKE IT AND VOMIT

- 1 part Vodka
- 1 part Peach Schnapps
- 1 part Blue Curaçao
- 1 part Grenadine
- 1 part Orange Juice
- Shot Glass

Shake with ice and strain

TANGAROA

- 3 parts Vodka
- 1 part Vanilla Liqueur
- Shot Glass

Shake with ice and strain

TANK FORCE

- 1 part Blue Curaçao
- 1 part Orange Juice
- 1 part Goldschläger®
- Shot Glass

Shake with ice and strain

TARTAN SPECIAL

- 1 part Glayva®
- 1 part Drambuie®
- 1 part Irish Cream Liqueur
- Shot Glass

Shake with ice and strain

TARZAN® SCREAM

- 2 parts Vodka
- 2 parts 151-Proof Rum
- 1 part Caramel Syrup
- splash Cream
- Shot Glass

Shake with ice and strain. Top with Cream.

T-BONE

- 1 part 151-Proof Rum
- splash Steak Sauce
- Shot Glass

Build in the glass with no ice

TEARDROP

- 3 parts Pepper-Flavored Vodka
- 1 part Triple Sec
- Shot Glass

Shake with ice and strain

TEEN WOLF

- 1 part Advocaat
- 1 part Kirschwasser
- Shot Glass

Shake with ice and strain

TEMPTATION ISLAND

- 1 part Coconut-Flavored Liqueur
- 1 part Frangelico®
- 1 part Peach Schnapps
- Shot Glass

Shake with ice and strain

TEN SNAKES IN A LAWNMOWER

- 1 part 151-Proof Rum
- 1 part Raspberry Liqueur
- 1 part Southern Comfort®
- 1 part Melon Liqueur
- Shot Glass

Shake with ice and strain

TEQUILA HEADFUCK

- 1 part Irish Cream Liqueur
- 2 parts Tequila
- Shot Glass

Shake with ice and strain

TEQUILA LEMON DROP

- 1 part Tequila
- 1 part Triple Sec
- 1 part Lemonade
- Shot Glass

Shake with ice and strain

TEQUILA PICKLE SHOOTER

- 1 part Tequila
- 1 part Pickle Juice
- Shot Glass

Build in the glass with no ice

TEQUILA POPPER

- 1 part Tequila Silver
- 1 part Lemon-Lime Soda
- Shot Glass

Build in the glass with no ice. Place your hand or a napkin over the glass and slam it down on the bar. Drink while it's still fizzing.

TEQUILA ROSE

- 1 part Tequila
- 1 part Triple Sec
- 1 part Cherry Juice
- 2 parts Sour Mix
- Shot Glass

Shake with ice and strain

TEQUILA SHOT

- 1 part Tequila
- 1 Lemon Wedge
- dash Salt
- Shot Glass

Rub the Lemon on the flesh between the thumb and forefinger of your left hand, cover the spot with Salt, then hold the Lemon between your thumb and forefinger. Lick the Salt, shoot the Tequila, and suck the Lemon.

TEQUILA SLAMMER

- 1 part Tequila
- 1 part Lemon-Lime Soda
- Shot Glass

Build in the glass with no ice

TERMINATOR

- 1 part Jägermeister®
- 1 part Southern Comfort®
- Shot Glass

Shake with ice and strain

TETANUS SHOT

- 1 part Irish Cream Liqueur
- 1 part Cherry Brandy
- 1 part Peach Schnapps
- Shot Glass

Shake with ice and strain

TEXAS ANTIFREEZE

- 1 part Coconut-Flavored Rum
- 1 part Citrus-Flavored Vodka
- 1 part Melon Liqueur
- Shot Glass

Shake with ice and strain

TEXAS RATTLESNAKE

- 1 part Yukon Jack®
- 1 part Cherry Brandy
- 1 part Southern Comfort®
- 1 part Sour Mix
- Shot Glass

Shake with ice and strain

THIRD AND GOAL

- 1 part Peach Schnapps
- 1 part Grand Marnier®
- 1 part Sour Mix
- Shot Glass

Shake with ice and strain

THIRD REICH

- 1 part Jägermeister®
- 1 part Rumple Minze®
- 1 part Goldschläger®
- Shot Glass

Shake with ice and strain

THONG

- 2 parts Vodka
- 1 part Triple Sec
- 1 part Cream
- 1 part Orange Juice
- 1 part Crème de Noyaux
- 1 part Grenadine
- Shot Glass

Shake with ice and strain. *Note: Because this recipe includes many ingredients, it's easier to make in volume, about 6 shots.

THORAZINE®

- 1 part Jägermeister®
- 1 part Rumple Minze®
- 1 part 151-Proof Rum
- Shot Glass

Shake with ice and strain

THORNY SITUATION

- 1 part Coconut-Flavored Liqueur
- 1 part Frangelico®
- 1 part Sour Mix
- Shot Glass

Shake with ice and strain

THREE SHEETS TO THE WIND

- 1 part Jägermeister®
- 1 part Rumple Minze®
- 1 part Tequila
- Shot Glass

Shake with ice and strain

THREE STAGES OF FRIENDSHIP

- 1 part Jack Daniel's®
- 1 part Tequila
- 1 part 151-Proof Rum
- Shot Glass

Shake with ice and strain

THREE WISE MEN

- 1 part Jack Daniel's®
- 1 part Johnnie Walker® Black Label
- 1 part Jim Beam®
- Shot Glass

Shake with ice and strain

THREE WISE MEN #2

- 1 part Jägermeister®
- 1 part Goldschläger®
- 1 part Rumple Minze®
- Shot Glass

Build in the glass with no ice

THE THREE WISE MEN AND THEIR MEXICAN PORTER

- 1 part Jack Daniel's®
- 1 part Rye Whiskey
- 1 part Scotch
- 1 part Tequila
- Shot Glass

Build in the glass with no ice

THREE WISE MEN ON A FARM

- 1 part Jack Daniel's®
- 1 part Jim Beam®
- 1 part Yukon Jack®
- 1 part Wild Turkey® Bourbon
- Shot Glass

Pour ingredients into glass neat (do not chill)

THREE-DAY WEEKEND

- 1 part Jägermeister®
- 1 part Malibu® Rum
- 1 part Pineapple Juice
- 1 part Grenadine
- Shot Glass

Shake with ice and strain

THREE-LEAF CLOVER

- 1 part Whiskey
- 1 part Irish Mist®
- Shot Glass

Shake with ice and strain

THREE-LEGGED MONKEY

- 2 parts Bourbon
- 1 part Cola
- 1 part Lemon Juice
- Shot Glass

Shake with ice and strain

THUMB PRESS

- 2 parts Vodka
- 2 parts Midori®
- 1 part 151-Proof Rum
- splash Grenadine
- Shot Glass

Shake with ice and strain

THUMBS UP

- 1 part Crème de Banana
- 1 part Cherry Brandy
- 1 part Mango Schnapps
- Shot Glass

Shake with ice and strain

THUMPER

- 1 part Cognac
- 1 part Amer Picon®
- Shot Glass

Shake with ice and strain

THUNDER AND LIGHTNING

- 1 part Rumple Minze®
- 1 part 151-Proof Rum
- Shot Glass

Shake with ice and strain

THUNDERCLOUD

- 2 parts Coffee Liqueur
- 1 part Southern Comfort®
- 1 part Peppermint Schnapps
- 1 part Rum
- splash Cream
- Shot Glass

Shake all but Cream with ice and strain into the glass. Place a few drops of Cream in the center of the drink.

THUNDERCLOUD SHOOTER

- 1 part Amaretto
- 1 part Irish Mist®
- 1 part 151-Proof Rum
- Shot Glass

Shake with ice and strain

THURSDAY SHOOTER

- 1 part Blue Curaçao
- 1 part Peach Schnapps
- 1 part Pineapple Juice
- Shot Glass

Shake with ice and strain

TIC TAC® SHOOTER

- 1 part Crème de Menthe (White)
- 1 part Ouzo
- Shot Glass

Shake with ice and strain

TIDY BOWL

- 4 parts Blue Curaçao
- 1 part Dr. McGillicuddy's® Mentholmint Schnapps
- 1 part Irish Cream Liqueur
- Shot Glass

Shake with ice and strain

TIE ME TO THE BEDPOST

- 1 part Midori®
- 1 part Citrus-Flavored Vodka
- 1 part Coconut-Flavored Rum
- 1 part Sour Mix
- Shot Glass

Shake with ice and strain

TIME BOMB

- 1 part Blue Curaçao
- 1 part Melon Liqueur
- Shot Glass

Shake with ice and strain

TIP ENERGIZER

- 1 part Passion Fruit Liqueur
- 1 part Blue Curaçao
- 1 part Lime Juice
- Shot Glass

Shake with ice and strain

TIRAMISU

- 1 part Coffee Liqueur
- 1 part Chocolate Mint Liqueur
- Shot Glass

Shake with ice and strain

TIRED PUSSY

- 3 parts Coconut-Flavored Rum
- 1 part Pineapple Juice
- 1 part Cranberry Juice Cocktail
- Shot Glass

Shake with ice and strain

TO THE MOON

- 1 part Coffee Liqueur
- 1 part Amaretto
- 1 part Irish Cream Liqueur
- 1 part 151-Proof Rum
- Shot Glass

Shake with ice and strain

TOFFEE APPLE

- 1 part Vodka
- 1 part Butterscotch Schnapps
- 1 part Apple Brandy
- Shot Glass

Shake with ice and strain

TOKYO ROSE

- 1 part Vodka
- 1 part Sake
- 1 part Melon Liqueur
- Shot Glass

Shake with ice and strain

TONGUE TWISTER

- 2 parts Dark Rum
- 1 part Coconut-Flavored Liqueur
- 1 part Triple Sec
- Shot Glass

Shake with ice and strain

TOOLKIT

- 1 part Crème de Cacao (White)
- 1 part Irish Cream Liqueur
- 1 part Amaretto
- 1 part Coffee Liqueur
- Shot Glass .

Shake with ice and strain

TOOTSIE ROLL®

- 1 part Coffee Liqueur
- 1 part Orange Juice
- Shot Glass

Shake with ice and strain

TOP BANANA SHOOTER

- 1 part Crème de Cacao (White)
- 1 part Vodka
- 1 part Coffee
- 1 part Crème de Banana
- Shot Glass

Shake with ice and strain

TORO

- 1 part Spiced Rum
- 1 part Vodka
- 1 part Sour Mix
- Shot Glass

Shake with ice and strain

TOXIC JELLY BEAN

- 2 parts Jägermeister®
- 1 part Ouzo
- 1 part Blackberry Brandy
- Shot Glass

Shake with ice and strain

TOXIC REFUSE

- 1 part Vodka
- 1 part Triple Sec
- 1 part Midori®

- splash Lime Juice
- Shot Glass

Shake with ice and strain

TRAFFIC LIGHT

- 1 part Orange Juice
- 1 part Peach Schnapps
- 1 part Grenadine

- 1 part Blue Curaçao
- 1 part Vodka
- Shot Glass

*Shake with ice and strain. *Note: Because this recipe includes many ingredients, it's easier to make in volume, about 6 shots.*

TRANSMISSION OVERHAUL

- 1 part Vodka
- 1 part Amaretto
- 1 part Southern Comfort®
- 1 part Mountain Dew®
- 1 part Orange Juice
- 1 part Grenadine
- Shot Glass

*Stir gently with ice and strain. *Note: Because this recipe includes many ingredients, it's easier to make in volume, about 6 shots.*

TREE FROG

- 1 part Citrus-Flavored Vodka
- 1 part Blue Hawaiian Schnapps
- 2 parts Grapefruit Juice
- Shot Glass

Shake with ice and strain

TRIPLESEX

- 1 part Vodka
- 1 part Triple Sec
- 1 part Sour Mix
- 1 part Pineapple Juice
- Shot Glass

Shake with ice and strain

TROPICAL HOOTER

- 1 part Citrus-Flavored Vodka
- 1 part Raspberry Liqueur
- 1 part Watermelon Schnapps
- 1 part Lemon-Lime Soda
- Shot Glass

Shake with ice and strain

TROPICAL PASSION

- 1 part Rum
- 1 part Peach Schnapps
- 1 part Sloe Gin
- 1 part Triple Sec
- splash Orange Juice
- Shot Glass

Shake with ice and strain

TROPICAL WATERFALL

- 1 part Wild Berry Schnapps
- 1 part Orange Juice
- Shot Glass

Shake with ice and strain

TRUE CANADIAN

- 1 part Vodka
- 1 part Maple Syrup
- Shot Glass

Shake with ice and strain

TUB THUMPER

- 1 part Apricot Brandy
- 1 part Irish Cream Liqueur
- 1 part Whiskey
- Shot Glass

Shake with ice and strain

TUBBOOCKI

- 2 parts Galliano®
- 1 part Sambuca
- 1 part Wild Turkey® Bourbon
- Shot Glass

Build in the glass with no ice

TURKEY SHOOT

- 3 parts Wild Turkey® Bourbon
- 1 part Anisette
- Shot Glass

Shake with ice and strain

TURKEYBALL

- 1 part Wild Turkey® Bourbon
- 1 part Amaretto
- 1 part Pineapple Juice
- Shot Glass

Shake with ice and strain

TURN UP THE VOLUME

- 1 part Citrus-Flavored Vodka
- 1 part Blue Curaçao
- 1 part Peach Schnapps
- Shot Glass

Shake with ice and strain

TWIN SISTERS

- 1 part Light Rum
- 1 part Spiced Rum
- splash Cola
- splash Sweetened Lime Juice
- Shot Glass

Shake with ice and strain

TWISTED JACK

- 1 part Amaretto
- 1 part Jack Daniel's®
- 1 part Sour Mix
- 1 part Southern Comfort®
- 1 part Raspberry Liqueur
- Shot Glass

Shake with ice and strain

TWISTER SHOOTER

- 1 part Vodka
- 1 part Cherry Brandy
- 1 part Ouzo
- Shot Glass

Shake with ice and strain

T-ZONE

- 1 part Sloe Gin
- 1 part 151-Proof Rum
- Shot Glass

Shake with ice and strain

U-2

- 1 part Crème de Menthe (White)
- 1 part Melon Liqueur
- Shot Glass

Shake with ice and strain

UARAPITO

- 2 parts Dark Rum
- 1 part Grenadine
- 1 part Apple Juice
- Shot Glass

Shake with ice and strain

UNABOMBER

- 1 part Gin
- 1 part Vodka
- 1 part Triple Sec
- 1 part Lime Juice
- Shot Glass

Shake with ice and strain

UNDER WATER

- 1 part Blue Curaçao
- 1 part Irish Cream Liqueur
- 1 part Peach Schnapps
- Shot Glass

Shake with ice and strain

THE UNDERTAKER

- 1 part Triple Sec
- 1 part 151-Proof Rum
- Shot Glass

Shake with ice and strain

UNDERTOW

- 1 part Blue Curaçao
- 1 part Raspberry Liqueur
- Shot Glass

Shake with ice and strain

UNHOLY WATER

- 1 part Gin
- 1 part Spiced Rum
- 1 part Tequila Silver
- 1 part Vodka
- Shot Glass

Shake with ice and strain

UNIVERSAL SHOOTER

- 1 part Grapefruit Juice
- 1 part Sweet Vermouth
- 1 part Maraschino Liqueur
- Shot Glass

Shake with ice and strain

UP CHUCK

- 1 part 151-Proof Rum
- 1 part Tequila
- 1 part Jägermeister®
- Shot Glass

Pour ingredients into glass neat (do not chill)

UPSIDE-DOWN APPLE PIE SHOT

- 1 part Apple Juice
- 1 part Cinnamon Schnapps
- 1 part Vodka
- Whipped Cream
- Shot Glass

Shake all but the Whipped Cream with ice and strain into a shot glass. Sit facing away from the bar and lean your head back onto the bar. Pour the shot into your mouth followed by a squirt of Whipped Cream and then sit up quickly. A towel might be handy.

UPSIDE-DOWN KAMIKAZE

- 2 parts Triple Sec
- 2 parts Vodka
- 1 part Lime Juice
- Whipped Cream
- Shot Glass

Shake with ice and strain into a shot glass. Sit facing away from the bar and lean your head back onto the bar. Pour the shot into your mouth followed by a squirt of Whipped Cream and then sit up quickly. A towel might be handy.

UPSIDE-DOWN MARGARITA

- 2 parts Tequila
- 2 parts Lime Juice
- 1 part Triple Sec
- Whipped Cream
- Shot Glass

Shake with ice and strain into a shot glass. Sit facing away from the bar and lean your head back onto the bar. Pour the shot into your mouth followed by a squirt of Whipped Cream and then sit up quickly. A towel might be handy.

UPSIDE-DOWN OATMEAL COOKIE

- 1 part Irish Cream Liqueur
- 1 part Goldschläger®
- Whipped Cream
- Shot Glass

Shake with ice and strain into a shot glass. Sit facing away from the bar and lean your head back onto the bar. Pour the shot into your mouth followed by a squirt of Whipped Cream and then sit up quickly. A towel might be handy.

URBAN COWBOY

- 1 part Grand Marnier®
- 1 part Jack Daniel's®
- 1 part Southern Comfort®
- Shot Glass

Shake with ice and strain

URINE SAMPLE SHOOTER

- 1 part Galliano®
- 1 part Midori®
- 1 part Vodka
- Shot Glass

Shake with ice and strain

VALIUM®

- 1 part Rye Whiskey
- 1 part Peach Schnapps
- 1 part Cranberry Juice Cocktail
- Shot Glass

Shake with ice and strain

VAMPIRE SLAYER

- 2 parts Southern Comfort®
- 1 part Cognac
- 1 part Rum
- 1 part Scotch
- 1 part Jägermeister®
- Shot Glass

Shake with ice and strain. *Note: Because this recipe includes many ingredients, it's easier to make in volume, about 6 shots.

VANILLA ICE

- 1 part Vanilla Liqueur
- 2 parts Blueberry Schnapps
- Shot Glass

Shake with ice and strain

VANILLA JACK

- 2 parts Jack Daniel's®
- splash Vanilla Extract
- fill with Root Beer
- Shot Glass

Build over ice and stir

VANILLA MILKSHAKE

- 1 part Crème de Cacao (Dark)
- 2 parts Vanilla-Flavored Vodka
- 2 parts Milk
- Shot Glass

Shake with ice and strain

VARADERO ESPECIAL

- 1 part Maraschino Liqueur
- 1 part Grapefruit Juice
- Shot Glass

Shake with ice and strain

VARICOSE VEINS

- 1 part Irish Cream Liqueur
- 1 part Crème de Menthe (White)
- Shot Glass

Shake with ice and strain

VEGAS BLOW JOB

- 2 parts Rum
- 2 parts Jägermeister®
- 1 part Banana Liqueur
- 1 part Orange Juice
- 1 part Pineapple Juice
- Shot Glass

*Shake with ice and strain. *Note: Because this recipe includes many ingredients, it's easier to make in volume, about 6 shots.*

VIAGRA® SHOOTER

- 1 part Vodka
- 1 part Blue Curaçao
- 1 part Irish Cream Liqueur
- Shot Glass

Shake with ice and strain

VIBRATOR

- 1 part After Shock® Cinnamon Schnapps
- 1 part Avalanche® Peppermint Schnapps
- 1 part Spiced Rum
- splash Ginger Ale
- Shot Glass

Build in the glass with no ice

VICTORIA'S SHOT

- 2 parts Vodka
- 2 parts Passion Fruit Liqueur
- 1 part Pineapple Juice
- splash Lime Juice
- pinch Powdered Sugar
- Shot Glass

Shake with ice and strain

VIGOR

- 1 part Peach Schnapps
- 1 part Crème de Cassis
- 1 part Cranberry Juice Cocktail
- 1 part Lemon Juice
- Shot Glass

Shake with ice and strain

VIKING FUNERAL

- 1 part Rumple Minze®
- 1 part Jägermeister®
- 1 part Goldschläger®
- Shot Glass

Shake with ice and strain

VILLAGE

- 1 part Vodka
- 1 part Passion Fruit Liqueur
- 1 part Pineapple Juice
- 1 part Aperol™
- Shot Glass

Shake with ice and strain

VINE CLIMBER

- 2 parts Vodka
- 2 parts Melon Liqueur
- 1 part Sour Mix
- Shot Glass

Shake with ice and strain

VIOLENT FUCK

- 1 part Grain Alcohol
- 1 part Cola
- Shot Glass

Build in the glass with no ice

VIPER

- 1 part Vodka
- 1 part Amaretto
- 1 part Malibu® Rum
- 1 part Midori®
- 1 part Pineapple Juice
- Shot Glass

Shake with ice and strain

VIRGIN BREAKER

- 1 part Vodka
- 1 part Whiskey
- 1 part Sambuca
- 1 part Orange Juice
- 1 part Grenadine
- Shot Glass

*Shake with ice and strain. *Note: Because this recipe includes many ingredients, it's easier to make in volume, about 6 shots.*

VIRGIN PUSSY

- 1 part Watermelon Schnapps
- 1 part Cinnamon Schnapps
- Shot Glass

Shake with ice and strain

VIRULENT DEATH

- 1 part Blue Curaçao
- 1 part Yukon Jack®
- 1 part Galliano®
- Shot Glass

Shake with ice and strain

VODKA PASSION

- 1 part Orange-Flavored Vodka
- 1 part Passion Fruit Juice
- Shot Glass

Shake with ice and strain

VOLVO®

- 1 part Cointreau®
- 1 part Grand Marnier®
- 1 part Vodka
- 1 part Cognac
- 1 part Apricot Brandy
- Shot Glass

*Shake with ice and strain. *Note: Because this recipe includes many ingredients, it's easier to make in volume, about 6 shots.*

VOODOO DOLL

- 1 part Vodka
- 1 part Raspberry Liqueur
- Shot Glass

Shake with ice and strain

VULCAN DEATH GRIP

- 1 part Goldschläger®
- 1 part Rum
- Shot Glass

Shake with ice and strain

VULCAN MIND MELD

- 1 part Ouzo
- 1 part 151-Proof Rum
- Shot Glass

Shake with ice and strain

WAFFLE

- 1 part Vodka
- 1 part Butterscotch Schnapps
- 1 part Orange Juice
- Shot Glass

Shake with ice and strain

WAHOO

- 1 part 151-Proof Rum
- 1 part Amaretto
- 1 part Pineapple Juice
- Shot Glass

Shake with ice and strain

WAK-WAK

- 1 part Crème de Cassis
- 1 part Absinthe
- Shot Glass

Shake with ice and strain

WALTZING MATILDA SHOOTER

- 2 parts Light Rum
- 1 part Blue Curaçao
- 1 part Pineapple Juice
- Shot Glass

Shake with ice and strain

WANDERING MINSTREL SHOOTER

- 1 part Crème de Menthe (White)
- 1 part Brandy
- 1 part Vodka
- 1 part Coffee
- Shot Glass

Shake with ice and strain

WARM AND FUZZY

- 1 part Triple Sec
- 1 part Southern Comfort®
- 1 part Cherry Brandy
- Shot Glass

Shake with ice and strain

WARM CARROT CAKE

- 1 part Butterscotch Schnapps
- 1 part Cinnamon Schnapps
- 1 part Irish Cream Liqueur
- Shot Glass

Shake with ice and strain

A WARM GLASS OF SHUT THE HELL UP

- 1 part Cinnamon Schnapps
- 1 part Peach Schnapps
- 1 part Southern Comfort®
- Shot Glass

Pour ingredients into glass neat (do not chill)

WARM LEATHERETTE

- 3 parts Black Sambuca
- 2 parts Amaretto
- 1 part Grenadine
- Shot Glass

Shake with ice and strain

WARP CORE BREACH

- 1 part Goldschläger®
- 1 part Tequila
- 1 part Jack Daniel's®
- Shot Glass

Shake with ice and strain

WASHINGTON RED APPLE

- 1 part Canadian Whiskey
- 1 part Sour Apple Schnapps
- 1 part Vodka
- 1 part Cranberry Juice Cocktail
- Shot Glass

Shake with ice and strain

WATER MOCCASIN

- 1 part Crown Royal® Whiskey
- 1 part Peach Schnapps
- 1 part Sour Mix
- Shot Glass

Shake with ice and strain

WATERLOO

- 2 parts Mandarine Napoléon® Liqueur
- 2 parts Spiced Rum
- 1 part Orange Juice
- Shot Glass

Shake with ice and strain

WATERMELON SHOT

- 1 part Vodka
- 1 part Amaretto
- 1 part Southern Comfort®
- 1 part Orange Juice
- Shot Glass

Shake with ice and strain

WAYNE'S WORLD

- 2 parts Jägermeister®
- 1 part Sambuca
- Shot Glass

Shake with ice and strain

WEASEL WATER

- 1 part Crème de Banana
- 1 part Cream
- Shot Glass

Shake with ice and strain

WEDGIE

- 2 parts Coffee Liqueur
- 1 part Crème de Cacao (Dark)
- 1 part Whiskey
- Shot Glass

Shake with ice and strain

WEEKEND ON THE BEACH

- 1 part Canadian Whiskey
- 1 part Sour Apple Schnapps
- 1 part Peach Schnapps
- 1 part Sour Mix
- Shot Glass

Shake with ice and strain

WENCH

- 1 part Amaretto
- 1 part Spiced Rum
- Shot Glass

Shake with ice and strain

WERTHER'S®

- 1 part Irish Cream Liqueur
- 1 part Butterscotch Schnapps
- 1 part Bourbon
- Shot Glass

Shake with ice and strain

WEST SIDE SPECIAL

- 1 part Southern Comfort®
- 1 part Peppermint Schnapps
- Shot Glass

Shake with ice and strain

WETBACK

- 1 part Coffee Liqueur
- 1 part Tequila
- Shot Glass

Shake with ice and strain

WET DREAM

- 1 part Southern Comfort®
- 1 part Coconut-Flavored Rum
- 1 part Cranberry Juice Cocktail
- 1 part Pineapple Juice
- 1 part Lemon-Lime Soda
- Shot Glass

Shake with ice and strain

WET MUFF

- 1 part Butterscotch Schnapps
- 2 parts Cointreau®
- 2 parts Tia Maria®
- 1 part Pineapple Juice
- Shot Glass

Shake with ice and strain

WHIP ME BABY

- 1 part Triple Sec
- 1 part Dry Vermouth
- 1 part Rémy Martin® VSOP
- Shot Glass

Shake with ice and strain

WHIPPERSNAPPER

- 1 part Melon Liqueur
- 1 part Apple Brandy
- 1 part Cranberry Juice Cocktail
- Shot Glass

Shake with ice and strain

WHISKER BISCUIT

- 1 part 151-Proof Rum
- 1 part Banana Liqueur
- 1 part Coconut-Flavored Rum
- 1 part Grenadine
- 2 parts Pineapple Juice
- Shot Glass

Shake with ice and strain. *Note: Because this recipe includes many ingredients, it's easier to make in volume, about 6 shots.

WHITE CAP

- 1 part Vodka
- 1 part Cream
- 1 part Coffee
- 1 part Port
- Shot Glass

Shake with ice and strain

WHITE CLOUD

- 1 part Milk
- 1 part Peppermint Schnapps
- Shot Glass

Shake with ice and strain

WHITE DEATH

- 1 part Crème de Cacao (White)
- 1 part Vodka
- 1 part Raspberry Liqueur
- Shot Glass

Shake with ice and strain

WHITE KNUCKLE RIDE

- 2 parts Coffee
- 1 part Vodka
- Shot Glass

Shake with ice and strain

WHITE MESS

- 1 part Light Rum
- 1 part Crème de Cassis
- 1 part Root Beer Schnapps
- 1 part Coconut-Flavored Rum
- 1 part Heavy Cream
- Shot Glass

*Shake with ice and strain. *Note: Because this recipe includes many ingredients, it's easier to make in volume, about 6 shots.*

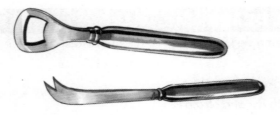

WHITE ORBIT

- 1 part Crème de Cacao (White)
- 1 part Melon Liqueur
- 1 part Glayva®
- 1 part Cream
- Shot Glass

Shake with ice and strain

WHITE SATIN SHOOTER

- 2 parts Tia Maria®
- 1 part Cream
- 1 part Frangelico®
- Shot Glass

Shake with ice and strain

WICKED SNOWSHOE

- 1 part Canadian Whiskey
- 1 part Goldschläger®
- 1 part Peppermint Schnapps
- 1 part Wild Turkey® 101
- Shot Glass

Shake with ice and strain

WICKED STEPMOTHER

- 2 parts Pepper-Flavored Vodka
- 1 part Amaretto
- Shot Glass

Shake with ice and strain

WIDGET

- 3 parts Peach Schnapps
- 1 part Gin
- Shot Glass

Shake with ice and strain

WIDOW MAKER

- 1 part Vodka
- 1 part Jägermeister®
- 1 part Coffee Liqueur
- splash Grenadine
- Shot Glass

Shake with ice and strain

WILD BERRY POP-TART®

- 1 part Wild Berry Schnapps
- 1 part Vodka
- 1 part Strawberry Liqueur
- Shot Glass

Shake with ice and strain

WILD CHILD

- 1 part Sour Apple Schnapps
- 1 part Vodka
- 1 part Lemon-Lime Soda
- Shot Glass

Build in the glass with no ice

WILD PEPPERTINI

- 1 part Wild Turkey® Bourbon
- 1 part Peppermint Schnapps
- Shot Glass

Shake with ice and strain

WILD THING SHOOTER

- 2 parts Vodka
- 1 part Apricot Brandy
- 1 part Lemon-Lime Soda
- Shot Glass

Build in the glass with no ice

WINDEX® SHOOTER

- 1 part Blue Curaçao
- 1 part Vodka
- Shot Glass

Shake with ice and strain

WINDY

- 1 part Vodka
- 1 part Blue Curaçao
- 1 part Pineapple Juice
- 1 part Sour Mix
- Shot Glass

Shake with ice and strain

WINTER GREEN DRAGON

- 2 parts Green Chartreuse®
- 1 part 151-Proof Rum
- 1 part Rumple Minze®
- Shot Glass

Shake with ice and strain

WOLF PUSSY

- 1 part Bourbon
- 1 part Cinnamon Schnapps
- Shot Glass

Pour ingredients into glass neat (do not chill)

WONKA

- 1 part Cherry Brandy
- 1 part Amaretto
- 1 part Sour Mix
- Shot Glass

Shake with ice and strain

WOO WOO SHOOTER

- 1 part Vodka
- 1 part Peach Schnapps
- 1 part Cranberry Juice Cocktail
- Shot Glass

Shake with ice and strain

WOOF

- 1 part Blue Curaçao
- 1 part Amaretto
- 1 part Parfait Amour
- Shot Glass

Shake with ice and strain

WOO-SHOO

- 2 parts Cranberry-Flavored Vodka
- 1 part Peach Schnapps
- Shot Glass

Shake with ice and strain

X

- 2 parts Amaretto
- 2 parts Wild Berry Schnapps
- 1 part Sour Mix
- 1 part Cola
- Shot Glass

Shake with ice and strain

XAIBALBA

- 1 part Vodka
- 1 part Butterscotch Schnapps
- 1 part Vanilla Liqueur
- 1 part Chocolate Syrup
- Shot Glass

Shake with ice and strain

Y2K SHOT

- 1 part Vodka
- 1 part Melon Liqueur
- 1 part Raspberry Liqueur
- Shot Glass

Shake with ice and strain

YAK MILK

- 1 part Crème de Cacao (Dark)
- 1 part Coconut-Flavored Rum
- Shot Glass

Shake with ice and strain

YAPS

- 1 part Yukon Jack®
- 1 part Sour Apple Schnapps
- Shot Glass

Shake with ice and strain

YELLOW BOW TIE

- 2 parts Vodka
- 2 parts Amaretto
- 1 part Triple Sec
- 1 part Fresh Lime Juice
- Shot Glass

Shake with ice and strain

YELLOW CAKE

- 1 part Vanilla-Flavored Vodka
- 1 part Triple Sec
- 1 part Pineapple Juice
- Shot Glass

Shake with ice and strain

YELLOW NUTTER

- 1 part Lemon-Lime Soda
- 1 part Bacardi® Limón Rum
- 1 part Sour Mix
- dash Sugar
- Shot Glass

Shake with ice and strain

YELLOW SNOW

- 3 parts Pineapple-Flavored Vodka
- 1 part Pineapple Juice
- Shot Glass

Shake with ice and strain

YING YANG

- 1 part Jägermeister®
- 1 part Rumple Minze®
- Shot Glass

Shake with ice and strain

YODA®

- 1 part Vodka
- 1 part Blue Curaçao
- 1 part Sour Mix
- 1 part Midori®
- 2 parts Sour Apple Schnapps
- Shot Glass

Shake with ice and strain

YOOHA

- 3 parts Whiskey
- 1 part Yoo-Hoo® Chocolate Drink
- Shot Glass

Shake with ice and strain

YUKON SNAKEBITE

- 3 parts Yukon Jack®
- 1 part Lime Juice
- Shot Glass

Shake with ice and strain

Z STREET SLAMMER

- 2 parts Crème de Banana
- 2 parts Pineapple Juice
- 1 part Grenadine
- Shot Glass

Shake with ice and strain

ZEKE'S SUPRISE

- 1 part Grand Marnier®
- 1 part Scotch
- 1 part Peppermint Schnapps
- Shot Glass

Shake with ice and strain

ZENMEISTER

- 1 part Jägermeister®
- 1 part Root Beer
- Shot Glass

Stir gently with ice and strain

ZOO STATION

- 1 part Amaretto
- 1 part Coffee Liqueur
- 1 part Irish Cream Liqueur
- 1 part Banana Liqueur
- 2 parts Cream
- Shot Glass

Shake with ice and strain

ZOOL

- 1 part Peach Schnapps
- 1 part Vodka
- 1 part Amaretto
- Shot Glass

Shake with ice and strain

ZOOT SUIT RIOT

- 1 part Apricot Brandy
- 1 part Blackberry Liqueur
- 1 part Cranberry Juice Cocktail
- 1 part Southern Comfort®
- Shot Glass

Shake with ice and strain

Layered Shots

4 HORSEMEN

- 1 part Goldschläger®
- 1 part Jägermeister®
- 1 part Rumple Minze©
- 1 part 151-Proof Rum
- Shot Glass

Layer in a shot glass

10W-40

- 1 part Black Sambuca
- 1 part Goldschläger®
- Shot Glass

Layer in a shot glass

401

- 1 part Coffee Liqueur
- 1 part Crème de Banana
- 1 part Irish Cream Liqueur
- 1 part Yukon Jack®
- Shot Glass

Layer in a shot glass

50-50 BAR

- 1 part Irish Cream Liqueur
- 1 part Coffee Liqueur
- splash 151-Proof Rum
- Shot Glass

Layer in a shot glass

69ER IN A POOL

- 1 part Vodka
- 1 part 151-Proof Rum
- splash Lemon Juice
- splash Tabasco® Sauce
- Shot Glass

Layer in a shot glass

A.T.B. (ASK THE BARMAN)

- 1 part Melon Liqueur
- 1 part Grenadine
- 1 part Blue Curaçao
- 1 part Amaretto
- 1 part Irish Cream Liqueur
- Shot Glass

Layer in a shot glass

ABC

- 1 part Amaretto
- 1 part Irish Cream Liqueur
- 1 part Cognac
- Shot Glass

Layer in a shot glass

ADIOS MOTHERFUCKER

- 1 part Coffee Liqueur
- 1 part Tequila

- Shot Glass

Layer in a shot glass

ADVOSARRY

- 3 parts Maraschino Liqueur
- 2 parts Advocaat

- Shot Glass

Layer in a shot glass

AEQUITAS

- 1 part After Shock® Cinnamon Schnapps
- 1 part 151-Proof Rum

- 1 part Jägermeister®
- 1 part Rumple Minze®
- Shot Glass

Layer in a shot glass

AFTER DARK

- 1 part Coffee Liqueur
- 1 part Irish Cream Liqueur
- 1 part Licor 43®
- Shot Glass

Layer in a shot glass

AFTER EIGHT®

- 1 part Coffee Liqueur
- 1 part Crème de Menthe (White)
- 1 part Irish Cream Liqueur
- Shot Glass

Layer in a shot glass

AFTER FIVE

- 1 part Coffee Liqueur
- 1 part Peppermint Schnapps
- 1 part Irish Cream Liqueur
- Shot Glass

Layer in a shot glass

AFTER FIVE #2

- 1 part Irish Cream Liqueur
- 1 part Peppermint Schnapps
- 1 part Coffee Liqueur
- Shot Glass

Layer in a shot glass

AFTERLANCHE

- 1 part After Shock® Cinnamon Schnapps
- 1 part Avalanche® Peppermint Schnapps
- Shot Glass

Layer in a shot glass

ALASKAN OIL SPILL

- 1 part Blue Curaçao
- 1 part Rumple Minze®
- splash Jägermeister®
- Shot Glass

Shake Blue Curaçao and Rumple Minze® together with ice and strain into a shot glass. Layer the Jägermeister® on top.

ALIEN NIPPLE

- 2 parts Butterscotch Schnapps
- 1 part Irish Cream Liqueur
- 1 part Melon Liqueur
- Shot Glass

Layer in a shot glass

ALLIGATOR BITE

- 1 part Jägermeister®
- 1 part Raspberry Liqueur
- 1 part Vodka
- splash Orange Juice
- 1 part Melon Liqueur
- Shot Glass

Layer in a shot glass

ALLIGATOR ON THE RAG

- 2 parts Melon Liqueur
- 1 part Raspberry Liqueur
- 1 part Jägermeister®
- Shot Glass

Layer in a shot glass

ALMOND JOY

- 1 part Amaretto
- 1 part Swiss Chocolate Almond Liqueur
- 1 part Irish Cream Liqueur
- Shot Glass

Layer in a shot glass

ALTERED STATE

- 1 part Golden Pear Liqueur
- 1 part Irish Cream Liqueur
- 1 part Coffee Liqueur
- Shot Glass

Layer in a shot glass

AMERICAN FLAG

- 1 part Grenadine
- 1 part Crème de Cacao (White)
- 1 part Blue Curaçao
- Shot Glass

Layer in a shot glass

AMOCO SHOT

- 1 part 151-Proof Rum
- 1 part Grain Alcohol
- splash Coffee Liqueur
- Shot Glass

Layer in a shot glass

AMY GIRL

- 1 part Banana Liqueur
- 1 part Butterscotch Schnapps
- 1 part Frangelico®
- Shot Glass

Layer in a shot glass

ANDY

- 1 part Cola
- 1 part Beer
- Shot Glass

Layer in a shot glass

ANGEL BLISS

- 3 parts Bourbon
- 1 part Blue Curaçao
- 1 part 151-Proof Rum
- Shot Glass

Layer in a shot glass

ANGEL'S DELIGHT

- 1 part Grenadine
- 1 part Triple Sec
- 1 part Sloe Gin
- 1 part Light Cream
- Pousse-Café Glass

Layer in a pousse-café glass

ANGEL'S KISS

- 1 part Coffee Liqueur
- 1 part Swiss Chocolate Almond Liqueur
- splash Irish Cream Liqueur
- Shot Glass

Layer in a shot glass

ANGEL'S TIT

- 1 part Crème de Cacao (White)
- 1 part Maraschino Liqueur
- 1 part Heavy Cream
- 1 Maraschino Cherry
- Shot Glass

Layer in a shot glass

ANGEL'S WING

- 1 part Crème de Cacao (White)
- 1 part Brandy
- splash Light Cream
- Pousse-Café Glass

Layer in a pousse-café glass

APACHE

- 1 part Coffee Liqueur
- 1 part Irish Cream Liqueur
- 1 part Melon Liqueur
- Shot Glass

Layer in a shot glass

APPLE PIE

- 1 part Vodka
- 1 part Apple Juice
- Shot Glass

Layer in a shot glass

APPLE SLAMMER

- 1 part Sour Apple Schnapps
- 1 part Lemon-Lime Soda
- Shot Glass

Layer in a shot glass. Cover with your hand, slam down against the bar, and drink while it fizzes.

AQUAFRESH

- 1 part After Shock® Cinnamon Schnapps
- 1 part Rumple Minze®
- 1 part Avalanche® Peppermint Schnapps
- Shot Glass

Layer in a shot glass

ASTROPOP

- 1 part Grenadine
- 1 part Amaretto
- 1 part Rumple Minze®
- Shot Glass

Layer in a shot glass

AUNT JEMIMA®

- 1 part Brandy
- 1 part Crème de Cacao (White)
- 1 part Benedictine®
- Pousse-Café Glass

Layer in a pousse-café glass

B AND B

- 1 part Brandy
- 1 part Benedictine®
- Cordial Glass

Layer in a cordial glass

B.B. GRAND

- 1 part Irish Cream Liqueur
- 1 part Banana Liqueur
- 1 part Grand Marnier®
- Shot Glass

Layer in a shot glass

B.B.C.

- 1 part Benedictine®
- 1 part Irish Cream Liqueur
- 1 part Cointreau®
- Shot Glass

Layer in a shot glass

B.B.G.

- 1 part Benedictine®
- 1 part Irish Cream Liqueur
- 1 part Grand Marnier®
- Shot Glass

Layer in a shot glass

B-52

- 1 part Grand Marnier®
- 1 part Coffee Liqueur
- 1 part Irish Cream Liqueur
- Shot Glass

Layer in a shot glass

BABY BEER

- 3 parts Licor 43®
- 1 part Cream
- Shot Glass

Layer in a shot glass

BABY GUINNESS®

- 3 parts Coffee Liqueur
- 1 part Irish Cream Liqueur
- Shot Glass

Layer in a shot glass

BACKFIRE

- 1 part Coffee Liqueur
- 1 part Irish Cream Liqueur
- 1 part Vodka
- Shot Glass

Layer in a shot glass

BAD STING

- 1 part Grenadine
- 1 part Anisette
- 1 part Grand Marnier®
- 1 part Tequila
- Shot Glass

Layer in a shot glass

BAGHDAD CAFÉ

- 1 part Coffee Liqueur
- 1 part Tia Maria®
- splash San Marco Cream
- Shot Glass

Layer in a shot glass

BAILEYS® CHOCOLATE-COVERED CHERRY

- 1 part Coffee Liqueur
- 1 part Grenadine
- 1 part Irish Cream Liqueur
- Shot Glass

Layer in a shot glass

BAILEYS® COMET

- 1 part Irish Cream Liqueur
- 1 part Goldschläger®
- splash 151-Proof Rum
- Shot Glass

Layer in a shot glass

BAKER'S DELITE

- 3 parts Crème de Cacao (White)
- 1 part Peach Schnapps
- Shot Glass

Layer in a shot glass

BALLISTIC MISSILE

- 1 part Amaretto
- 1 part Grand Marnier®
- 1 part Pineapple Juice
- Shot Glass

Layer in a shot glass

BANANA CREAM PIE

- 1 part Coffee Liqueur
- 1 part 99-Proof Banana Liqueur
- 1 part Licor 43®
- Shot Glass

Layer in a shot glass

BANANA DROP

- 1 part Crème de Banana
- 1 part Irish Cream Liqueur
- ½ part Cream
- ½ part Chocolate Mint Liqueur
- Shot Glass

Layer in a shot glass

BANANA SLIP

- 1 part Crème de Banana
- 1 part Irish Cream Liqueur
- Cordial Glass

Layer in a cordial glass

BATTERED, BRUISED, AND BLEEDING

- 1 part Grenadine
- 1 part Melon Liqueur
- 1 part Blue Curaçao
- Shot Glass

Layer in a shot glass

BAZOOKA JOE®

- 1 part Parfait Amour
- 1 part Crème de Banana
- 1 part Irish Cream Liqueur
- Shot Glass

Layer in a shot glass

BEAM ME UP SCOTTY

- 1 part Coffee Liqueur
- 1 part Banana Liqueur
- 1 part Irish Cream Liqueur
- Shot Glass

Layer in a shot glass

BEAUTY AND THE BEAST

- 3 parts Jägermeister®
- 1 part Tequila Rose®
- Shot Glass

Layer in a shot glass

BELFAST CAR BOMB

- 1 part Coffee Liqueur
- splash Irish Cream Liqueur
- splash Irish Whiskey
- ½ pint Guinness® Stout
- Shot Glass

Layer Coffee Lixqueur, Irish Cream Liqueur, and Irish Whiskey in a shot glass. Drop the shot into a ½-filled pint of Guinness® and drink all at once.

BELLEVUE GANGBANG

- 1 part Cinnamon Schnapps
- 1 part Black Sambuca
- Shot Glass

Layer in a shot glass

BERTIE BICHBERG

- 1 part Vodka
- 1 part Crème de Banana
- 1 Maraschino Cherry
- Shot Glass

Layer in a shot glass

BEVERLY HILLS

- 1 part Swiss Chocolate Almond Liqueur
- 1 part Irish Cream Liqueur
- 1 part Grand Marnier®
- Shot Glass

Layer in a shot glass

BIG 'O'

- 1 part Peppermint Schnapps
- 1 part Irish Cream Liqueur
- Shot Glass

Layer in a shot glass

BIPPLE

- 1 part Butterscotch Schnapps
- 1 part Irish Cream Liqueur
- Shot Glass

Layer in a shot glass

BIT-O-HONEY® SHOT

- 1 part Apple Brandy
- 1 part Frangelico®
- Shot Glass

Layer in a shot glass

BLACK ARMY

- 1 part Galliano®
- 1 part Jägermeister®
- Shot Glass

Layer in a shot glass

BLACK BITCH

- 3 parts Black Sambuca
- 3 parts Irish Cream Liqueur
- 2 parts 151-Proof Rum
- Shot Glass

Layer in a shot glass

BLACK BULLET

- 1 part Peppermint Schnapps
- 1 part Jägermeister®
- Shot Glass

Layer in a shot glass

BLACK DRAGON

- 1 part Crème de Menthe (White)
- 1 part Coffee Liqueur
- 1 part Scotch
- Shot Glass

Layer in a shot glass

BLACK FOREST

- 1 part Coffee Liqueur
- 1 part Grand Marnier®
- 1 part Cherry Whiskey
- Shot Glass

Layer in a shot glass

BLACK KNIGHT

- 1 part Coffee Liqueur
- 1 part Irish Cream Liqueur
- 1 part Sambuca
- splash Advocaat
- splash Grenadine
- Shot Glass

Layer in a shot glass

BLACK MAGIC CREAM

- 1 part Coffee Liqueur
- 1 part Crème de Cacao (White)
- 1 part Amarula® Crème Liqueur
- Shot Glass

Layer in a shot glass

BLACK RAIN

- 1 part Black Sambuca
- 2 parts Champagne
- Shot Glass

Layer in a shot glass

BLACK SAND

- 1 part Coffee Liqueur
- 1 part Sambuca
- 1 part Amaretto
- Shot Glass

Layer in a shot glass

BLACK TIE

- 1 part Drambuie®
- 1 part Scotch
- 1 part Amaretto
- Shot Glass

Layer in a shot glass

BLACK UNICORN

- 1 part Coffee Liqueur
- 1 part Butterscotch Schnapps
- 1 part Irish Cream Liqueur
- Shot Glass

Layer in a shot glass

BLACK WOLF

- 1 part Black Sambuca
- 1 part Green Chartreuse
- splash Tabasco® Sauce
- Shot Glass

Layer in a shot glass

BLACKBERRY BLOSSOM

- 1 part Blackberry Liqueur
- 1 part Irish Cream Liqueur
- Shot Glass

Layer in a shot glass

BLASTER

- 1 part Banana Liqueur
- 1 part Triple Sec
- 1 part Coffee Liqueur
- Shot Glass

Layer in a shot glass

BLEACHER'S TWIST

- 1 part Coffee Liqueur
- 1 part Raspberry Liqueur
- 1 part Irish Cream Liqueur
- Shot Glass

Layer in a shot glass

BLOOD CLOT

- 2 parts Southern Comfort®
- 1 part Grenadine
- Shot Glass

Layer in a shot glass

BLOOD OF SATAN

- 1 part Jägermeister®
- 1 part Goldschläger®
- 1 part Irish Whiskey
- 1 part Jack Daniel's®
- Shot Glass

Layer in a shot glass

BLOODEYE

- ½ part Raspberry Liqueur
- 1 part Citrus-Flavored Vodka
- ½ part Cranberry Liqueur
- Shot Glass

Layer in a shot glass

BLOODY FROG CUM

- 1 part Grenadine
- splash 151-Proof Rum
- 1 part Melon Liqueur
- splash Irish Cream Liqueur
- Shot Glass

Layer in a shot glass

BLOODY PSYCHO

- splash Orange Liqueur
- splash 151-Proof Rum
- 1 part Irish Cream Liqueur
- Shot Glass

Layer in a shot glass

BLOW IN THE JAW

- splash Goldschläger®
- splash Calvados Apple Brandy
- 1 part Spiced Rum
- Shot Glass

Layer in a shot glass

BLOW JOB

- 1 part Irish Cream Liqueur
- 1 part Coffee Liqueur
- Shot Glass

Layer in a shot glass. Top with Whipped Cream. Drink without using your hands.

BLUE ICE BREATHE

- 1 part Citrus-Flavored Vodka
- 1 part Blue Curaçao
- 1 part Bitter Lemon
- Shot Glass

Layer in a shot glass

BLUE KISOK

- 2 parts Blue Curaçao
- 1 part Vodka
- splash Lime Juice
- fill with Lemon-Lime Soda
- Shot Glass

Layer in a shot glass

BLUE MOON SHOOTER

- 1 part Amaretto
- 1 part Irish Cream Liqueur
- 1 part Blue Curaçao
- Shot Glass

Layer in a shot glass

BLUE NEON

- 3 parts Goldschläger®
- 1 part Rum
- splash Blue Curaçao
- Shot Glass

Layer in a shot glass

BOB MARLEY

- 1 part Melon Liqueur
- 1 part Jägermeister®
- 1 part Goldschläger®
- Shot Glass

Layer in a shot glass

BONFIRE

- 1 part Irish Cream Liqueur
- splash Goldschläger®
- dash Cinnamon
- Shot Glass

Layer in a shot glass

BONONO

- 1 part Banana Liqueur
- 1 part Triple Sec
- 1 part Grand Marnier®
- Shot Glass

Layer in a shot glass

BONSAI PIPELINE

- 1 part Wild Turkey® 101
- 1 part Melon Liqueur
- splash 151-Proof Rum
- Shot Glass

Layer in a shot glass

BOTTOM BOUNCER

- 1 part Irish Cream Liqueur
- 1 part Butterscotch Schnapps
- Shot Glass

Layer in a shot glass

BRAIN TEASER

- 2 parts Sambuca
- 2 parts Irish Cream Liqueur

- 1 part Advocaat
- Shot Glass

Layer in a shot glass

BRANDED NIPPLE

- 1 part Butterscotch Schnapps
- 1 part Irish Cream Liqueur
- 1 part Goldschläger®

- splash 151-Proof Rum
- Shot Glass

Layer in a shot glass

BREAK

- 1 part Coffee Liqueur
- 1 part Crème de Banana

- 1 part Anisette
- Shot Glass

Layer in a shot glass

BRIMFUL RAINBOW

- 1 part Blue Curaçao
- 1 part Amaretto
- 1 part Grenadine
- 1 part Melon Liqueur
- Shot Glass

Layer in a shot glass

BRUSH FIRE

- 1 part Tequila
- splash Tabasco® Sauce
- Shot Glass

Layer in a shot glass

BUCKSHOT

- 1 part Tequila
- 1 part Jack Daniel's®
- 1 part Irish Cream Liqueur
- dash Ground Pepper
- Shot Glass

Layer in a shot glass

BULGARIA UNITED

- 1 part Grenadine
- 1 part Crème de Menthe (Green)
- 1 part Vodka
- Shot Glass

Layer in a shot glass

BUMBLE BEE

- 1 part Irish Cream Liqueur
- 1 part Coffee Liqueur
- 1 part Sambuca
- Shot Glass

Layer in a shot glass

BUTTER BABY

- 1 part Butterscotch Schnapps
- 1 part Irish Cream Liqueur
- Shot Glass

Layer in a shot glass

BUTTERY JÄGER RIPPLE

- 1 part Jägermeister®
- 1 part Irish Cream Liqueur
- 1 part Butterscotch Schnapps
- Shot Glass

Layer in a shot glass

BUTTERY NIPPLE WITH A CHERRY KISS

- 1 part Butterscotch Schnapps
- 1 part Irish Cream Liqueur
- splash Cherry Liqueur
- Shot Glass

Layer in a shot glass

CAMEL HUMP

- 2 parts Butterscotch Schnapps
- 1 part Irish Cream Liqueur
- Shot Glass

Layer in a shot glass

CAMEL'S SNOT

- 1 part Red Wine
- 1 part Irish Cream Liqueur
- Shot Glass

Layer in a shot glass

CANDY CANE

- 1 part Grenadine
- 1 part Crème de Menthe (White)
- 1 part Peppermint Schnapps
- Shot Glass

Layer in a shot glass

CANDY CORN

- 1 part Licor 43®
- 1 part Blue Curaçao
- 1 part Cream
- Shot Glass

Layer in a shot glass

CANDY RACCOON

- 1 part Cinnamon Schnapps
- 1 part Black Sambuca
- Shot Glass

Layer in a shot glass

CARE BEAR®

- 1 part Raspberry Liqueur
- 1 part Chocolate Liqueur
- Shot Glass

Layer in a shot glass

CEMENT MIXER

- 2 parts Irish Cream Liqueur
- 1 part Sweetened Lime Juice
- Shot Glass

Layer in a shot glass. Shake liquid in your mouth before you swallow.

CEREBELLUM

- 4 parts Vodka
- 1 part Grenadine
- 1 part Irish Cream Liqueur
- Shot Glass

Layer in a shot glass

CEREBRAL HEMORRHAGE

- 1 part Strawberry Liqueur
- splash Irish Cream Liqueur
- splash Grenadine
- Shot Glass

Layer in a shot glass

CHANNEL 64

- 1 part Crème de Banana
- 1 part Irish Cream Liqueur
- 1 part Advocaat
- Shot Glass

Layer in a shot glass

CHASTITY BELT

- 1 part Tia Maria®
- 1 part Frangelico®
- 1 part Irish Cream Liqueur
- 1 part Cream
- Shot Glass

Layer in a shot glass

CHILL OUT SHOCK

- 1 part Butterscotch Schnapps
- 1 part Espresso
- Shot Glass

Layer in a shot glass

CHINA WHITE

- 3 parts Crème de Cacao (White)
- 1 part Irish Cream Liqueur
- dash Cinnamon
- Shot Glass

Layer in a shot glass

CHOCOLATE ALMOND

- 1 part Amaretto
- 1 part Crème de Cacao (Dark)
- 1 part Irish Cream Liqueur
- Shot Glass

Layer in a shot glass

CHOCOLATE CHERRY BOMB

- 1 part Crème de Cacao (White)
- 1 part Cream
- 1 part Grenadine
- Shot Glass

Layer in a shot glass

CHOCOLATE CHIMP

- 1 part Crème de Cacao (White)
- 1 part Coffee Liqueur
- 1 part Crème de Banana
- Shot Glass

Layer in a shot glass

CHOCOLATE SUNDAE

- 1 part Irish Cream Liqueur
- 1 part Crème de Cacao (White)
- 1 part Coffee Liqueur
- Shot Glass

Layer in a shot glass. Top with Whipped Cream.

CHOCORANGE

- 2 parts Crème de Cacao (Dark)
- 1 part Raspberry Liqueur
- 1 part Grand Marnier®
- Shot Glass

Layer in a shot glass

CHRISTMAS SHOTS

- 1 part Melon Liqueur
- 1 part Raspberry Liqueur
- Shot Glass

Layer in a shot glass

CHRISTMAS TREE

- 1 part Crème de Menthe (White)
- 1 part Grenadine
- 1 part Irish Cream Liqueur
- Shot Glass

Layer in a shot glass

CINN'S STOP LIGHT

- 1 part Melon Liqueur
- 1 part Grenadine
- 1 part Irish Cream Liqueur
- Shot Glass

Layer in a shot glass

CITY HOT SHOT

- 1 part Blue Curaçao
- 1 part Triple Sec
- 1 part Grenadine
- Shot Glass

Layer in a shot glass

CLEAR LAYERED SHOT

- 1 part Lemon-Lime Soda
- 1 part Grain Alcohol
- 1 part Grenadine
- Shot Glass

Layer in a shot glass. The Grenadine will settle in the middle.

COBRA

- 1 part Irish Cream Liqueur
- 1 part Jägermeister®
- 1 part Rumple Minze®
- Shot Glass

Layer in a shot glass

COCK SUCKING COWBOY

- 2 parts Butterscotch Schnapps
- 1 part Irish Cream Liqueur
- Shot Glass

Layer in a shot glass

THE COLOMBIAN

- 1 part Coffee Liqueur
- 1 part Amaretto
- 1 part Hennessy®
- Shot Glass

Layer in a shot glass

CONCRETE

- 1 part Vodka
- 1 part Irish Cream Liqueur
- Shot Glass

Layer in a shot glass

CYPRESS

- 1 part Crème de Cacao (White)
- 1 part Light Cream
- Shot Glass

Layer in a shot glass

CYRANO

- 1 part Irish Cream Liqueur
- 1 part Grand Marnier®
- splash Raspberry Liqueur
- Shot Glass

Layer in a shot glass

DAGGER

- 1 part Tequila
- 1 part Crème de Cacao (White)
- 1 part Peach Schnapps
- Shot Glass

Layer in a shot glass

DANCIN' COWBOY

- 1 part Banana Liqueur
- 1 part Coffee Liqueur
- 1 part Irish Cream Liqueur
- Shot Glass

Layer in a shot glass

DANCING MEXICAN

- 2 parts Tequila
- 1 part Milk
- Shot Glass

Layer in a shot glass

DECADENCE

- 1 part Coffee Liqueur
- 1 part Frangelico®
- 1 part Irish Cream Liqueur
- Shot Glass

Layer in a shot glass

DESERT WATER

- 1 part Tabasco® Sauce
- fill with Tequila

- Shot Glass

Layer in a shot glass

DIRTY BIRD

- 1 part Tequila Reposado
- 1 part Wild Turkey® 101

- Shot Glass

Layer in a shot glass

DIRTY NIPPLE

- 1 part Sambuca
- 1 part Irish Cream Liqueur

- Shot Glass

Layer in a shot glass

DIRTY OATMEAL

- 1 part Jägermeister®
- 1 part Irish Cream Liqueur
- Shot Glass

Layer in a shot glass

DOG BOWL

- 1 part Amarula® Crème Liqueur
- 1 part Banana Liqueur
- 1 part Frangelico®
- Shot Glass

Layer in a shot glass

DON QUIXOTE

- 1 part Guinness® Stout
- 1 part Tequila
- Shot Glass

Layer in a shot glass

DRAGON SLAYER

- 1 part Green Chartreuse®
- 1 part Tequila

- Shot Glass

Layer in a shot glass

DRAGOON

- 1 part Black Sambuca
- 1 part Coffee Liqueur

- 1 part Irish Cream Liqueur
- Pousse-Café Glass

Layer in a pousse-café glass

DUCK SHIT INN

- 1 part Coffee Liqueur
- 1 part Melon Liqueur
- 1 part Irish Cream Liqueur

- 1 part Tequila
- Shot Glass

Layer in a shot glass

E.T.

- 1 part Melon Liqueur
- 1 part Irish Cream Liqueur
- 1 part Vodka
- Shot Glass

Layer in a shot glass

EL REVOLTO

- 1 part Peppermint Schnapps
- 1 part Irish Cream Liqueur
- 1 part Cointreau®
- Shot Glass

Layer in a shot glass

ELECTRIC BANANA

- 1 part Tequila
- 1 part Banana Liqueur
- Shot Glass

Layer in a shot glass

ELIPHINO

- 1 part Sambuca
- 1 part Grand Marnier®
- Shot Glass

Layer in a shot glass

ESKIMO KISS

- 1 part Chocolate Liqueur
- 1 part Cherry Liqueur
- 1 part Amaretto
- Shot Glass

Layer in a shot glass. Top with Whipped Cream.

FACE OFF

- 1 part Grenadine
- 1 part Crème de Menthe (White)
- 1 part Parfait Amour
- 1 part Sambuca
- Shot Glass

Layer in a shot glass

FAHRENHEIT 5,000

- 1 part Fire Water®
- 1 part Absolut® Peppar Vodka
- 3 splashes Tabasco® Sauce
- Shot Glass

Layer in a shot glass

FEATHER DUSTER

- 1 part Whiskey
- splash Blackberry Liqueur
- Shot Glass

Layer in a shot glass

FERRARI® SHOOTER

- 1 part Sambuca
- 1 part Tia Maria®
- Shot Glass

Layer in a shot glass

FIFTH AVENUE

- 1 part Crème de Cacao (Dark)
- 1 part Apricot Brandy
- splash Light Cream
- Shot Glass

Layer in a shot glass

FIGHTIN' IRISH GOLD SHOT

- 1 part Irish Cream Liqueur
- 1 part Goldschläger®
- Shot Glass

Layer in a shot glass

FISHERMAN'S WHARF

- 1 part Grand Marnier®
- 1 part Courvoisier©
- 1 part Amaretto
- Shot Glass

Layer in a shot glass

THE FLAG

- 1 part Grenadine
- 1 part Maraschino Liqueur
- 1 part Chartreuse®
- Shot Glass

Layer in a shot glass

FLAMBOYANCE

- ½ part Apricot Brandy
- 1 part Vodka
- splash Grand Marnier®
- Shot Glass

Layer in a shot glass

FLAME THROWER

- 2 parts Crème de Cacao (White)
- 1 part Benedictine®
- 1 part Brandy
- Shot Glass

Layer in a shot glass

FLAMING DIAMOND

- 1 part Strawberry Liqueur
- 1 part Peppermint Schnapps
- 1 part Grand Marnier®
- Shot Glass

Layer in a shot glass

FLATLINER

- 1 part Sambuca
- splash Tabasco® Sauce
- 1 part Tequila
- Shot Glass

Layer in a shot glass

FLYING MONKEY

- 1 part Coffee Liqueur
- 1 part Banana Liqueur
- 1 part Irish Cream Liqueur
- Shot Glass

Layer in a shot glass

FOOL'S GOLD

- 1 part Coffee Liqueur
- 1 part Goldschläger®
- 1 part Jägermeister®
- Shot Glass

Layer in a shot glass

FOURTH OF JULY

- 1 part Grenadine
- 1 part Cream
- 1 part Blue Curaçao
- Shot Glass

Layer in a shot glass

FRANCIS DRAKE

- 1 part Coffee Liqueur
- 1 part Spiced Rum
- Shot Glass

Layer in a shot glass

FREDDIE'S NAUGHTY NEOPOLITAN

- 1 part Coffee Liqueur
- 1 part Crème de Cacao (White)
- 1 part Tequila Rose®
- Pousse-Café Glass

Layer in a pousse-café glass

FRENCH KISS

- 1 part Amaretto
- 1 part Crème de Cacao (White)
- 1 part Irish Cream Liqueur
- Shot Glass

Layer in a shot glass

FRENCH POUSSE-CAFÉ

- 1 part Cognac
- 1 part Grenadine
- 1 part Maraschino Liqueur
- Shot Glass

Layer in a shot glass

FROZEN BIRD

- 1 part Wild Turkey® Bourbon
- 1 part Rumple Minze®
- Shot Glass

Layer in a shot glass

FULL MOON

- 1 part Amaretto
- 1 part Grand Marnier®
- Shot Glass

Layer in a shot glass

GERMAN BLOW JOB

- 1 part Irish Cream Liqueur
- 1 part Jägermeister®
- 1 part Rumple Minze®
- Shot Glass

Layer in a shot glass. Top with Whipped Cream and drink without using your hands.

GINGERBREAD

- 1 part Irish Cream Liqueur
- 1 part Goldschläger®
- 1 part Butterscotch Schnapps
- Shot Glass

Layer in a shot glass

GODFATHER SHOOTER

- 1 part Amaretto
- 1 part Scotch
- Shot Glass

Layer in a shot glass

GOLD RUSH

- 1 part Swiss Chocolate Almond Liqueur
- 1 part Vodka
- 1 part Yukon Jack®
- Shot Glass

Layer in a shot glass

GOLDEN FLASH

- 1 part Sambuca
- 1 part Triple Sec
- 1 part Amaretto
- Shot Glass

Layer in a shot glass

GOLDEN NIGHT

- 1 part Swiss Chocolate Almond Liqueur
- 1 part Irish Cream Liqueur
- 1 part Frangelico®
- Shot Glass

Layer in a shot glass

GOLDEN NIPPLE

- 1 part Goldschläger®
- 1 part Butterscotch Schnapps
- 1 part Irish Cream Liqueur
- Shot Glass

Layer in a shot glass

GONE IN 60 SECONDS

- 1 part Strawberry Liqueur
- 1 part Vanilla Liqueur
- 1 part Cream
- Shot Glass

Layer in a shot glass

GORILLA SNOT

- 1 part Port
- 1 part Irish Cream Liqueur
- Shot Glass

Layer in a shot glass

GRAND BAILEYS®

- 1 part Irish Cream Liqueur
- 1 part Grand Marnier®
- Shot Glass

Layer in a shot glass

GRAND SLAM

- 1 part Crème de Banana
- 1 part Irish Cream Liqueur
- 1 part Grand Marnier®
- Shot Glass

Layer in a shot glass

GREAT BALLS OF FIRE

- 1 part Goldschläger®
- 1 part Cinnamon Schnapps
- 1 part Cherry Brandy
- Shot Glass

Layer in shot glass

GREAT WHITE NORTH

- 1 part Coffee Liqueur
- 1 part Irish Cream Liqueur
- 1 part Anisette
- Shot Glass

Layer in a shot glass

GREEN EMERALD

- 1 part Crème de Menthe (White)
- 1 part Swiss Chocolate Almond Liqueur
- Shot Glass

Layer in a shot glass

GREEN MONKEY

- 1 part Crème de Menthe (White)
- 1 part Banana Liqueur
- Shot Glass

Layer in a shot glass

GREEN WITH ENVY

- 1 part Crème de Menthe (Green)
- 1 part Irish Cream Liqueur
- Shot Glass
- 1 part Sambuca

Layer in a shot glass

GUILLOTINE

- 1 part Butterscotch Schnapps
- 1 part After Shock® Peppermint Schnapps
- 1 part Irish Cream Liqueur
- Shot Glass

Layer in a shot glass

GUILTY CONSCIENCE

- 1 part Melon Liqueur
- splash Grenadine
- 1 part Gold Tequila
- Shot Glass

Layer in a shot glass

HARD ON

- 1 part Coffee Liqueur
- 1 part Amaretto
- 1 part Irish Cream Liqueur
- Shot Glass

Layer in a shot glass

HARD ROCKA

- 1 part Vodka
- 1 part Melon Liqueur
- 1 part Irish Cream Liqueur
- Shot Glass

Layer in a shot glass

HEARTBREAKER

- 1 part Amaretto
- 1 part Irish Cream Liqueur
- 1 part Peach Schnapps
- Shot Glass

Layer in a shot glass

HOT JIZZ

- 1 part Melon Liqueur
- 1 part Hot Damm!® Cinnamon Schnapps
- 1 part Grain Alcohol
- 1 part Lemon-Lime Soda
- Shot Glass

Layer in a shot glass

ICARUS

- 1 part Crème de Cacao (White)
- 1 part Irish Cream Liqueur
- 1 part Plum Brandy
- Shot Glass

Layer in a shot glass

ILICIT AFFAIR

- 1 part Irish Cream Liqueur
- 1 part Peppermint Schnapps
- Shot Glass

Layer in a shot glass. Top with Whipped Cream.

INHALER

- 1 part Courvoisier®
- 1 part Amaretto
- Shot Glass

Layer in a shot glass

INNOCENT EYES

- 1 part Coffee Liqueur
- 1 part Sambuca
- 1 part Irish Cream Liqueur
- Shot Glass

Layer in a shot glass

IRISH FLAG

- 1 part Irish Cream Liqueur
- 1 part Crème de Menthe (Green)
- 1 part Brandy
- Shot Glass

Layer in a shot glass

IRISH GOLD

- 1 part Irish Cream Liqueur
- 1 part Goldschläger®
- Shot Glass

Layer in a shot glass

IRISH HEADLOCK

- 1 part Brandy
- 1 part Amaretto
- 1 part Irish Whiskey
- 1 part Irish Cream Liqueur
- Shot Glass

Layer in a shot glass

IRISH MONK

- 1 part Frangelico®
- 1 part Peppermint Schnapps
- 1 part Irish Cream Liqueur
- Shot Glass

Layer in a shot glass

JEDI® MIND TRICK

- 1 part Goldschläger®
- splash Irish Cream Liqueur
- splash Melon Liqueur
- splash 151-Proof Rum
- Shot Glass

Layer in a shot glass

JOE HAZELWOOD

- 1 part Rumple Minze®
- 1 part Jägermeister®
- Shot Glass

Layer in a shot glass

KAHBULA

- 1 part Coffee Liqueur
- 1 part Irish Cream Liqueur
- 1 part Tequila Reposado
- Shot Glass

Layer in a shot glass

KILTED BLACK LEPRECHAUN

- 1 part Irish Cream Liqueur
- 1 part Coconut-Flavored Rum
- 1 part Drambuie®
- Shot Glass

Layer in a shot glass

KING ALPHONSE

- 1 part Crème de Cacao (Dark)
- 1 part Coffee Liqueur
- 1 part Cream
- Shot Glass

Layer in a shot glass

KOKOPA

- 1 part Coffee Liqueur
- 1 part Peppermint Schnapps
- Shot Glass

Layer in a shot glass

KUBA LOLLIPOP

- 1 part Peppermint Liqueur
- 1 part Ponche Kuba®
- Shot Glass

Layer in a shot glass

L.A.P.D. NIGHTSHIFT

- 1 part Grenadine
- 1 part Blue Curaçao
- 1 part Tequila
- Shot Glass

Layer in a shot glass

LANDSLIDE

- 1 part Irish Cream Liqueur
- 1 part Apricot Brandy
- 1 part Banana Liqueur
- 1 part Coffee Liqueur
- Shot Glass

Layer in a shot glass

LATE BLOOMER

- 1 part Triple Sec
- 1 part Apricot Brandy
- 1 part Rum
- Shot Glass

Layer in a shot glass

LAVA LAMP

- 1 part Coffee Liqueur
- 1 part Strawberry Liqueur
- 1 part Frangelico®
- 1 part Irish Cream Liqueur
- splash Advocaat
- Shot Glass

In a shot glass, pour the Coffee Liqueur, Strawberry Liqueur, and Frangelico®. Layer the Irish Cream Liqueur and place 2 to 3 drops of Advocaat in the center.

LAYER CAKE

- 1 part Crème de Cacao (Dark)
- 1 part Apricot Brandy
- 1 part Heavy Cream
- Shot Glass

Layer in a shot glass

LEATHER AND LACE

- 1 part Swiss Chocolate Almond Liqueur
- 1 part Peach Schnapps
- Shot Glass

Layer in a shot glass

LEWD LEWINSKY

- 1 part Jägermeister®
- 1 part Cream
- Shot Glass

Layer in a shot glass

LIBERACE

- 1 part Coffee Liqueur
- 1 part Milk
- 1 part 151-Proof Rum
- Shot Glass

Layer in a shot glass

LICKITY CLIT

- 1 part Irish Cream Liqueur
- 1 part Butterscotch Schnapps
- Shot Glass

Layer in a shot glass

LICORICE HEART

- 1 part Strawberry Liqueur
- 1 part Sambuca
- 1 part Irish Cream Liqueur
- Shot Glass

Layer in a shot glass

LIZARD SLIME

- 3 parts Jose Cuervo© Mistico
- 1 part Melon Liqueur
- Shot Glass

Layer in a shot glass

LONESTAR

- 1 part Parfait Amour
- 1 part Cherry Liqueur
- 1 part Rum
- Shot Glass

Layer in a shot glass

LSD

- 1 part Cherry Brandy
- 1 part Vodka
- 1 part Passoã®
- Shot Glass

Layer in a shot glass

LUBE JOB

- 1 part Vodka
- 1 part Irish Cream Liqueur
- Shot Glass

Layer in a shot glass

MACHINE SHOT

- 1 part 151-Proof Rum
- splash Mountain Dew®
- Shot Glass

Layer in a shot glass

MARIJUANA MILKSHAKE

- 1 part Crème de Cacao (White)
- 1 part Melon Liqueur
- 1 part Milk
- Shot Glass

Layer in a shot glass

MARTIAN HARD-ON

- 1 part Crème de Cacao (White)
- 1 part Melon Liqueur
- 1 part Irish Cream Liqueur
- Shot Glass

Layer in a shot glass

MEET THE PARENTS

- 1 part Raspberry Liqueur
- 1 part Coconut Liqueur
- 2 parts Cream
- Shot Glass

Layer in a shot glass

MELON POUSSE-CAFÉ

- 1 part Crème de Almond
- 1 part Crème de Cacao (White)
- 1 part Melon Liqueur
- Shot Glass

Layer in a shot glass

MENAGE À TROIS SHOOTER

- 1 part Coffee Liqueur
- 1 part Frangelico®
- 1 part Grand Marnier®
- Shot Glass

Layer in a shot glass

MEXICAN BERRY

- 1 part Coffee Liqueur
- 1 part Strawberry Liqueur
- 1 part Tequila
- Shot Glass

Layer in a shot glass

MEXICAN FLAG

- 1 part Grenadine
- 1 part Crème de Menthe (Green)
- 1 part Tequila
- Shot Glass

Layer in a shot glass

MEXICAN MOTHERFUCKER

- 1 part Tequila
- 1 part Irish Cream Liqueur
- 1 part Frangelico®
- 1 part Coffee Liqueur
- Shot Glass

Layer in a shot glass

MIDNIGHT MADNESS

- 1 part Triple Sec
- 1 part Coffee Liqueur
- 1 part Brandy
- Shot Glass

Layer in a shot glass

MILES OF SMILES

- 1 part Amaretto
- 1 part Peppermint Schnapps
- 1 part Rye Whiskey
- Shot Glass

Layer in a shot glass

MILK OF AMNESIA

- 1 part Jägermeister®
- 1 part Irish Cream Liqueur
- Shot Glass

Layer in a shot glass

MINI GUINNESS®

- 3 parts Coffee Liqueur
- 1 part Irish Cream Liqueur

- Shot Glass

Layer in a shot glass

MODEL T

- 1 part Coffee Liqueur
- 1 part Swiss Chocolate Almond Liqueur

- 1 part Crème de Banana
- Shot Glass

Layer in a shot glass

MOIST AND PINK

- 1 part Sambuca
- 1 part Tequila Rose®

- Shot Glass

Layer in a shot glass

MOM'S APPLE PIE

- 3 parts Sour Apple Schnapps
- 1 part Cinnamon Schnapps
- Shot Glass

Layer in a shot glass

MONKEY BALLS

- 1 part 99-Proof Banana Liqueur
- 3 parts Tequila Rose®
- Shot Glass

Layer in a shot glass

MUSHROOM

- 1 part Grenadine
- 1 part Irish Cream Liqueur
- 1 part Melon Liqueur
- Shot Glass

Layer in a shot glass

NAPALM DEATH

- 1 part Cointreau®
- 1 part Coffee Liqueur
- 1 part Drambuie®
- 1 part Irish Cream Liqueur
- Shot Glass

Layer in a shot glass

NECROPHILIAC

- 1 part Blue Curaçao
- 1 part Advocaat
- Shot Glass

Layer in a shot glass

NIPPLE ON FIRE

- 1 part Fire Water®
- 1 part Butterscotch Schnapps
- 1 part Irish Cream Liqueur
- Shot Glass

Layer in a shot glass

NORWEGIAN ORGASM

- 1 part Crème de Menthe (White)
- 1 part Irish Cream Liqueur
- Shot Glass

Layer in a shot glass

NOSE OPENER

- 3 parts Cinnamon Schnapps
- 1 part Irish Cream Liqueur
- Shot Glass

Layer in a shot glass

NUDE BOMB

- 1 part Coffee Liqueur
- 1 part Amaretto
- 1 part Crème de Banana
- Shot Glass

Layer in a shot glass

NUTTY BUDDY

- 1 part Frangelico®
- 1 part Swiss Chocolate Almond Liqueur
- 1 part Peppermint Schnapps
- Shot Glass

Layer in a shot glass

NUTTY IRISHMAN

- 1 part Frangelico®
- 1 part Irish Cream Liqueur
- Shot Glass

Layer in a shot glass

OKANAGAN

- 1 part Apricot Brandy
- 1 part Strawberry Liqueur
- 1 part Blueberry Schnapps
- Shot Glass

Layer in a shot glass

OLD GLORY

- 1 part Grenadine
- 1 part Heavy Cream
- 1 part Blue Curaçao
- Shot Glass

Layer in a shot glass

OREO® COOKIE

- 1 part Coffee Liqueur
- 1 part Crème de Cacao (White)
- 1 part Irish Cream Liqueur
- splash Vodka
- Shot Glass

Layer in a shot glass

P.D.C.

- 1 part Crème de Menthe (White)
- 2 parts Black Sambuca
- 2 parts Green Chartreuse®
- 1 part Irish Cream Liqueur
- Shot Glass

Layer in a shot glass

PASEDENA LADY

- 1 part Swiss Chocolate Almond Liqueur
- 1 part Amaretto

- 1 part Brandy
- Shot Glass

Layer in a shot glass

PASSION MAKER

- 1 part Raspberry Liqueur
- 1 part Irish Cream Liqueur

- Shot Glass

Layer in a shot glass

THE PATRIOT

- 1 part Blue Curaçao
- 1 part Crème de Cacao (White)

- 1 part Grenadine
- Shot Glass

Layer in a shot glass

PATRIOTIC BLOW

- 1 part Sloe Gin
- 1 part Blue Curaçao
- 1 part Cream
- Shot Glass

Layer in a shot glass

PENALTY SHOT

- 1 part Crème de Menthe (White)
- 1 part Tia Maria®
- 1 part Peppermint Schnapps
- Shot Glass

Layer in a shot glass

PERUVIAN JUNGLE FUCK

- 1 part Chocolate Banana Liqueur
- 1 part Cafe Orange Liqueur
- 1 part Half and Half
- Shot Glass

Layer in a shot glass

PIPELINE

- 1 part Tequila
- 1 part Vodka
- Shot Glass

Layer in a shot glass

PLACENTA

- 1 part Amaretto
- 1 part Irish Cream Liqueur
- splash Grenadine
- Shot Glass

Layer the Amaretto then the Irish Cream in a shot glass. Place a few drops of Grenadine in the center of the drink.

PLEASURE DOME

- 1 part Brandy
- 1 part Crème de Cacao (White)
- 1 part Benedictine®
- Shot Glass

Layer in a shot glass

PORT AND STARBOARD

- 1 part Grenadine
- 1 part Crème de Menthe (Green)
- Shot Glass

Layer in a shot glass

POUSSE-CAFÉ

- 1 part Crème de Menthe (White)
- 1 part Crème Yvette®
- 1 part Grenadine
- 1 part Chartreuse®
- Shot Glass

Layer in a shot glass

POUSSE-CAFÉ AMERICAN

- 1 part Red Curaçao
- 1 part Cognac
- 1 part Maraschino Liqueur
- Shot Glass

Layer in a shot glass

PRIMORDIAL

- 1 part Melon Liqueur
- 1 part Black Sambuca
- Shot Glass

Layer in a shot glass

PUMPING STATION

- 1 part Coffee Liqueur
- 1 part Amaretto
- 1 part 151-Proof Rum
- Shot Glass

Layer in a shot glass

QUICK KARLO

- 1 part Amaretto
- 1 part Whiskey
- Shot Glass

Layer in a shot glass

QUICK TANGO

- 1 part Coffee Liqueur
- 1 part Irish Cream Liqueur
- 1 part Melon Liqueur
- Shot Glass

Layer in a shot glass

RACE WAR

- 1 part Crème de Cacao (White)
- 1 part Irish Cream Liqueur
- 1 part Vodka
- Shot Glass

Layer in a shot glass

RAGING BULL

- 1 part Coffee Liqueur
- 1 part Sambuca
- 1 part Tequila
- Shot Glass

Layer in a shot glass

RAIDER

- 1 part Irish Cream Liqueur
- 1 part Grand Marnier®
- 1 part Cointreau®
- Shot Glass

Layer in a shot glass

RAINBOW COCKTAIL

- 1 part Blue Curaçao
- 1 part Crème de Menthe (Green)
- 1 part Cognac
- 1 part Maraschino Liqueur
- 1 part Blackberry Liqueur
- 1 part Crème de Cassis
- Shot Glass

Layer in a shot glass

RASPBERRY'S ROMANCE

- 1 part Raspberry Liqueur
- 1 part Coffee Liqueur
- 1 part Irish Cream Liqueur
- Shot Glass

Layer in a shot glass

RATTLESNAKE

- 1 part Irish Cream Liqueur
- 1 part Crème de Cacao (White)
- 1 part Coffee Liqueur
- Shot Glass

Layer in a shot glass

THE RED AND BLACK

- 1 part Coffee Liqueur
- 1 part Grenadine
- Shot Glass

Layer in a shot glass

RED, WHITE, AND BLUE

- 1 part Cinnamon Schnapps
- 1 part Goldschläger®
- 1 part Peppermint Schnapps
- Shot Glass

Layer in a shot glass

REDBACK SHOOTER

- 2 parts Sambuca
- 1 part Advocaat
- Shot Glass

Layer in a shot glass

REDHEAD'S NIPPLE

- 1 part Vanilla Liqueur
- 1 part Irish Cream Liqueur
- Shot Glass

Layer in a shot glass

RETURN OF THE YETI

- 1 part Lychee Liqueur
- 1 part Parfait Amour
- 1 part Goldschläger®
- Shot Glass

Layer in a shot glass

RHINO

- 1 part Coffee Liqueur
- 1 part Amarula® Crème Liqueur
- 1 part Cointreau®
- Shot Glass

Layer in a shot glass

RHUBARB AND CUSTARD

- 1 part Advocaat
- 1 part Raspberry Liqueur
- Shot Glass

Layer in a shot glass

ROCK LOBSTER

- 1 part Irish Cream Liqueur
- 1 part Crème de Cacao (White)
- 1 part Amaretto
- Shot Glass

Layer in a shot glass

ROCK 'N' ROLL

- 1 part Chocolate Mint Liqueur
- 1 part Vodka
- Shot Glass

Layer in a shot glass

ROLY-POLY SHOOTER

- 1 part Triple Sec
- 1 part Irish Cream Liqueur
- 1 part Peach Liqueur
- Shot Glass

Layer in a shot glass

ROY HOB SPECIAL

- 1 part Jack Daniel's®
- 1 part Irish Cream Liqueur
- 1 part Peppermint Schnapps
- Shot Glass

Layer in a shot glass

RUM ROLLER

- 1 part Frangelico®
- 1 part Dark Rum
- 1 part Espresso
- Shot Glass

Layer in a shot glass

RUNNY NOSE

- 1 part Coffee Liqueur
- 1 part Irish Cream Liqueur
- 1 part Cherry Advocaat
- Shot Glass

Layer in a shot glass

RUSSIAN CANDY

- 1 part Vodka
- 1 part Peach Schnapps
- 1 part Grenadine
- Shot Glass

Layer in a shot glass

RUSTY SPIKE

- 1 part Drambuie®
- 1 part Scotch
- Shot Glass

Layer in a shot glass

SAIPA

- 1 part Banana Liqueur
- 1 part Vodka
- Shot Glass

Layer in a shot glass

SANTA SHOT

- 1 part Grenadine
- 1 part Crème de Menthe (Green)
- 1 part Peppermint Schnapps
- Shot Glass

Layer in a shot glass

SAVOY HOTEL

- 1 part Benedictine®
- 1 part Crème de Cacao (White)
- 1 part Brandy
- Shot Glass

Layer in a shot glass

SCREAMING LIZARD

- 1 part Tequila
- 1 part Chartreuse®
- Shot Glass

Layer in a shot glass

SEA MONKEY

- 2 parts Goldschläger®
- 1 part Blue Curaçao
- Shot Glass

Layer in a shot glass

SEDUCTION

- 1 part Frangelico®
- 1 part Crème de Banana
- 1 part Irish Cream Liqueur
- Shot Glass

Layer in a shot glass

SHAMROCK SHOOTER

- 1 part Crème de Menthe (White)
- 1 part Irish Cream Liqueur
- 1 part Crème de Cacao (White)
- Shot Glass

Layer in a shot glass

SHORTY SEX HOUSE

- 2 parts Ouzo
- 2 parts Crème de Menthe (Green)
- 1 part Passion Fruit Nectar
- Shot Glass

Layer in a shot glass

SILVER THREAD

- 1 part Banana Liqueur
- 1 part Irish Cream Liqueur
- 1 part Peppermint Schnapps
- Shot Glass

Layer in a shot glass

SLEIGH RIDE

- 1 part Grenadine
- 1 part Green Chartreuse®
- 1 part Tequila Silver
- Shot Glass

Layer in a shot glass

SLIPPERY SIN

- 1 part Coconut-Flavored Liqueur
- 1 part Irish Cream Liqueur
- Shot Glass

Layer in a shot glass

SNAP SHOT

- 1 part Peppermint Schnapps
- 1 part Irish Cream Liqueur
- Shot Glass

Layer in a shot glass

SNOW CAP

- 1 part Irish Cream Liqueur
- 1 part Tequila
- Shot Glass

Layer in a shot glass

SOFT PORN

- 1 part Crème de Cassis
- 1 part Raspberry Liqueur
- 1 part Irish Cream Liqueur
- Shot Glass

Layer in a shot glass

SOLAR PLEXUS

- 2 parts Vodka
- 1 part Cherry Brandy
- 1 part Campari®
- Shot Glass

Layer in a shot glass

SOUTHERN BELLE

- 1 part Brandy
- 1 part Crème de Cacao (White)
- 1 part Benedictine®
- Shot Glass

Layer in a shot glass

SOUTHERN RATTLER

- 1 part Crème de Banana
- 1 part Southern Comfort®
- 1 part Gold Tequila
- Shot Glass

Layer in a shot glass

SPOT SHOOTER

- 1 part Vodka
- 1 part Coffee
- splash Irish Cream Liqueur
- Shot Glass

Layer in a shot glass. Place a few drops of Irish Cream in the center of the drink.

SPRING FEVER

- 1 part Swiss Chocolate Almond Liqueur
- 1 part Drambuie®
- Shot Glass

Layer in a shot glass

SPRINGBOK

- 3 parts Crème de Menthe (White)
- 1 part Cream
- 2 parts Amarula® Crème Liqueur
- Shot Glass

Layer in a shot glass

STARS AND STRIPES

- 1 part Blue Curaçao
- 1 part Heavy Cream
- 1 part Grenadine
- Shot Glass

Layer in a shot glass

STINKY BEAVER

- 1 part Jägermeister®
- 1 part Goldschläger®
- Pousse-Café Glass

Shake with ice and strain

STORM

- 1 part Light Rum
- 1 part Blue Curaçao

- 1 part Irish Cream Liqueur
- Shot Glass

Layer in a shot glass

STORM CLOUD

- 2 parts Rum
- 1 part Tequila

- 1 part Amaretto
- Shot Glass

Layer in a shot glass

STRAWBERRY FREDDO

- 1 part Irish Cream Liqueur
- 1 part Coffee Liqueur

- 1 part Strawberry Liqueur
- Shot Glass

Layer in a shot glass

STRAWBERRY KISS

- 1 part Coffee Liqueur
- 1 part Strawberry Liqueur
- 1 part Irish Cream Liqueur
- Shot Glass

Layer in a shot glass

STREET CAR

- 1 part Crème de Cacao (Dark)
- 1 part Irish Cream Liqueur
- 1 part Apricot Brandy
- Shot Glass

Layer in a shot glass

SUMMER FLING

- 1 part Blue Curaçao
- 1 part Irish Cream Liqueur
- Shot Glass

Layer in a shot glass

SUN AND SURF

- 1 part Coffee Liqueur
- 1 part Grand Marnier®
- 1 part Tequila
- Shot Glass

Layer in a shot glass

SUNRISE SHOOTER

- 1 part Parfait Amour
- 1 part Grenadine
- 1 part Chartreuse®
- 1 part Cointreau®
- Shot Glass

Layer in a shot glass

SWEET BULL

- 2 parts Tequila Reposado
- 2 parts Lychee Liqueur
- 1 part Grenadine
- Shot Glass

Layer in a shot glass

SWEET BURNING ERUPTION

- 1 part Triple Sec
- 1 part Butterscotch Schnapps
- 1 part Irish Cream Liqueur
- splash Grenadine
- Shot Glass

Layer all but Grenadine in a shot glass. Place a few drops of Grenadine in the center of the drink.

SWISS AND WHOOSH

- 1 part Tia Maria®
- 1 part Frangelico®
- 1 part Irish Cream Liqueur
- Shot Glass

Layer in a shot glass

SWISS HIKER

- 1 part Swiss Chocolate Almond Liqueur
- 1 part Crème de Banana
- 1 part Irish Cream Liqueur
- Shot Glass

Layer in a shot glass

T-52

- 1 part Coffee Liqueur
- 1 part Tequila Rose®
- 1 part Grand Marnier®
- Shot Glass

Layer in a shot glass

TAMPA POND SCUM

- 1 part Peach Schnapps
- 1 part Melon Liqueur
- 1 part Rum
- 1 part Milk
- Shot Glass

Layer in a shot glass

TECHNICAL KNOCKOUT

- 1 part Ouzo
- 1 part Coffee Liqueur
- 1 part Tequila
- Shot Glass

Layer in a shot glass

TEQUILA KNOCKOUT

- 3 parts Tequila Silver
- 1 part Grenadine
- Shot Glass

Layer in a shot glass

TEXAS CHAINSAW MASSACRE

- 1 part Strawberry Liqueur
- 1 part Vodka
- Shot Glass

Layer in a shot glass

TEXAS THUNDERSTORM

- 1 part Amaretto
- splash 151-Proof Rum
- splash Irish Cream Liqueur
- Shot Glass

Layer in a shot glass

THIN BLUE LINE

- 1 part Vodka
- 1 part Triple Sec
- splash Blue Curaçao
- Shot Glass

Layer the Triple Sec on top of the Vodka then gently drip the Blue Curaçao. It will settle between the Vodka and Triple Sec, forming a thin blue line.

THORNY ROSE

- 1 part Tequila Rose®
- 1 part Peppermint Schnapps
- 1 part Coffee Liqueur
- Shot Glass

Layer in a shot glass

THREE'S COMPANY

- 1 part Courvoisier®
- 1 part Grand Marnier®
- 1 part Coffee Liqueur
- Shot Glass

Layer in a shot glass

TIGER TAIL

- 1 part Tia Maria®
- 1 part Grand Marnier®
- 1 part Peppermint Schnapps
- Shot Glass

Layer in a shot glass

TORONTO MAPLE LEAFS

- 1 part Blue Curaçao
- 1 part Irish Cream Liqueur
- Shot Glass

Layer in a shot glass

TRAP DOOR

- 1 part Swiss Chocolate Almond Liqueur
- 1 part Rum Crème Liqueur
- Shot Glass

Layer in a shot glass

TRIAL OF THE CENTURY

- 1 part Jägermeister®
- 1 part Goldschläger®
- 1 part Grenadine
- Shot Glass

Layer in a shot glass

TRICOLORE

- 1 part Crème de Menthe (White)
- 1 part Apricot Brandy
- 1 part Maraschino Liqueur
- Shot Glass

Layer in a shot glass

TRIPLE IRISH SHOOTER

- 1 part Irish Whiskey
- 1 part Irish Cream Liqueur
- 1 part Irish Mist®
- Shot Glass

Layer in a shot glass

UNCLE SAM

- 1 part After Shock® Cinnamon Schnapps
- 1 part Rumple Minze®
- 1 part Avalanche® Peppermint Schnapps
- Shot Glass

Layer in a shot glass

UNDERTAKER

- 1 part Jägermeister®
- 1 part Cointreau®
- 1 part 151-Proof Rum
- Shot Glass

Layer in a shot glass

V-2 SCHNIEDER

- 1 part Coffee Liqueur
- 1 part Irish Cream Liqueur
- 1 part Frangelico®
- Shot Glass

Layer in a shot glass

VIBRATOR

- 2 parts Southern Comfort®
- 1 part Irish Cream Liqueur
- Shot Glass

Layer in a shot glass

VICE VERSA

- 1 part Pisang Ambon® Liqueur
- 1 part Passion Fruit Liqueur
- 1 part Green Chartreuse®
- Shot Glass

Layer in a shot glass

WELL-GREASED DWARF

- 1 part Crème de Cacao (White)
- 1 part Sambuca
- 1 part Irish Cream Liqueur
- Shot Glass

Layer in a shot glass

WET KISS

- 1 part Amaretto
- 1 part Sour Mix
- 1 part Watermelon Schnapps
- Shot Glass

Layer in a shot glass

WHICK

- 1 part Sambuca
- 1 part Black Sambuca
- Shot Glass

Layer in a shot glass

WHIPSTER

- 1 part Crème de Cacao (White)
- 1 part Apricot Brandy
- 1 part Triple Sec
- Shot Glass

Layer in a shot glass

WHISTLE STOP

- 1 part Grand Marnier®
- 1 part Jack Daniel's®
- Shot Glass

Layer in a shot glass

WHISTLING GYPSY

- 1 part Tia Maria®
- 1 part Irish Cream Liqueur
- 1 part Vodka
- Shot Glass

Layer in a shot glass

WHITE LIGHTNING

- 1 part Crème de Cacao (White)
- 1 part Tequila
- Shot Glass

Layer in a shot glass

WHITE TORNADO

- 3 parts Sambuca
- 1 part Tequila Rose®
- Shot Glass

Layer in a shot glass

WINDSURFER

- 1 part Coffee Liqueur
- 1 part Triple Sec
- 1 part Yukon Jack®
- Shot Glass

Layer in a shot glass

WINTER BREAK

- 1 part Peach Schnapps
- 1 part Banana Liqueur
- 1 part Southern Comfort®
- Shot Glass

Layer in a shot glass

WOBBLE WALKER

- 1 part Crème de Banana
- 2 parts Irish Cream Liqueur
- 1 part 151-Proof Rum
- Shot Glass

Layer in a shot glass

YANKEE'S POUSSE-CAFÉ

- 1 part Brandy
- 1 part Red Curaçao
- 1 part Grenadine
- 1 part Maraschino Liqueur
- 1 part Vanilla Liqueur
- Shot Glass

Layer in a shot glass

ZIPPER SHOOTER

- 1 part Grand Marnier®
- 1 part Tequila

- 1 part Irish Cream Liqueur
- Shot Glass

Layer in a shot glass

ZOWIE

- 1 part Banana Liqueur
- 1 part Irish Cream Liqueur

- 1 part Coconut Flavored Rum
- Shot Glass

Layer in a shot glass

Flaming Shots

A.S.S. ON FLAMES

- 1 part Amaretto
- 1 part Sour Apple Schnapps
- 1 part Southern Comfort®
- splash 151-Proof Rum
- Shot Glass

Layer in a shot glass. Light the Rum with a lighter or match. Extinguish by placing an empty shot glass over the shot. Always extinguish the flame before consuming.

BURNING AFRICA

- 1 part Jägermeister®
- 1 part 151-Proof Rum
- Shot Glass

Layer in a shot glass. Light the Rum with a lighter or match. Extinguish by placing an empty shot glass over the shot. Always extinguish the flame before consuming.

CONCORD

- 1 part Coffee Liqueur
- 1 part Irish Cream Liqueur
- splash 151-Proof Rum
- Shot Glass

Layer in a shot glass. Light the Rum with a lighter or match. Extinguish by placing an empty shot glass over the shot. Always extinguish the flame before consuming.

EVERYBODY'S IRISH

- 2 parts Whiskey
- ½ part Crème de Menthe (Green)
- Shot Glass

Pour ingredients into a glass neat (do not chill). Light the Whiskey with a lighter or a match. Extinguish by placing an empty shot glass over the shot. Always extinguish the flame before consuming.

FEEL THE BURN

- 1 part Coffee Liqueur
- 1 part Irish Cream Liqueur
- 1 part Ouzo
- 1 part Wild Turkey® Bourbon
- 1 part 151-Proof Rum
- Shot Glass

Pour ingredients into glass neat (do not chill). Light the Rum with a lighter or match. Extinguish by placing an empty shot glass over the shot. Always extinguish the flame before consuming.

FIERY BALLS OF DEATH

- 1 part 151-Proof Rum
- 1 part Triple Sec
- Shot Glass

Pour ingredients into glass neat (do not chill). Light the Rum with a lighter or match. Extinguish by placing an empty shot glass over the shot. Always extinguish the flame before consuming.

FIERY BLUE MUSTANG

- 1 part Banana Liqueur
- 1 part Blue Curaçao
- 1 part 151-Proof Rum
- Shot Glass

Pour ingredients into glass neat (do not chill). Light the Rum with a lighter or match. Extinguish by placing an empty shot glass over the shot. Always extinguish the flame before consuming.

FLAMBE

- 1 part Grenadine
- 1 part Crème de Menthe (White)
- 1 part Vodka
- 1 part 151-Proof Rum
- Shot Glass

Layer in a shot glass. Light the Rum with a lighter or match. Extinguish by placing an empty shot glass over the shot. Always extinguish the flame before consuming.

FLAMING ARMADILLO

- 1 part Tequila
- 1 part Amaretto
- 1 part Rum
- Shot Glass

Pour ingredients into glass neat (do not chill). Light the Rum with a lighter or match. Extinguish by placing an empty shot glass over the shot. Always extinguish the flame before consuming.

FLAMING BLAZER

- 1 part Crème de Cacao (White)
- 1 part Southern Comfort®
- 1 part 151-Proof Rum
- Shot Glass

Pour ingredients into glass neat (do not chill). Light the Rum with a lighter or match. Extinguish by placing an empty shot glass over the shot. Always extinguish the flame before consuming.

FLAMING BLUE

- 1 part Anisette
- 1 part Dry Vermouth
- 1 part 151-Proof Rum
- Shot Glass

Pour ingredients into glass neat (do not chill). Light the Rum with a lighter or match. Extinguish by placing an empty shot glass over the shot. Always extinguish the flame before consuming.

FLAMING BLUE FUCK

- 3 parts Sambuca
- 1 part Blue Curaçao
- Shot Glass

Pour ingredients into glass neat (do not chill). Light the Sambuca with a lighter or match. Extinguish by placing an empty shot glass over the shot. Always extinguish the flame before consuming.

FLAMING BLUE JESUS

- 1 part Peppermint Schnapps
- 1 part Southern Comfort®
- 1 part Tequila
- 2 parts 151-Proof Rum
- Shot Glass

Pour ingredients into glass neat (do not chill). Light the Rum with a lighter or match. Extinguish by placing an empty shot glass over the shot. Always extinguish the flame before consuming.

FLAMING COURAGE

- 1 part Cinnamon Schnapps
- 1 part Peppermint Schnapps
- 1 part Melon Liqueur
- splash 151-Proof Rum
- Shot Glass

Pour ingredients into glass neat (do not chill). Light the Rum with a lighter or match. Extinguish by placing an empty shot glass over the shot. Always extinguish the flame before consuming.

FLAMING DRAGON

- 1 part Green Chartreuse®
- 1 part 151-Proof Rum
- Shot Glass

Pour ingredients into glass neat (do not chill). Light the Rum with a lighter or match. Extinguish by placing an empty shot glass over the shot. Always extinguish the flame before consuming.

FLAMING DRAGON SNOT

- 1 part Crème de Menthe (White)
- 1 part Irish Cream Liqueur
- 1 part 151-Proof Rum
- Shot Glass

Pour ingredients into glass neat (do not chill). Light the Rum with a lighter or match. Extinguish by placing an empty shot glass over the shot. Always extinguish the flame before consuming.

FLAMING FART

- 1 part Cinnamon Schnapps
- 1 part 151-Proof Rum
- Shot Glass

Pour ingredients into glass neat (do not chill). Light the Rum with a lighter or match. Extinguish by placing an empty shot glass over the shot. Always extinguish the flame before consuming.

FLAMING FRUIT TREES

- 1 part Peach Schnapps
- 1 part Banana Liqueur
- 1 part 151-Proof Rum
- Shot Glass

Pour ingredients into glass neat (do not chill). Light the Rum with a lighter or match. Extinguish by placing an empty shot glass over the shot. Always extinguish the flame before consuming.

FLAMING GIRAFFE

- 2 parts Coffee Liqueur
- 1 parts Butterscotch Schnapps
- 1 parts 151-Proof Rum
- Shot Glass

Pour ingredients into glass neat (do not chill). Light the Rum with a lighter or match. Extinguish by placing an empty shot glass over the shot. Always extinguish the flame before consuming.

FLAMING GLACIER

- 1 part Cinnamon Schnapps
- 1 part Rumple Minze®
- Shot Glass

Pour ingredients into glass neat (do not chill). Light the Schnapps with a lighter or match. Extinguish by placing an empty shot glass over the shot. Always extinguish the flame before consuming.

FLAMING GORILLA

- 1 part Peppermint Schnapps
- 1 part Coffee Liqueur
- 1 part 151-Proof Rum
- Shot Glass

Pour ingredients into glass neat (do not chill). Light the Rum with a lighter or match. Extinguish by placing an empty shot glass over the shot. Always extinguish the flame before consuming.

FLAMING GORILLA TITTIES

- 1 part 151-Proof Rum
- 1 part Coffee Liqueur
- Shot Glass

Pour ingredients into glass neat (do not chill). Light the Rum with a lighter or match. Extinguish by placing an empty shot glass over the shot. Always extinguish the flame before consuming.

FLAMING JESUS

- 1 part Vodka
- 1 part Lime Juice
- 1 part Grenadine
- 1 part 151-Proof Rum
- Shot Glass

Pour ingredients into glass neat (do not chill). Light the Rum with a lighter or match. Extinguish by placing an empty shot glass over the shot. Always extinguish the flame before consuming.

FLAMING LICORICE

- 1 part Jägermeister®
- 1 part Sambuca
- 1 part 151-Proof Rum
- Shot Glass

Pour ingredients into glass neat (do not chill). Light the Rum with a lighter or match. Extinguish by placing an empty shot glass over the shot. Always extinguish the flame before consuming.

FLAMING NAZI

- 1 part Goldschläger®
- 1 part Rumple Minze®
- 1 part 151-Proof Rum
- Shot Glass

Pour ingredients into glass neat (do not chill). Light the Rum with a lighter or match. Extinguish by placing an empty shot glass over the shot. Always extinguish the flame before consuming.

FLAMING RASTA

- 1 part Amaretto
- 1 part Grenadine
- 1 part 151-Proof Rum
- Shot Glass

Layer in a shot glass. Light the Rum with a lighter or match. Extinguish by placing an empty shot glass over the shot. Always extinguish the flame before consuming.

FREAKIN' FLAMIN' FRUIT

- 1 part Melon Liqueur
- 1 part Crème de Banana
- 1 part Golden Pear Liqueur
- 1 part 151-Proof Rum
- Shot Glass

Pour ingredients into glass neat (do not chill). Light the Rum with a lighter or match. Extinguish by placing an empty shot glass over the shot. Always extinguish the flame before consuming.

GREEN LIZARD

- 4 parts Green Chartreuse®
- 1 part 151-Proof Rum
- Shot Glass

Layer in a shot glass. Light the Rum with a lighter or match. Extinguish by placing an empty shot glass over the shot. Always extinguish the flame before consuming.

HARBOR LIGHT

- 1 part Coffee Liqueur
- 1 part Irish Cream Liqueur
- 1 part 151-Proof Rum
- Shot Glass

Layer in a shot glass. Light the Rum with a lighter or match. Extinguish by placing an empty shot glass over the shot. Always extinguish the flame before consuming.

LIGHTHOUSE

- 1 part Coffee Liqueur
- 1 part Irish Cream Liqueur
- 1 part 151-Proof Rum
- Shot Glass

Layer in a shot glass. Light the Rum with a lighter or match. Extinguish by placing an empty shot glass over the shot. Always extinguish the flame before consuming.

MORPHINE DRIP

- 1 part Amaretto
- 1 part Butterscotch Schnapps
- splash 151-Proof Rum
- Shot Glass

Pour ingredients into glass neat (do not chill). Light the Rum with a lighter or match. Extinguish by placing an empty shot glass over the shot. Always extinguish the flame before consuming.

NAPALM

- 1 part Cinnamon Schnapps
- 1 part Fire & Ice®
- 1 part 151-Proof Rum
- Shot Glass

Pour ingredients into glass neat (do not chill). Light the Rum with a lighter or match. Extinguish by placing an empty shot glass over the shot. Always extinguish the flame before consuming.

NAPALM CREMATORIUM

- 1 part Cinnamon Schnapps
- 1 part Rumple Minze®
- 1 part 151-Proof Rum
- Shot Glass

Layer in a shot glass. Light the Rum with a lighter or match. Extinguish by placing an empty shot glass over the shot. Always extinguish the flame before consuming.

PYRO

- 1 part Vodka
- 1 part Fire Water®
- splash 151-Proof Rum
- Shot Glass

Build in the glass with no ice. Light the Rum with a lighter or match. Extinguish by placing an empty shot glass over the shot. Always extinguish the flame before consuming.

ROCK STAR

- 1 part Cinnamon Schnapps
- 1 part Sloe Gin
- 1 part Triple Sec
- 1 part Jägermeister®
- 1 part 151-Proof Rum
- Shot Glass

Build in the glass with no ice. Light the Rum with a lighter or match. Extinguish by placing an empty shot glass over the shot. Always extinguish the flame before consuming.

SOUTHERN BOUND METEOR

- 1 Maraschino Cherry
- 1 part Southern Comfort®
- 1 part Goldschläger®
- splash 151-Proof Rum
- Shot Glass

Remove the stem from a cherry and drop it in a shot glass. Pour in the Southern Comfort® and Goldschläger®. Top with a splash of 151-Proof Rum. Light the Rum with a lighter or match. Extinguish by placing an empty shot glass over the shot. Always extinguish the flame before consuming.

THRILLER SHOOTER

- 1 part Strawberry Liqueur
- 1 part Dark Rum
- Shot Glass

Build in the glass with no ice. Light the Rum with a lighter or match. Extinguish by placing an empty shot glass over the shot. Always extinguish the flame before consuming.

VESUVIUS

- 3 parts Crème de Cacao (Dark)
- 1 part Green Chartreuse®
- Shot Glass

Layer in a shot glass. Light the Chartreuse with a lighter or match. Extinguish by placing an empty shot glass over the shot. Always extinguish the flame before consuming.

Tabasco Shots

911 OUCH

- 1 part Cinnamon Schnapps
- 1 part 100-Proof Peppermint Schnapps
- splash Tabasco® Sauce
- Shot Glass

Pour ingredients into glass neat (do not chill)

ABSOLUTION

- 1 part Vodka
- dash Tabasco® Sauce

- Shot Glass

Pour ingredients into glass neat (do not chill)

ABUSE MACHINE

- 1 part Tequila
- ½ part Whiskey
- ½ part Sambuca

- splash Tabasco® Sauce
- splash Worcestershire Sauce
- Shot Glass

Shake with ice and strain

AFTERBURNER

- splash Tabasco® Sauce
- 1 part Tequila Silver
- dash Salt
- 1 Lime slice
- Shot Glass

Pour enough Tabasco® Sauce into the shot glass to cover the bottom completely. Fill the rest of the shot glass with Tequila. Lick your hand and pour some Salt on it. Lick the Salt, slam the shot, then suck the Lime.

AFTERBURNER #2

- 1 part Vodka
- ½ part Tabasco® Sauce
- Shot Glass

Pour ingredients into glass neat (do not chill)

ANUS BURNER

- 1 Jalapeño Pepper Slice
- 1 part Tequila
- splash Tabasco® Sauce
- Shot Glass

Place slice of Jalapeño in shot glass. Add Tequila and enough Tabasco® to make deep red in color.

THE ANTICHRIST

- 1 part Grain Alcohol
- 1 part 151-Proof Rum
- 1 part Absolut® Peppar Vodka
- 3 splashes Tabasco® Sauce
- Shot Glass

Shake with ice and strain

AQUA DEL FUEGO

- 1 part Tequila
- 1 part Tabasco® Sauce
- Shot Glass

Pour ingredients into glass neat (do not chill)

BLOODY CHICKEN

- 1 part Wild Turkey® Bourbon
- ½ part Tequila
- ¼ splash Tabasco® Sauce
- Shot Glass

Pour ingredients into glass neat (do not chill)

BRAVE BULL

- 1 part Tequila
- 1 part Tabasco® Sauce
- Shot Glass

Pour ingredients into glass neat (do not chill)

BUFFALO BALL SWEAT

- 3 parts Yukon Jack®
- 3 splashes Tabasco® Sauce
- Shot Glass

Pour ingredients into glass neat (do not chill)

BUFFALO PISS

- 1 part Tequila
- 1 part Tabasco® Sauce
- Shot Glass

Pour ingredients into glass neat (do not chill)

BURN IN HELL AND PRAY FOR SNOW!

- 2 parts Rum
- 2 parts Whiskey
- 1 part Tabasco® Sauce
- 12 Hot Peppers
- Shot Glass

Combine all ingredients in a blender with ice. Blend until smooth. Pour into shot glasses and top with a splash of Irish Cream.

BURNING ANGEL

- 1 part Vodka
- 1 part Jägermeister®
- splash Tabasco® Sauce
- dash Salt
- Shot Glass

Pour ingredients into glass neat (do not chill)

CHUCK WAGON

- 1 part Jägermeister®
- ½ splash Tabasco® Sauce
- Shot Glass

Pour ingredients into glass neat (do not chill)

DEAD DOG

- 1 part Bourbon
- 1 part Beer
- 3 splashes Tabasco® Sauce
- Shot Glass

Pour ingredients into glass neat (do not chill)

DEATH BY FIRE

- 1 part Peppermint Schnapps
- 1 part Cinnamon Schnapps
- 1 part Tabasco® Sauce
- Shot Glass

Pour ingredients into glass neat (do not chill)

DEVIL DRINK

- 1 part Irish Cream Liqueur
- 1 part Sambuca
- 1 part Vodka
- 3 splashes Tabasco® Sauce
- Shot Glass

Pour ingredients into glass neat (do not chill)

DIABLO!

- 1 part 151-Proof Rum
- splash Tabasco® Sauce
- Shot Glass

Pour ingredients into glass neat (do not chill)

ESTONIAN FOREST FIRE

- 1 part Vodka
- 6 splashes Tabasco® Sauce
- 1 Kiwi Slice
- Shot Glass

Combine the Tabasco® with a shot of Vodka. Chase it with a slice of Kiwi.

FENCE JUMPER

- 1 part Tequila
- 1 part Rum
- splash Tabasco® Sauce
- Shot Glass

Pour ingredients into glass neat (do not chill)

FIRE IN THE HOLE

- 1 ½ parts Ouzo
- 3 splashes Tabasco® Sauce
- Shot Glass

Pour ingredients into glass neat (do not chill)

FIREBALL

- 1 part Fire Water®
- splash Tabasco® Sauce
- Shot Glass

Pour ingredients into glass neat (do not chill)

FIREBALL #2

- 1 part Sambuca
- 1 part Tequila
- splash Tabasco® Sauce
- Shot Glass

Pour ingredients into glass neat (do not chill)

FIREBALL #3

- 1 part Cinnamon Schnapps
- splash Tabasco® Sauce
- Shot Glass

Pour ingredients into glass neat (do not chill)

FIREBALL SHOOTER

- 1 part Cinnamon Schnapps
- 1 part 151-Proof Rum
- 2 splashes Tabasco® Sauce
- Shot Glass

Pour ingredients into glass neat (do not chill)

FIRECRACKER SHOT

- 2 parts Tequila
- 1 part Tabasco® Sauce
- Shot Glass

Pour ingredients into glass neat (do not chill)

FIST FUCK

- 1 part Tabasco® Sauce
- 1 part Tequila
- Shot Glass

Pour ingredients into glass neat (do not chill)

GALAXY

- 1 part Sambuca
- 1 part Tequila
- 3 splashes Tabasco® Sauce
- Shot Glass

Pour ingredients into glass neat (do not chill)

GREAT WHITE SHARK

- 1 part Jack Daniel's®
- 1 part Tequila
- splash Tabasco® Sauce
- Shot Glass

Pour ingredients into glass neat (do not chill)

GREEN CHILLI

- 1 part Cinnamon Schnapps
- 2 splashes Tabasco® Sauce
- Shot Glass

Shake with ice and strain

GUT BOMB

- 1 part Rum
- splash Tabasco® Sauce
- Shot Glass

Pour ingredients into glass neat (do not chill)

HELL'S GATE

- 2 parts Brandy
- 1 part Tabasco® Sauce
- dash Wasabi
- splash Butterscotch Schnapps
- Shot Glass

Pour ingredients into glass neat (do not chill)

HELLFIRE

- 2 parts Rye Whiskey
- 1 part Tabasco® Sauce
- Shot Glass

Pour ingredients into glass neat (do not chill)

HOT BITCH

- 1 part Vodka
- 1 part Whiskey
- 1 part Gin
- splash Tabasco® Sauce
- Shot Glass

Pour ingredients into glass neat (do not chill)

HOT SHOT

- 1 part Vodka
- 1 part Peppermint Schnapps
- splash Tabasco® Sauce
- Shot Glass

Shake with ice and strain

HOT SHOT #2

- 1 part Crème de Menthe (White)
- 1 part Vodka
- splash Tabasco® Sauce
- Shot Glass

Shake with ice and strain

HOT SPOT

- 1 part Vodka
- 1 part Tequila
- 1 part Tabasco® Sauce
- Shot Glass

Pour ingredients into glass neat (do not chill)

INCINERATOR

- 2 parts Black Sambuca
- 1 part 151-Proof Rum
- splash Tabasco® Sauce
- Shot Glass

Pour ingredients into glass neat (do not chill)

IRONMAN

- 1 part Green Chartreuse®
- 1 part Sambuca
- 1 part Scotch
- 3 parts Tabasco® Sauce
- 1 part Tequila
- Shot Glass

Pour ingredients into glass neat (do not chill)

JAWBREAKER

- 1 part Goldschläger®
- splash Tabasco® Sauce
- Shot Glass

Pour ingredients into glass neat (do not chill)

KENTUCKY HOT TUB

- 1 part Jim Beam®
- 1 part Cointreau®
- 1 part Blue Curaçao
- splash Tabasco® Sauce
- Shot Glass

Shake with ice and strain

KICKSTARTER

- 1 part Jack Daniel's®
- 1 part Fire Water®
- splash Tabasco® Sauce
- Shot Glass

Build in the glass with no ice

LABIA LICKER

- 1 part Rum
- splash Tabasco® Sauce
- Shot Glass

Build in the glass with no ice

LAVA

- 1 part Fire Water®
- 1 part Grain Alcohol
- 2 splashes Tabasco® Sauce
- Shot Glass

Pour ingredients into glass neat (do not chill)

LEGGS

- 1 part Tequila
- 1 part Jägermeister®
- splash Tabasco® Sauce
- Shot Glass

Pour ingredients into glass neat (do not chill)

LOUISIANA SHOOTER

- 1 part Tequila
- 1 Raw Oyster
- ¼ dash Horseradish
- splash Tabasco® Sauce
- Shot Glass

Pour ingredients into glass neat (do not chill)

MAD DOG

- 1 part Vodka
- 1 part Cherry Juice
- splash Tabasco® Sauce
- Shot Glass

Shake with ice and strain

MEXICAN JUMPING BEAN

- 1 part Tequila
- splash Tabasco® Sauce
- splash Worcestershire Sauce
- Shot Glass

Pour ingredients into glass neat (do not chill)

MEXICAN MISSILE

- 1 part Tequila Silver
- splash Tabasco® Sauce
- Shot Glass

Shake with ice and strain

MONKEY FART

- 1 part Vodka
- 1 part Coffee Liqueur
- splash Tabasco® Sauce
- Shot Glass

Pour ingredients into glass neat (do not chill)

NAPALM TACO

- 1 part Jägermeister®
- 1 part Tequila
- 1 part Tabasco® Sauce
- Shot Glass

Shake with ice and strain

OKLAHOMA RATTLER

- 1 part Tequila Silver
- splash Tabasco® Sauce
- Shot Glass

Pour ingredients into glass neat (do not chill)

OYSTER SHOT

- 1 Raw Oyster
- 1 part Tequila
- splash Tabasco® Sauce
- Shot Glass

Build in the glass with no ice

PRAIRIE DOG

- 1 part 151-Proof Rum
- 3 splashes Tabasco® Sauce
- Shot Glass

Pour ingredients into glass neat (do not chill)

PRAIRIE FIRE

- 1 part Tequila
- 5 splashes Tabasco® Sauce
- Shot Glass

Pour ingredients into glass neat (do not chill)

PSYCHO TSUNAMI

- 1 part Tequila Reposado
- 1 part Blue Curaçao
- 1 part Fresh Lime Juice
- splash Tabasco® Sauce
- Shot Glass

Build in the glass with no ice

RED HOT

- 1 part Cinnamon Schnapps
- splash Tabasco® Sauce
- Shot Glass

Build in the glass with no ice

ROSWELL

- 1 part Tabasco® Sauce
- 1 part Tequila Reposado
- 1 part Red Bull® Energy Drink
- Shot Glass

Build in the glass with no ice

RUSSIAN BLOODY MARY

- 1 part Vodka
- splash Tabasco® Sauce
- Shot Glass

Build in the glass with no ice

SATAN'S PISS

- 1 part 151-Proof Rum
- 3 splashes Tabasco® Sauce
- Shot Glass

Pour ingredients into glass neat (do not chill)

SATAN'S REVENGE

- 1 part Tequila
- 1 part Jack Daniel's®
- 1 part Goldschläger®
- splash Tabasco® Sauce
- Shot Glass

Pour ingredients into glass neat (do not chill)

SATAN'S SPAWN

- 1 part Fire Water®
- 4 splashes Tabasco® Sauce
- Shot Glass

Pour ingredients into glass neat (do not chill)

SCRATCHY ASSHOLE

- 2 parts Jägermeister®
- 2 parts Peach Schnapps
- 1 part Tabasco® Sauce
- 1 part Lemon-Lime Soda
- Shot Glass

Shake with ice and strain

SHARPSHOOTER

- 1 part Ouzo
- 1 part Vodka
- splash Tabasco® Sauce
- Shot Glass

Pour ingredients into glass neat (do not chill)

SHOT OF HELL

- 1 part Vodka
- splash Tabasco® Sauce
- Shot Glass

Pour ingredients into glass neat (do not chill)

SHOT OF RESPECT

- 1 part Tequila
- 1 part 151-Proof Rum
- 1 splash Tabasco® Sauce
- Shot Glass

Pour ingredients into glass neat (do not chill)

SQUARE FURNACE

- 1 part Jim Beam®
- 1 part Tequila
- 1 part Irish Cream Liqueur
- 1 part 151-Proof Rum
- 1 part Tabasco® Sauce
- Shot Glass

Shake with ice and strain. *Note: Because this recipe includes many ingredients, it's easier to make in volume, about 6 shots.

STOMACHACHE

- 1 part Jägermeister®
- 2 splashes Tabasco® Sauce
- Shot Glass

Pour ingredients into glass neat (do not chill)

SWEATY GOAT'S ASS

- 3 parts Tequila Silver
- splash Tabasco® Sauce
- 1 part Cream
- Shot Glass

Build in the glass with no ice

SWEATY IRISHMAN

- 1 part Irish Whiskey
- 1 part Cinnamon Schnapps
- splash Tabasco® Sauce
- Shot Glass

Build in the glass with no ice

SWEATY LUMBERJACK

- 1 part 151-Proof Rum
- 1 part Tabasco® Sauce
- 1 part Tequila
- Shot Glass

Build in the glass with no ice

SWEATY MELON

- 1 part Watermelon Schnapps
- 1 part Vodka
- splash Tabasco® Sauce
- Shot Glass

Build in the glass with no ice

SWEATY MEXICAN LUMBERJACK

- 3 parts Yukon Jack®
- 1 part Tequila
- splash Tabasco® Sauce
- Shot Glass

Build in the glass with no ice

T2

- 1 part Tequila
- 1 part Tabasco® Sauce
- dash Black Pepper
- Shot Glass

Pour ingredients into glass neat (do not chill)

TENEMENT FIRE

- 1 part Vodka
- splash Tabasco® Sauce
- Shot Glass

Build in the glass with no ice

TEQUILA FIRE

- 1 part Tequila
- ½ splash Tabasco® Sauce
- Shot Glass

Build in the glass with no ice

TEXAS PRAIRIE FIRE

- 1 part Tequila
- splash Lime Juice
- splash Tabasco® Sauce
- Shot Glass

Build in the glass with no ice

TEXAS ROADKILL

- 1 part Wild Turkey® Bourbon
- 1 part Vodka
- 1 part Gin
- 1 part 151-Proof Rum
- splash Tabasco® Sauce
- Shot Glass

Shake with ice and strain

TOBY WALLBANGER

- 1 part Melon Liqueur
- 1 part Banana Liqueur
- 1 part Tequila
- 1 part Gin
- 1 part Dark Rum
- dash Bitters
- splash Tabasco® Sauce
- Shot Glass

*Shake with ice and strain. *Note: Because this recipe includes many ingredients, it's easier to make in volume, about 6 shots.*

TRIPLE RED

- 1 part Sloe Gin
- 1 part Amaretto
- splash Tabasco® Sauce
- Shot Glass

Build in the glass with no ice

ZHIVAGO'S REVENGE

- 1 part Cinnamon Schnapps
- 1 part Pepper-Flavored Vodka
- 1 part Tabasco® Sauce
- Shot Glass

Shake with ice and strain

Index

Index of Drinks
by Main Ingredients

INDEX OF DRINKS BY MAIN INGREDIENTS |

INDEX OF DRINKS BY MAIN INGREDIENTS | **769**